The Merlion & Mt. Fuji

50 Years of Singapore–Japan Relations

The Merlion & Mt. Fuji

50 Years of Singapore–Japan Relations

Tai Wei Lim

UniSIM, Singapore & East Asian Institute, NUS, Singapore

World Scientific

NEW JERSEY · LONDON · SINGAPORE · BEIJING · SHANGHAI · HONG KONG · TAIPEI · CHENNAI · TOKYO

Published by

World Scientific Publishing Co. Pte. Ltd.

5 Toh Tuck Link, Singapore 596224

USA office: 27 Warren Street, Suite 401-402, Hackensack, NJ 07601

UK office: 57 Shelton Street, Covent Garden, London WC2H 9HE

National Library Board, Singapore Cataloguing in Publication Data
Name(s): Lim, Tai Wei, author.
Title: The Merlion and Mt. Fuji : 50 years of Singapore-Japan Relations /
    Tai Wei Lim, UiSim, Singapore & East Asian Institute, NUS.
Other title(s): Merlion and Mount Fuji | Fifty years of Singapore-Japan relations
Description: Singapore : World Scientific Publishing Co. Pte. Ltd., [2016]
Identifier(s): OCN 956397923 | ISBN 978-981-31-4570-2 (paperback) |
    ISBN 978-981-31-4569-6 (hardcover)
Subject(s): LCSH: Singapore--Relations--Japan. | Japan--Relations--Singapore. |
    Japan--Social life and customs. | Cultural relations.
Classification: DDC 303.4825957052--dc23

British Library Cataloguing-in-Publication Data
A catalogue record for this book is available from the British Library.

Desk Editor: Philly Lim

Typeset by Stallion Press

Email: enquiries@stallionpress.com

Foreword

by H.E. Kenji Shinoda, Ambassador of Japan to Singapore

The year 2016 marks the 50th anniversary of diplomatic relations between Japan and Singapore. To celebrate and commemorate this remarkable year in both nations, "The 50th Anniversary of Singapore-Japan Diplomatic Relations (SJ50)" book project was conceptualised and realised by an array of stakeholders. At the heart of the book is the rich tapestry of bilateral relations between the two countries and how they have actively interacted with each other over 50 years.

Japan and Singapore have a lot in common. Their economies also have a few similarities. Both countries are maritime nations with hardly any natural resources and are dependent on high-quality human resources to manage their economies. Both are also dependent on import of raw materials. Japan shared its development experiences with Singapore, and Singapore in turn selectively indigenised some of them (for example, concepts like *Kaizen*, the Japanese business philosophy of continuous improvement and personal efficiency, as applied in the productivity movement, as well as other aspects such as "just-in-time production"). These and other economic features were developed and served as useful references for Japan and other Asian countries.

Beyond economics, both countries play important roles in cultural fields, and have shared much together. The establishment of the Japan

Creative Centre (JCC) of Embassy of Japan in Singapore is indeed the most visible symbol of the collaborative initiatives that Prime Minister Shinzo Abe and Prime Minister Lee Hsien Loong jointly started in 2007. Cooperation in educational institutions (such as the setting up of the Japan-Singapore Training Centre (JSTC) and the Department of Japanese Studies at the National University of Singapore) were also actualised. In non-institutional areas, the "osmosis" of Japanese popular culture into Singapore is also featured in this publication. A chapter on the creative nucleus of the Japanese cultural production, *Akihabara*, is included.

Intellectuals, academics and Singaporeans who know Japan well have also contributed to this book. They relate their cross-cultural experiences and narrate them from personal perspectives, including those tinged with fond nostalgia. Some selected perspectives of Singaporeans who have spent time in Japan on exchange programmes and as tourists are also included. Their contributions piece together a multi-faceted picture of Japan-Singapore relations. I would particularly thank Mr Tai Wei Lim who dedicated his time in combining this commemorative book.

On the occasion of half a century of bilateral interactions between Japan and Singapore, I congratulate the publisher, chapter contributors and editor/author for putting together this volume. And I truly wish that this book will be widely read not only by people in both countries to celebrate "SJ50" but also by many more readers globally, as a reference for future generations so that they can learn how these two island countries achieved so much economic prosperity and cultural enrichment together.

Foreword

by Professor Yoshihisa Godo,
Professor of Economics, Meiji Gakuin University, Japan

Every time I arrive at Changi Airport, I remind myself of my core research purpose. While my regular workplace, Meiji Gakuin University, is in Tokyo, Singapore is where I go for encouragement and training. I am so happy to get a chance to write a foreword to this book, which was prepared to celebrate the 50th anniversary of the Singapore–Japan diplomatic relationship.

I first visited Singapore in February 2012. At that time, I was privileged to have Meiji Gakuin University grant me a one-year research sabbatical at a foreign university for the 2013 Japanese school year (from 1 April, 2013 to 31 March, 2014). I was thinking of spending the year at a university in Singapore, which is an emerging country in both the business and academic fields. The purpose of my first Singapore visit was to observe the research conditions and atmosphere in Singaporean universities.

Before I came to Singapore, a friend of mine, who had previously worked in Singapore as a resident reporter of a Japanese publishing company, strongly suggested that I should meet Yoichi Suzuki, then Ambassador Extraordinary and Plenipotentiary of Japan to the Republic of Singapore. According to my friend, many Singaporeans appreciated Mr Suzuki's cheery and genial personality. He kindly sent an email to

Mr Suzuki to arrange an exclusive meeting with me at the Japanese Embassy in Singapore on the first day of my Singapore visit.

At the beginning of the meeting at the Japanese Embassy in Singapore, I briefly mentioned that I was looking for a Singaporean professor who would be a good reference when I applied for a one-year stay at a university in Singapore. However, given his high diplomatic rank, I did not expect Mr Suzuki's particular support for me. In spite of his busy schedule, he spared time for a meeting with me. It was already more than enough for me.

During the meeting, Mr Suzuki and I mainly talked about agricultural trade issues. Mr Suzuki has rich experience in international trade negotiations, and my major research field is agricultural policy. I enjoyed a fruitful discussion with him.

After a nearly 30-minute discussion, it seemed a good time to leave the Embassy. Before saying "good-bye", I wanted to leave a message with Mr. Suzuki. I told him:

Almost one year has passed since the Great East Japan Earthquake. I learnt a lot from the disaster. One of the most important lessons is about foreign peoples' hospitality. They expressed their sympathy with us over the massive deaths from the tsunami. Many countries, including ASEAN members, offered various forms of support for Japan's reconstruction from the disaster. I would like to return my thanks to all of them by promoting mutual understanding through research projects. This is the biggest motivation for my research activities. You are a diplomat and I am an academic. While our positions differ, I am totally sure that you and I share the same feeling. Today, I am so pleased to get a chance to talk with you.

As I was about to say "good-bye", I changed my mind and waited for Mr Suzuki's response because I found that the expression of his eyes had changed. He called his secretary and asked her to list Singaporean professors with whom I should make contact. While waiting for her list, Mr Suzuki spoke to me gently but seriously:

Do you know why so many top leaders in ASEAN countries ardently supported Japan's recovery from the damages of the Great East Japan

Earthquake? This is a carryover from the 1950s and '60s. At that time, Japan made various contributions to economic development in Asian countries. For example, Japan constructed social infrastructure such as bridges and roads. In addition, Japan sent many experts to train local people. Japan was not aggressive in advertising those contributions worldwide. However, those who received benefits appreciated Japan so much and have not forgotten the kind things Japan had done for them. Now they are in leading positions in the business, academic, and political spheres in ASEAN countries. Last year, Japan was damaged by the Great East Japan Earthquake. For them, it was the right time to return their thanks to Japan. As a teacher, you should tell this story to your students. We should have countries exchange thanks from generation to generation.

I was impressed with Mr Suzuki's faithfulness and passion for promoting international friendship. Nearly 10 minutes later, the secretary came back with a memo of the names and emails of Singaporean professors. Mr Suzuki received it and attached to the memo a document recommending the order in which the professors should be contacted. Handing it to me, Mr Suzuki said, "At first, you should make contact with them according to this order. If you receive any positive response from some of them, I will write a letter of recommendation for you."

As soon as I got to the hotel, I sent emails as Mr Suzuki had suggested. First on Mr Suzuki's list was a professor of the East Asian Institutes (EAI) at the National University of Singapore. The EAI professor responded quickly, saying "the EAI will consider seriously accepting you if we receive Mr Suzuki's recommendation letter." In this way, I got a chance to stay with the EAI for my one-year research sabbatical.

The EAI was founded in 1997. The EAI mainly focuses on current issues in the People's Republic of China, while North and South Korea, and Japan are also included in the EAI's research scope. Previously, there were no Japanese in the EAI's research team. However, this does not mean that the EAI underrates the importance of studying Japan. In fact, throughout my one-year stay at the EAI, its members often came to my cubicle to talk about Japan's current issues. Even after my research sabbatical ended, I kept close contact with the EAI. I occasionally visit the EAI to carry out analyses on Japan's current issues.

I believe that Singapore is the best place for free discussions on Japan's current issues. In Japan, there is a tendency, the so-called "wrap-up phenomenon", whereby discussion on current issues mostly conforms to a single pattern. For example, Japanese mass media often describe the domestic agricultural industry as one of the most promising industries by presenting farmers only in a good light. This is probably because Japanese citizens are thirsty for rosy stories about agriculture, while famous Japanese companies in the manufacturing and commercial sectors, such as Panasonic, Sharp and Sony, have faced difficulties during the prolonged recession since the 1990s. In other words, populism and escapism are growing in Japan. In that sense, those who do not follow a routine pattern of thinking tend to receive cold treatment in Japan.

In contrast, Singaporean researchers want to have information that is not available in Japanese newspapers and journals. Thus, in presenting my own findings and views on Japan's current issues, I am more comfortable in Singapore than in Japan.

There are many harsh realities of Japanese society that Japanese researchers like me should present in Singapore. For example, in my recent paper published by the EAI, I warned that Japan is heading in a dangerous direction where the Japanese government strongly controls and monitors all citizens and that Japanese citizens are becoming obedient to the government. This kind of assertion is politically so touchy that non-Japanese researchers would hesitate to hazard it.

Immediately after the Second World War, many Singaporeans had hostile feelings towards the Japanese because Singaporean society was badly devastated under Japan's military occupation. However, the two countries made many efforts to form a friendly post-war relationship. As a result, most Singaporeans today have a positive sentiment toward Japan. Japanese culture, namely cartoons, dishes, music, etc., are now Singaporeans' favourites. Japanese love Singapore, too. Singapore is one of the most popular cities among Japanese sightseers. In addition, Singapore is known as one of the top three cities for family members of Japanese businesspersons to reside in (the others are San Francisco and Sydney; Japanese businesspersons call these three cities the "three S's").

The relationship between Singapore and Japan over these 50 years can be considered among the finest examples of how warm friendship was fostered between the two countries despite their unhappy history of tense relations.

I am considering how the next 50 years of relations between Singapore and Japan should be conducted. My suggestion is that we should graduate from being "good friends" to "trusted partners". To do so, we should focus on both each other's beautiful and ugly sides. This can be compared to a relationship between two persons. As long as they are ordinary friends, they should look at each other's virtues only. However, if they want to be responsible long-term partners, they should also point out each other's faults and consider how to cope with them.

Considering the rapid development of communication and transportation technologies, it is easy to expect that economies in the Asia-Pacific area will become more and more integrated. Japan and Singapore are the top two countries in terms of *per capita* GDP. Thus, Japan and Singapore should collaborate closely in taking an initiative to create a framework of a common economic market in the Asia-Pacific area. If, in doing so, Singapore and Japan become "trusted partners", it will benefit not only both countries but also all countries in the Asia-Pacific area.

About the Author

Tai Wei Lim is a Senior Lecturer at SIM University (UniSIM) and a Research Fellow Adjunct at the National University of Singapore (NUS) East Asian Institute. His research interests are in the energy histories of China and Japan and modern/contemporary East Asian history in general. He graduated from Cornell University with a PhD in history and teaches the world history course in UniSIM. He also conducts policy research on contemporary Sino-Japanese relations, popular culture and the soft power influence of the creative industries in Japan as well as Sino-Hong Kong relations. His latest co-authored book is *Contextualizing Occupy Central in Contemporary Hong Kong* published by Imperial College Press in 2015.

Contents

1

Introduction

The year 2016 marks the 50th anniversary of diplomatic relations between Japan and Singapore. In order to celebrate this remarkable year in both nations, the 50th Anniversary of Singapore–Japan Diplomatic Relations Executive Committee, which was established in January 2015, has decided to approve and support those projects which meet the purpose of promoting the mutual understanding and the exchange between two countries as "The 50th Anniversary of Singapore–Japan Diplomatic Relations (SJ50) project". The central theme of this publication is how two of the most important economies in East Asia collaborated in the past half century. Japan was the first country to modernise in East Asia in 1868 and its development was shared with Singapore from the 1970s onwards as the Japanese growth model was selectively emulated by the four tiger economies (including Singapore). The success of Singapore then became an important economic inspiration for other East Asian economies to learn from, including Chinese economic reforms starting from 1979 that gradually transformed it from a central-planning command economy to a market economy.

Singapore and Japan continues to play important roles in all fields, including collaboration in the socio-cultural field (through the initiation of the Japan Creative Centre or JCC), in military/defence ties as ally and strategic partner to the US (in the case of Japan and Singapore, respectively), in the field of education (setting up the Japan–Singapore Training Centre (JSTC) and the Department of Japanese Studies in the National University of Singapore, for example), and in terms of economic exchanges (productivity drive, just-in-time). The publication is divided into two equal portions: (1) one section will be analysing 50 years of bilateral relations from the viewpoint of Singapore; (2) and the other section will be the analysis of bilateral relations from the perspective of Japan. For the Singapore portion, the author worked with some Singapore-based scholars and writers for their contributions to the volume. For the Japanese portion, the author is tapping into the resources within the Japanese embassy education or cultural divisions, JETRO, JCCI and JCC, for example. The author gathers materials related to Singapore's view on these bilateral ties by going through a literature collection, and also translate Japanese-language materials for the same purpose. Using interpretative work, textual analysis, archival work, unstructured interviews, corroboration of different sources and media materials collection/analysis, the author will piece together five decades of relations between the two countries.

Milestones Leading to SJ50

As Singapore and Japan celebrate their 50th anniversary of bilateral relations (SJ50) in 2016, it is useful to recall some important historical milestones in bilateral relations that had helped to cement that relationship. Singapore–Japan relations can be divided into three phases. The first phase is from 1966 to the 1980s when Japan became a dominant investor in Singapore and also served as a model for Singaporean economic development as one of the famed four tiger economies. The second phase starts from the 1990s to 2002 when Singapore becomes a developed economy and the relationship between the two becomes a collaborative one culminating in Singapore signing an economic partnership agreement with Japan (the first country that has succeeded in working out a free trade agreement (FTA) with Japan). From 2000s to the current period, the relationship has become an equal one in which not only does Singapore continue to learn from Japan but Japan has started observing Singapore's best practices such as its success in the finance and banking sector, running integrated resorts and attraction of global talents. These three phases are now capped by SJ50, the 50th year marker of Singaporean–Japanese relations. This volume is not a comprehensive account of the three historical phases in bilateral relationship but serves as a historical survey of its milestones, current achievements and future orientations. There is a regional and global dimension to this relationship as both countries have tapped into their collective resources to work with other countries in capacity building activities. In other words, the external dimension of this relationship has benefitted other countries in Southeast Asia and beyond. Given Singapore's role as what has been described by some analysts as the "brain" of Southeast Asia, Japanese cooperation with Singapore may likely end up benefitting the ASEAN Economic Community (AEC) as well.

At the apex of political power in both states, personal rapport between the current two prime ministers (PMs) contributed to the close working relationships between them. In the political sphere, the current PM of Japan Shinzo Abe has been a proactive driver of bilateral relations between Singapore and Japan since taking office in early 2013 when he won the election in late 2012. Mr Abe has been advocating peace and security in the region as one of his foreign policy priorities. Realising the importance of the security platform of the Shangri-La Dialogue, Japanese PM Mr Shinzo Abe accepted Singapore's invitation in 2013 to make the keynote speech at the Singapore-hosted Shangri-La Dialogue on 15 December 2013. The two countries are pro-peace in the region and conveyed this message in the Dialogue as early as 2013. Both PM Lee and PM Abe are known regionally as statesmen with leadership styles that endure the rigour of parliamentary elections and democracy. Singapore and Japan reiterated their strong working relationship when the PM of Japan Mr Abe congratulated the Singapore PM's strong showing in Singapore's September 2015 election. In that particular significant year of SG50 (Singapore's 50th anniversary after its founding), Mr Abe also attended the funeral of Singapore's founding father Mr Lee Kuan Yew while Deputy PM Taro Aso attended the SG50 National Day Parade (NDP). Both leaders reaffirmed Japan's important regional role when Mr Abe explained his new security legislative initiatives and when Mr Lee noted the successful organisation of the trilateral meeting late 2015. In recognition of Japan's contribution, Singapore supports Japan's aspirations to become a permanent member of the United Nations Security Council (UNSC).

Other than the legislators, the heads of state of Singapore and Japan also visited each other's countries in the recent past. At the head of state level, the Japanese Emperor Akihito and Empress Michiko carried out an official visit to Singapore in June 2006 and, in return, former President

SR Nathan and the first lady went to Japan in May 2009 in their official capacities. The examples above indicate that the legislature and executive have been working closely together with each other at all levels. In the years following the SJ50 anniversary, both countries are likely to witness an intensification of bilateral relations with a regional perspective, especially with the gradual progress made by the AEC.

Economics appears to be a binding force for Singapore–Japan ties. After Singapore's independence in 1965, Japan was the largest investor in Singapore during the fast-growth period in the 1970s and 1980s. This was a historical period when Singapore and the four tiger economies (Hong Kong, South Korea, Taiwan) started studying the positive features of the Japanese model of development. In 1980, Singapore implemented the "Learn from Japan" campaign that saw certain successful features of Japanese management practices such as company unions indigenised in the Singapore context. The subsequent chapters provide some examples of indigenised features of the Japanese social and economic systems in Singapore. This includes items like *koban*, on-the-job training by *senpai* or upper-study, one-stop mall retailing and other Japanese management features.

In the decade after Singaporean independence, in the 1970s, Japan became Singapore's biggest external investor and trading partner, and in 2002, history was again in the making when the Lion City was the inaugural country to ink an FTA with Japan in 2002. In the subsequent lap of economic cooperation, bilateral negotiations between Singapore and Japan on an FTA known later as the Japan–Singapore Economic Agreement for a New Age Partnership (JSEPA) was held on 31 January 2001. Mr Lim Chin Beng, a private sector leader and former Singapore Ambassador to Japan represented the Singapore side for the negotiations. The JSEPA became effective on 30 November 2007. Singapore became the first state with whom Japan signed an economic partnership, in the further advancement of free trade. The next lap in economic destiny between the two countries lies in their common stakeholder interests in the success of the Trans-Pacific Partnership (TPP). The TPP is likely to bind both countries closer to their major working partner, the United States.

In the near future, we are likely to see a more equitable partnership between Singapore and Japan since the former has evolved from a learner economy adapting from Japanese management practices and economic features to a model from which Japanese could pick out best practices for indigenisation. This is especially the case in the financial sector where Singapore has become a leading financial centre in the region and a successful advocate of free trade with other nations in the world. Japan is known to have an interest in studying these integrated resort. Singapore's ability to attract global foreign talents as a migrant and heterogeneous society is also a case study for Japan's homogenous society seeking for solutions to cope with an ageing society that needs more manpower. With economic development came responsibilities and obligations for Singapore and Japan. Singapore and Japan have also dispensed their capacity-building responsibility to the region under the Japan–Singapore Partnership Programme for the 21st Century (JSPP21) by channelling technical help to other developing economies.

Popular culture is a strong component of the SJ50 celebrations. The Singapore Tourism Board announced that celebrity director Eric Khoo is producing a film on the topic of *ramen* together with counterparts from Japan that includes film stars from both countries and scheduled for screening in late 2016.[1] Khoo is the director of iconic art films like *Mee Pok Man*, an art film that is also a social commentary on the marginalised sections of Singapore society. The title of the film is also named after a popular noodle dish in Singapore and so the theme of *ramen* returns Khoo to yet another noodle-themed film. SJ50 in this sense is mobilising celebrity power for its celebration, adding an element of glamour to the diplomatic event. In the chapter on cultural exchanges between the two countries for this volume, I will analyse and discuss the significance of popular culture, traditional cultures and food culture in the context of bilateral relationship. I will examine the concept of cultural soft power in a bidirectional manner — cultural exchanges that Japan has with Singapore and how the latter is indigenising aspects of Japanese cultures and then hybridising them with local and Western cultures to create new fusion varieties. A good example here is local interpretations and introduction of Japanese foods into local catering menus.

---

[1] Yeo, Lionel. "JNTO-STB MOC signing — Message by Lionel Yeo, Chief Executive, Singapore Tourism Board" dated 18 Jan 2016 in the Singapore Tourism Board (STB) website [downloaded on 22 Jan 2016], available at https://www.stb.gov.sg/news-and-publications/lists/newsroom/dispform.aspx?ID=638.

Besides intangible factors like cultural exchanges and fashion trends, Singapore–Japan ties are also built on tangible institutional foundations. The actors for bilateral ties involve multi-stakeholders with pluralistic interests. They include both state and non-state actors, multinational corporations (MNCs) and business associations, political elites and the masses. The volume does not pretend to be comprehensive in listing out all these actors but surveys and profiles some of them in promoting bilateral relations between the two countries. The involvement of multiple stakeholders is the reason why bilateral ties are highly intertwined, complex and deeply rooted and intensely bound together. It ensures that different sectors of the relationship have open and common platforms for communications between the peoples of both countries. This volume's chapters on Singapore–Japan economic and political exchanges provide some examples of these institutional actors working with individuals to foster closer relations. Perhaps that is a possible reason why organisations who are celebrating half a century of close ties between the two countries are keen to apply for the official SJ50 logo for their events. The SJ50 anniversary has been touted by some in the international media as a "sequel" to SG50.[2] SJ50 has a comprehensive approval process for using the SJ50 logo. Its executive committee is headed by Japan's ambassador to Singapore, Haruhisa Takeuchi, and other Japanese organisations advocating friendship between the two countries and official logo approvals must be sought before firms can attain the status of official SJ50 supporters.[3] This appears to be a sound quality control over SJ50 marketing and product endorsement.

Methodology

The methodology for this volume is multi-faceted in nature. I scoured the electronic archives set up by the Ministry of Foreign Affairs Japan to search and locate older documents related to bilateral relations at the official state level. I have also scanned archived media pieces for

---

[2] Sile, Aza Wee, "SG50 sequel: Singapore, Japan to launch SJ50 to celebrate bilateral ties" dated 31 Dec 2015 in CNBC AsiaOne website [downloaded on 1 Jan 2016], available at http://business.asiaone.com/news/sg50-sequel-singapore-japan-launch-sj50-celebrate-bilateral-ties.
[3] *Ibid.*

journalistic reporting on Singapore–Japan relations. As a Singaporean who was born about a decade after Singapore and Japan established official ties, I have also added my own standpoint and an experiential perspective to the narrative. I also researched online resources, including the official websites of the Japanese and Singaporean organisations that have established their roots in Singapore or have working relationships with Singaporean organisations to reconstruct their histories and understand their mission statements and activities in Singapore. Besides textual documents, material artefacts, observation studies and policy statements, I have also analysed and examined narratives from different stakeholders and commentators in this bilateral relationship for this writing. I was interested in the external gazes from individuals who are not necessarily Singaporeans or experts in Singapore but interested in the bilateral relationship from different angles and perspectives. This includes the gazes of ordinary Singaporeans from all walks of life who experienced Japan in various ways, as tourists, students, businessmen, etc. Their unstructured dialogues, conversations and commentaries about Japan shed light on how Singaporeans view the Land of the Rising Sun.

Several books have been written in the Japanese language on Singapore–Japan ties. I collected a number of them during my fieldtrips to Japan and acquired compiled volumes of past issues of *The Southern Cross* published by the Japanese Association in Singapore. The Japanese-language books were useful for understanding the writers' expert views about Singapore. It offers glimpses of Japanese views about Singapore. For example *The Southern Cross* volumes are useful primary sources of information about the Japanese expatriate community in Singapore and their observations of all things Singapore. The 30th anniversary volume published in 1997 begins with an extensive collection of photos on Chinatown and Boat Quay as well as Clarke Quay taken in the 1970s and 1980s. The first section of the publication features a number of speakers recalling the past 10 years' (1985–1995) worth of Singaporean events and milestones. For example, one of the interviewers in this section of the volume revealed how the Japanese expatriate community had grown from approximately 8,000 individuals in 1985 to 20,000 people in 1995.[4]

---

[4] The Japanese Association, Singapore editorial team (*Henshuu iinkai*), The Southern Cross 30th anniversary issue (*Minamijuujise soukan sanjuushuunen kinengou*) (Singapore: The Japanese Association), 1997, p. 19.

The anniversary volumes are packed with dense information about Singapore from its flora and fauna to practical information about settling in Singapore. The volumes provide a glimpse into Japanese expatriates' perspective of life in Singapore. Unlike previous publications, however, this book is one of its kind as it commemorates something significant in over half a century. It can potentially serve as an important reference for the large numbers of individuals in both countries responsible for or have played a part in contributing to a bilateral relationship that have the hallmarks of contributing to regional peace, economic development and cultural diversity. As the most advanced economies in Southeast and Northeast Asia respectively, Singapore and Japan will continue to be demonstrative case studies for economic development in the region.

Contents Layout

In terms of chapterisation, my contents are laid out as follows. In the next chapter, Singapore and Japan's pivotal roles in the East Asian region are discussed. In international relations (IR), Singapore and Japan are disproportionate in sizes of population, land area and GDP. Singapore is a small state in terms of both geographical and demographic sizes, while Japan is a major global economic power, a regional power in geopolitical terms, an advanced developed economy with technologically-sophisticated industries. Yet, the two states did not let size get in the way due to commonalities in outlook, interests and economic complementarity. The chapter surveys the milestones and achievements that both countries have made so far in promoting interdependence, economic development, peace and stability in the region.

After the chapter on politics, the volume surveys economic ties between Singapore and Japan. While political and security represent the "hard" aspects of bilateral cooperation, both-countries are also engaged in "ofter" economic cooperation which had catalysed economic-development in the region, with Singapore as a nimble, fast-mover promoter of FTAs in East Asia and Japan as a major builder of production networks in the Southeast Asia. Both roles contribute to the formation of an economic community in Southeast Asia. This chapter surveys the economic ties between

Singapore and Japan in this context. Both past and present milestones are discussed. Singapore and Japan are likely to intensify their respective roles as nodes within the East Asian economies that can provide economic developmental training to other economies in the region, promote free trade by institutionalising structures and regulations to break down barriers, stimulate technological cooperation to disseminate technological knowhow to the Southeast Asian region in the latter's industrialisation process, enhance connectivity between economies in the region through encouraging production networking first set up by Japan in the past few decades.

After the contextualisation of Japan's role in Singapore's economic development, the following chapter is a case study written by an author **Kong Tuan Yuen**, who used to work at a Japanese MNC in Malaysia which moved from Singapore in 1988 to conduct business management, financial and planning analysis for four years. During his service with the MNC, he was sent to Japan to learn about Toyota's production system and manufacturing automation. He also conducted research on several case studies about Japanese manufacturing companies to compare the business management style. The applied aspects of Japanese business management will be discussed as a case study in this chapter. In addition to experienced veterans in the industry, it is also important to have a non-comprehensive peek at some selective perspectives of Japanese business management through the eyes of young Singaporeans.

To get an individual glimpse of how Singaporeans who are still schooling view Japan's economy, business management methodologies and the prospects of learning from Japan, the subsequent chapter takes the form of an experiential writing by a young Singaporean (**Aomi Poh**) who made a visit to Japan on a study trip specifically designed to immerse in Japan's corporate culture, understand Japanese business practices and interact with Japanese business executives. It is not designed to be comprehensive but raises some points that may possibly shed some thoughts on about future economic and business cooperation from the standpoint and perspective of a young Singaporean.

The next two chapters discuss about consumption of Japanese products in Singapore. **Janice Kam**'s chapter is a journalistic/

column-style meditation on the perspective, very much subjective, of a Singaporean encountering Japan as she appears in Singapore, as an experiential consumer who has grown up and lived in a country which is the recipient of Japanese FDI. Kam also describes the increasing sophistication of consumption of Japanese products that comes with development, with Singapore as a society very open to experience and consumption, where multi-culturalism beyond the customary ethnic composition of Singapore serves as an indicator of development, sophistication and cosmopolitanism. In brief, she reflects on a child-hood and adulthood where Japanese stores and services were and still remain a ubiquitous presence on my mental geography. This is followed by the writing of another young Singaporean (**Soh Hui Shi**) who writes about her impressions of working in a Japanese retail outlet based in Singapore. She provides a standpoint and perspective of Japanese service quality and also interesting observations on how Singaporean and Japanese employees interact with each other in a mixed setting with both nationals present in the same workplace. This chapter rounds up the collection of writings related to Japanese economy and business management.

The previous chapters discussed Singapore and Japan's bilateral political and economic exchanges. The two platforms, particularly economic exchanges, are traditional prisms in which the media and state view official ties. But an important aspect of relations between the two countries is neither state-led nor market-driven, instead people-to-people exchange is interest-driven and motivated by more altruistic goals compared to political-institutional and commercial ties. Two societies can only reach long-term understanding if their peoples are engaged culturally, linguistically and morally. These qualities are expressed through volunteerism, personal motivation to pick up the language of communication and acts of compassion and mutual help. The following chapter is an account of some recent and past examples of exchanges between the people of both Singapore and Japan. Much of the exchanges mentioned in this chapter are ethically conscious and purposeful, e.g. directed towards natural disaster recovery or law enforcement. They are also functional, like the world of the Japanese expatriate community in Singapore, i.e. salarymen who bring their families along to conduct productive business activities for their companies and firms. The subsequent chapter will examine people-to-people exchanges from a leisure-based, recreational perspective, including personal tours taken by Singaporeans including myself to Japan to explore Japan by trekking, backpacking, taking road trips and train rides. An undergraduate at a local Singaporean university, **Hilda Tan**, studying Human Resources presented her individual account of a university exchange program to Japan to reflect upon her own life experiences with the country: its culture, symbolisms and lifestyle trends. She looked back on her recollection and realised that "Japan" has been in her life in more ways than expected. Her chapter is an account of a Singaporean's thoughts, recollection, views and opinions of an exchange program between Singapore and Japan. This is her story.

For the volume's chapter on cultural exchanges, I am adopting several approaches to examine the topical matter. First in this chapter, I will examine selective impressions that Singaporeans have of Japan through travels, food experiences (particularly since food is almost a national pastime for Singaporeans), popular cultural performances, etc. I am including personal observation studies and impressions from my own travels to Japan as well as culinary experiences as a foodie. The chapter immediately following this examines popular cultural consumption in Akihabara, a district in Tokyo that has been the trendsetter for Japanese popular culture since the 1990s, the widely-recognised Mecca of Japanese pop culture in Japan in terms of both consumption and generation of ideas. This chapter is followed by my latest observation studies in my travels to Akihabara and other Japanese popular cultural sites in Tokyo related to its creative economy. This is then followed by a Singaporean *otaku*'s (**Yeo Kai Yeat**) account of his experiences and encounters with Japanese popular culture. By including this three-pronged approach to examining Singapore–Japan cultural exchanges, I hope to provide a pluralistic diversity of glimpses into the bilateral exchanges, but it does not pretend to be comprehensive. The actual exchanges are even more intense, in-depth, multi-faceted, multi-layered and cosmopolitan than what is portrayed here. The next chapter, also written by a fan (**Sim Zhi Ya**), argues from the gender perspective that, as an avid reader of romance *shoujo manga*, she feels that the greatest appeal of these category of *manga* is how female readers can relate to the storylines and contents. The final chapter written by a Japanese popular culture fan (**Alvin Teo**) details how Japanese pop culture influenced him throughout his life. In his chapter, he also noted that cultural differences are visible through how different countries interpret the concept of *anime* and produce animation.

In the concluding remarks, the volume argues that both countries will continue to tackle common challenges together in the future in common areas such as an ageing population, changing geopolitical realities, mature economies, environmental challenges and, in the process, strengthen their relations for the next 50 years.

2

Political Exchanges

SJ50: Historical Background and its Milestones

Like all political relationships, Singapore and Japan initiated their bilateral relations based on national interests. Throughout the postwar period in bilateral relations, both countries and their leaders were able to locate issues of common interests to strengthen the relationship. On the 50th year of bilateral ties between the two countries, it may be useful to review the bilateral relationship between the two countries. In some ways, the subtext of this chronology is also Singapore's nation-building story and its legacy in regional diplomacy. I will survey the chronological events below though it does not pretend to be comprehensive. I divide the half a century worth of diplomatic relationship into three phases.

In the first phase, external crises appear to push the two nations closer together. Two years after the independence of the Republic of Singapore, the joint communique between Singapore and Japan stated that, at the invitation of the Singaporean government, then Prime Minister (PM) of Japan Eisaku Sato visited Singapore between 25 September 1967 and 26 September 1967, and they interacted and exchanged views on global affairs. The official communique records this historic meeting as "cordial" and "contributed to deepening of mutual understanding". The unfolding Vietnam conflict was on the minds of the two leaders who hoped for peace in that region.

In the next decade, the subsequent external crisis to confront the leaders of both countries was energy-related. In the 1970s, Japanese PM Mr Kakuei Tanaka met with Singapore's founding father and PM Mr Lee Kuan Yew. The meeting took place against the backdrop of an oil crisis in Japan in January 1974. Mr Tanaka expressed worries about the impact of the oil crisis on Japan's fertiliser supply which in turn impacted on agricultural output. The Singaporean leader told his counterpart about the impact of reduced oil supply affecting the island nation's refinery industries and the impact of a cutback on production and manufacturing activities in the Japanese factories based in Singapore.

Mr Tanaka reassured Mr Lee that any export reduction in Japan will be met proportionately by a decrease in imports. This was probably the first instance of a regional role that Japan assumed in stabilising the economies of East Asia, including Singapore. Japan's regional role also reached out into the people-to-people exchanges and cultural sphere. To promote friendship amongst Japan and Southeast Asia, Mr Tanaka revealed plans to retrofit a ship for hosting Southeast Asian youths and transport them to Japan for exchanges and studies. Both economic and cultural outreaches represented Japan's growing regional soft power.

By the late 1970s, under the Japanese administration of Takeo Fukuda, then Singapore PM Mr Lee highlighted the fact that Japanese investments and technological dissemination to Southeast Asia have become contributive factors to regional development and economic stability. A regional dimension of bilateral relations was opened up with the increasing institutionalisation of Association of Southeast Asian Nations (ASEAN). Singapore and Japan were also getting closer together by working with the regional body of ASEAN. Bilateral economic cooperation and regional capacity-building efforts characterised the second phase of Singapore–Japan relations.

By the end of the 1970s, Singapore was quickly emerging as an economic model for the region, just as Japan had been after the fast-growth economic period of the 1960s. On 22 October 1979, the then PM of Japan, Mr Masayoshi Ohira and his wife welcomed Mr Lee to Tokyo. Here, the setting up of the Singapore–Japan Training Centre highlighted the increasing institutionalisation of bilateral ties between the two countries. Skills dissemination and capacity-building was taking place at a fast rate between the two countries during this period of time. Singapore's growing economic prosperity is also visible when the island economy began exporting manufactured products to Japan. It had acquired manufacturing capabilities of its own. Again, the transferability of this experience to other ASEAN economies was reiterated at the welcome dinner.

The 1980s was a period of economic prosperity for both Singapore and Japan. In 1981, the ethos of Japanese work ethics started to emerge in Singapore's narrative at the state dinner hosted by Mr Lee for the then PM of Japan Mr Zenko Suzuki. This was the start of the period of selective and careful study of the Japanese model of development by the Singaporean government. By the middle of the decade, both economies were sufficiently economically mature enough to contribute to regional efforts to combat contagion effects of cyclical economic slowdowns. Arriving in Japan at the height of its economic prosperity, Mr Lee visited Japanese PM Yasuhiro Nakasone on 14 October 1986 to seek cooperation in managing Singapore and ASEAN's slowing economic growth at that point of time.

Singapore by then was more economically dependent on Japan than on the US and other major economies in the world during Japan's economic bubble period. Japan's global prominence grew through the decade, until its world's second largest economic status necessitated it to reassure others in the region of its benign economic policies. In the latter part of the 1980s, on a regional tour of Southeast Asia, then Japanese PM Mr Noboru Takeshita sat down with Mr Lee in Singapore to reassure the latter that Japan intended to avoid a trade conflict between the world's two largest economic powers.

At the meeting, the following items were announced. Mr Takeshita increased the availability of scholarships to Southeast Asian students, upgraded the loans to regional economies and also started playing a global role by sending non-military personnel to help out with the Namibian crisis. At this point of time, both Singapore and Japan were now fully playing global roles in international affairs with Singapore contributing police officers to help oversee the Namibian elections. The regional role of Japan in linking up with ASEAN became clear in 1988 when it set up a fund for investing in ASEAN in 1988. Then Japanese

Foreign Minister Mr Sosuke Uno who later became PM made this known during his visit to Southeast Asia which included Singapore.

With its global role, Japan's market access became a regional issue. According to the next PM Mr Toshiki Kaifu's policy address in Singapore in May 1991, Mr Kaifu noted that Japan was prepared to offer access to its market. In response, Mr Lee said in his conversation with the visiting Japanese PM that the rise of East Asia was built on US-initiated open free market worldviews and any regional initiatives should include the US. Singapore and Japan at this time were quickly becoming fast-movers on free trade advocacy in the region and also promoted open and inclusive economic regionalism in East Asia.

With increasing complexities between the two economies, in the 1990s, Singapore and Japan instituted symposiums to accommodate plurality of views from different sectors of both societies. Then former PM Goh Chok Tong and the Japanese PM Mr Tomiichi Murayama started the first Japan–Singapore Symposium in 1995 and the forum has been ongoing since 1995. Such forums became useful as the two countries had become economic drivers in the East Asian region. In 1998, then Japanese Foreign Minister Keizo Obuchi (who later became PM from 1998 to 2000) visited Singapore on 4 and 5 May 1998 and spoke on Japan and East Asian relations at the Institute of Policy Studies (IPS) while exchanging views on regional development. Through greater understanding, the two countries had also become casual and at ease with bilateral visits. Against the backdrop of a severe economic financial crisis in 1997, then Japanese PM Ryutaro Hashimoto visited Singapore in January 1997 and then the Singaporean PM returned the visit in August 1997. These two years saw a flurry of diplomatic visits between the two countries in rapid succession.

Entering into the 21st century, in the year 2000, Mr Goh visited Japan and was hosted by then Japanese PM Yoshiro Mori on 22 October 2000. Here, an important milestone in bilateral relationship was initiated with the conclusion of the study and its report on the Japan–Singapore Economic Agreement for a New Age Partnership (JSEPA). This paved the way for eventual signing of the pact with the subsequent Japanese PM. The all-important came two years later when Mr

Goh welcomed PM Mr Junichiro Koizumi to the Istana on 13 January 2002 and the milestone JSEPA was inked marking closer integration of the trade, investments and economic cooperation between Singapore and Japan. Mr Koizumi's administration also coincided with the Japanese Emperor and Empress' visit to Singapore in June 2006.

Hitherto, economic and political relations characterised bilateral ties. The third phase of bilateral relationship goes beyond an economic focus. But, in the next year in 2007, environmental progress was achieved when PM Yasuo Fukuda of Japan adopted the Singapore Declaration on Climate Change, Energy and the Environment in the run up to the G8 Hokkaido Lake Toya Summit held in 2008. Environment and sustainability are foregrounded in the bilateral relations of great importance. This was a visit that was reciprocated by the then Singapore President SR Nathan who went to Japan in May 2009 during Japanese PM Taro Aso's administration. Besides the field of the environment, the creative sector between the two countries also received more bilateral exchanges. In the first Shinzo Abe administration, yet another milestone was achieved when PM Lee Hsien Loong officially inaugurated the Japan Creative Centre in Singapore in November 2009.

The two countries continued to clock new achievements outside the economic sphere when PM Yukio Hatoyama unfurled regional initiatives in 2010 when he initiated a *yu-ai* fraternity ship to dispense medical aid and foster cultural exchanges in Southeast Asia. The Singaporean PM Lee then held talks with Japanese PM Naoto Kan on October 2010 to reaffirm good ties and welcomed the US and Russia into the East Asia Summit, a major forum in the East Asian region. The relations also covered the important angle of disaster relief. On 31 August 2011, PM Lee wrote to incoming Japanese PM Yoshihiko Noda and assured the latter that Singapore would support Japanese recovery and reconstruction process in the Tohoku north-eastern region of Japan.

In 2016, Singapore and Japan are preparing for the 50th anniversary of bilateral ties with celebrations. PM Lee is once again reacquainted with PM Shinzo Abe's second administration. The current multi-dimensional nature of bilateral ties is likely to experience deepening in intensity in the coming years. Reflecting the pluralistic complexity of this bilateral relationship, the planned celebration events with joint movie productions, high-level visits, photographic exhibitions of disaster relief efforts and other traditional and popular cultural events symbolises this multi-faceted relationship.

International Relations (IR) Perspectives

In IR, Singapore and Japan are disproportionate in sizes of population, land area and GDP. Singapore is a small state in terms of both geographical and demographic sizes while Japan is a major global economic power, a regional power in geopolitical terms, an advanced developed economy with technologically-sophisticated industries. Yet, the two states did not let size get in the way due to commonalities in outlook, interests and economic complementarity. Both are friendly towards the US. Singapore also has friendly ties with other major powers in the region like European Union (EU), Australia, China, India and Indonesia as well as other ASEAN countries. Japan-US has been the cornerstone alliance in East Asia forming the foundation of peace and security in the region in the post-war era. Singapore is a close strategic partner of both members of this alliance. At the same time, Singapore plays an important role as a neutral platform for all major powers to develop cooperative ties, including China, India, Australia, EU, Russia and ASEAN member states. Because of this ability to agglomerate regional interests, Singapore becomes a useful platform for bilateral cooperation with Japan in organising capacity-building activities with third parties, dispensing loans, aids, training and funding to Southeast Asia and beyond.

The two countries are known to be constructivist and functionalist. They have been promoting interdependence between economies while promoting peace in the region. Singapore practices pragmatism as a small state. It is in favour of free trade agreements (FTAs) (in fact the Japan–Singapore Economic Partnership Agreement is a good example) and reaches out to all states, regardless of size and political ideology. Often characterising itself as a "little red dot", Singapore's influence reaches beyond what its small size connotes. Sometimes described by others as a "brain of ASEAN", Singapore is a fast mover in advocating the removal trade barriers within ASEAN in the region's aspirations to institutionalise the ASEAN Economic Community (AEC). In terms of regional affairs, it is in favour of a Code of Conduct for maritime territorial management in a bid to strengthen peace and security in the region. Reflective of its central position in serving as a neutral platform for discussing regional affairs, Singapore is located within a seven hour flight radius of the capital cities of all major economies in East Asia, making it an ideal location for major regional conferences in the region.

Like Singapore, Japan has symbolised peace and cooperation in the region through morale legitimacy. From 1960s onwards, Japan promoted production networking in East Asia, something complementary to Singapore's position of advocating free trade. Since the 1990s, Japan has also been participating in United Nations (UN) peacekeeping missions, and played a major role in Cambodia's transition to peace after a civil war. For Japan, domestically, the Act on Cooperation with United Nations Peacekeeping Operations and Other Operations (the International Peace Cooperation Act) in June 1992 started Japan on a track towards contribution to peace and order in the international community in initiatives led by the UNs. Since then, Japan's Self-Defense Forces (SDF) has been deployed to Cambodia, Mozambique, Golan Heights, East Timor, Sudan and Haiti, and police personnel to Cambodia and East Timor. The SDF contingents have also been dispatched to manage operations related to Rwandan, East Timorese, Afghan and Iraqi refugees. Japanese domestic public opinion is strongly in favour of deploying SDF soldiers for such international obligations. The "Public Opinion Survey on Foreign Affairs" carried out by the Cabinet Office in October 2014 showed that about 80% of Japanese people surveyed are keen to have Japan's involvement in UN Peacekeeping Operations. With wide public support, Japan is making important contributions to PKO through the new security bill. Under the Abe administration, Japan has instituted a new security law that permits Japan to send armed soldiers to assist UN peacekeepers who may sometimes come under hostile fire. Sometimes, some of these peacekeepers were killed. This opens the way for Japan to contribute in both non-combat roles as well as combat engagements. These are all part of Mr Abe's initiative known as "Proactive Contribution to Peace".

Japan's contributions are much needed because of increasing sectarian, militant, ethnic and religious conflicts that have broken out in politically volatile parts of the world. New democracies also need help in election monitoring while impoverished communities need access to medicines and basic necessities. Japan's highly trained and highly skilled armed personnel are an asset to enhancing the security and other needs of UN headquarters and mission headquarters. Its experts and instructors have been involved in the UN Training of Trainers Course held in Tokyo. Japan is also indicating full support for its major ally in the Pacific, the US and US initiatives like the US–African Peacekeeping Rapid Response Partnership. Japan has been accepted almost universally as a player on the international stage with high integrity, pro-peace orientation and a long history of providing aids, loans, capacity-building help to other nations. As the world's third largest economy and a model for economic development, Japan has obligations to contribute to the international community. Japanese procedures for approving peacekeeping operations include an intense assessment of the needs of the countries in question and Japan's capabilities. Thereafter, the PM himself requests for his Cabinet's approval on deployment with all the details of the dispatch clearly spelt out before it sends its International Peace Cooperation Corps.

In terms of future deployment, Japan also intends to send more female peacekeepers overseas, an indication of its desire for gender parity. They are particularly crucial for managing cases of discrimination and acts of violence against women and children. Japan is also likely to increase cooperation with Troop Contributing Countries (TCCs) from Asia and work with the UN, other TCCs, the permanent as well as the non-permanent members of the Security Council. This latest development on new security laws facilitate Japanese peacekeepers to protect other peacekeepers if necessary for self-defence and protection. It could open a new chapter for Japan in peacekeeping activities. This could be an additional role for Japanese peacekeepers in addition to offering technical expertise knowledge, infrastructure capacity-building and support roles that they are already performing too well.

In all, both countries have some complementary roles in regional peace and economic development. The current PM of Japan Shinzo Abe has been a proactive driver of bilateral relations since taking office in early 2013 when he won the election in late 2012. Mr Abe has been advocating peace and security in the region as one of his foreign policy priorities. In this area, Singapore has been hosted a Track 1.5 half-governmental, semi non-state premium security forum, the Shangri-La Dialogue, in the East Asian region. Realising the important and crucial security platform that the Dialogue represents, Japanese PM Mr Shinzo Abe accepted Singapore's invitation in 2013 to make the keynote speech at the Singapore-hosted Shangri-La Dialogue on 15 December 2013. Both countries affirmed their desire to manage territorial disputes peacefully and in line with international laws.[1] The two countries are pro-peace in regional affairs. With this common outlook on geopolitical matters, as early as 2013, both countries had already mentioned preparations for the 50th anniversary celebration of bilateral ties. "In 2016, Singapore and Japan celebrate the 50th anniversary of diplomatic relations. PM Lee and I are likely to meet on many occasions next year, and I firmly believe the partnership between the two countries will deepen," said Mr Abe.[2]

Both PM Lee and PM Abe are known regionally as statesmen with leadership styles that endure the rigour of parliamentary elections and democracy. Singapore and Japan reiterated their strong working relationship when the PM of Japan Mr Abe congratulated the Singapore PM's strong showing in Singapore's September 2015 election. The year 2015 was an eventful year. In that particular significant year of SG50 (Singapore's 50th anniversary after its founding), Mr Abe also attended the funeral of Singapore's founding father Mr Lee Kuan Yew while Deputy PM Taro Aso attended the SG50 National Day Parade (NDP). Both leaders reaffirmed Japan's important regional role when Mr Abe explained his new security legislative initiatives and when Mr Lee noted the successful organisation of the trilateral meeting late 2015. In recognition of Japan's contribution, Singapore supports Japan's aspirations to become a permanent member of the United Nations Security Council (UNSC).

---

[1] Channelnewsasia, "PM Lee, Abe affirm relations between Japan and Singapore" dated 16 December 2013 in Today Online [downloaded on 1 Jan 2016], available at http://www.todayonline.com/singapore/pm-lee-abe-affirm-relations-between-japan-and-singapore.

[2] *Ibid.*

Besides the ruling party, other political parties have also kept up their relationship-building with the Singaporean political establishment. For example, in 2014, New Komeito Chief Natsuo Yamaguchi visited Singapore from 16–19 July 2014 and met with Singaporean Prime Minister Lee Hsien Loong, Emeritus Senior Minister Goh Chok Tong and Minister in the Prime Minister's Office (PMO) and Second Minister for Foreign Affairs Grace Fu while Former Japanese Deputy Prime Minister Katsuya Okada made a trip to Singapore from 1–5 September 2013 as the 39th Lee Kuan Yew Exchange Fellow.[3] When the current opposition party Minshuto (Democratic Party of Japan or DPJ) was in power, its politicians also visited Singapore. Former Prime Minister Yukio Hatoyama went to Singapore in November 2009 and inaugurated the Japan Creative Centre (JCC).[4]

Other than the legislators, the heads of state of Singapore and Japan also visited each other's countries. At the head of state level, the Japanese Emperor Akihito and Empress Michiko carried out an official visit to Singapore in June 2006 and, in return, former President SR Nathan and the first lady went to Japan in May 2009 in their official capacities.[5] The examples above indicated that the legislature and executive have been working closely together with each other at all levels.

Besides diplomatic protocols and state visits, Singapore and Japan have also been cooperating in the field of non-traditional security (NTS). Besides security arrangements that directly impact the geopolitical makeup of the region through the US–Japan alliance, Japan also engages the Southeast Asian region in the softer aspects of security. Both are collaborating in the areas of mitigating infectious diseases (e.g. SARS and avian influenza) and anti-piracy manoeuvres carried out by the coast

---

[3] Ministry of Foreign Affairs (MFA), "Recent bilateral highlights" undated in the Ministry of Foreign Affairs website [downloaded on 1 Jan 2016], available at http://www.mfa.gov.sg/content/mfa/countries_and_region/northeast_asia/japan.html.
[4] GlobalSecurity.org, "Singapore — Foreign Relations" dated 16 Feb 2016 (updated) in the Global Security website [downloaded on 17 Feb 2016], available at http://www.globalsecurity.org/military/world/singapore/forrel.htm.
[5] *Ibid.*

guards of both states.[6] In fact, Japan has a large role in funding and cooperating with the Regional Cooperation Agreement on Combating Piracy and Armed Robbery against Ships in Asia (ReCaap), founded in 2004 and based in Singapore to manage the rise in piracy from 70 attacks in 2010 to 144 in 2014.[7] According to Nishihara, security cooperation between Singapore and Japan is the "oldest" in Southeast Asia and this was pushed one step higher when the two states concluded the Memorandum of Understanding (MOU) on defence cooperation and officer personnel exchanges as part of Japan's overall tightening outreach to ASEAN states to enhance relations through non-combat ways.[8] Other than piracy, Japan is also cooperating with Singapore and ASEAN to stem the spread of terrorist ideology. ASEAN including Singapore as well as Japan are working hard to mitigate extremism and spread of radical ideologies and so in 2015, Singapore organised an East Asian Summit symposium on religious rehabilitation and social reintegration with Japan as a dialogue partner joining in the conversations on these ASEAN priorities.[9]

Overall, Japan is aware of the importance of ASEAN diplomacy, including ties with Singapore. End 2015 marks a flurry of ASEAN diplomacy for all major powers in the East Asian region and Japan is no exception. At APEC Manila, the bilateral summit between the Japanese PM Mr Shinzo Abe and Filipino President Benigno Aquino III discussed security and defence matters. Mrs Abe also took the opportunity to visit

---

[6] GlobalSecurity.org, "Singapore — Foreign Relations" dated 16 Feb 2016 (updated) in the Global Security website [downloaded on 17 Feb 2016], available at http://www.globalsecurity.org/military/world/singapore/forrel.htm.

[7] Nishihara, Masashi, "Japan's emerging security role in Southeast Asia" dated 12 Jan 2016 in Institute of Southeast Asian Studies (ISEAS) Discussion Papers [downloaded on 1 Jan 2016] in the ISEAS Yusof Ishak Institute Regional Outlook Forum 2016 website, available at http://www.iseas-rof.sg/sites/live.rof2016.site.gsi.sg/files/ROF%20Session%202a.pdf.

[8] *Ibid.*

[9] Kawai, Masahiro, Moe Thuzar and Bill Hayton, "ASEAN's regional role and relations with Japan: The challenges of deeper integration" dated Feb 2016 in Chatham House Research Paper [downloaded on 1 March 2016], available at https://www.chathamhouse.org/sites/files/chathamhouse/publications/research/2016-02-18-asean-regional-role-kawai-thuzar-hayton.pdf.

the capacity-building not-for-profit organisation (NPO) Salt Payatas Foundation that has provided help for the women in Quezon City. Mrs Abe was emotional and teary when she visited a facility for housing street-bound kids in Manila. Whether in terms of hard diplomacy like defence or soft first lady diplomacy, the Japanese leader had a productive time in Manila. After the Manila APEC round, the Japanese leader left for Kuala Lumpur (KL) for the ASEAN summit, yet another flurry of diplomatic interactions.

In the economic realm, realising the significance of a combined 600 million-strong consumer market, a young workforce, increasing foreign direct investments, greater net connectivity and tourist arrivals, and Asia's third largest economy, Japan which has production networks in the region for decades is working with ASEAN partners to strengthen cooperation. The AEC was set up on 31 December 2015, an important step that is the start of a long journey to forming a regional economic community. Japanese investments and aid/loans can help the AEC harmonise its standards for a smoother transition to become a regional organisation. The ASEAN Community has three arms: AEC, Political Security Community and the Socio-Cultural Community. Japan, which is East Asia's oldest democracy with harmonious civil society–state relations, has much to offer in terms of experience for the Socio–Cultural Community. The impetus for hastening the Regional Cooperation for Economic Partnership (RCEP) comes from the successfully-concluded Trans Pacific Partnership (TPP) talks although challenges remaining for the ambitious regional plan, including harmonising the standards of a FTA between ASEAN+6 countries and between economies that do not yet have a bilateral FTA. Japan is a stakeholder in both TPP and RCEP. Currently, the TPP seems to be running faster as President Obama is pushing through a Trade Promotion Bill that allows him to gain powers that can accelerate the process of inking FTAs with minimal interference from the US Congress.

On the security front, one month before the ASEAN Summit and APEC Manila on 1 October 2015, Japan led by Cabinet Minister Eriko Yamatani who is the current chairperson of the National Public Safety Commission held the ministerial meeting between Japan and ASEAN on the issues of terrorism and cyber security. Both ASEAN and Japanese

Ministers present at the meeting vowed to have greater information exchanges and conversations between them and the cornerstone of this conversation will be the ASEAN–Japan Cybercrime Dialogue founded in 2014. Japan also asked for ASEAN support in resolving the abduction issue whereby North Korean kidnapped Japanese nationals three to four decades ago. KL will host the Japan–ASEAN dialogue on terrorism and cybercrime early 2016. It is here that KL hopes its information and data on extremists and terrorists can be offered in exchange for help in Japan-developed tracking technologies for human trafficking and cyber-security. KL information may be useful since Japanese citizens had been held hostage and/or executed in the conflict zones in the Middle East.

Singapore and Japan have a close political, geopolitical and security relationship in the region. This relationship is intertwined with the common interests of the East Asian region, which is the maintenance of peace and security for economic development. The relationship is also beneficial to ASEAN, with Singapore as a platform to express the concerns, worries, anxieties, suspicions and friendship of all major powers, middle powers and small states in the region. While political and security represent the "hard" aspects of bilateral cooperation, both countries are also engaged in "softer" economic co-operation which had catalysed economic development in the region, with Singapore as a nimble, fast-mover promoter of FTAs in East Asia and Japan as a major builder of production networks in the Southeast Asia. Both roles are contributive to the formation of an economic community in Southeast Asia. The next chapter surveys the economic ties between Singapore and Japan in this context.

3

Economic Cooperation between Singapore and Japan

Economic relations between Singapore and Japan began shortly after the young nation of the Republic of Singapore was formed. Two years after Singapore's independence, Japan agreed to provide economic assistance to Singapore and Malaysia, starting the path towards bilateral economic co-operation.[1] Japan's influence on Singapore's economic nation building was tremendous, investing in local industries, supplying household items via Japanese-operated mall concepts, concluding Free Trade Agreements (FTAs) with Singapore and transferring skills and technologies and cooperating in the finance sector. After Singapore's independence in 1965, Japan became the largest investor in Singapore during the economic fast-growth period in the 1970s and 1980s. Much of the Japanese investments headed towards Singapore at this point of time were found in the electronics and petrochemical industries.[2] This was a historical period when the four tiger economies (Hong Kong, South Korea, Taiwan and Singapore) started Learning from Japan.

---

[1] Furuoka, Fumitaka, Mikio Oisho and Iwao Kato, "From aid recipient to aid donor tracing the historical transformation of Japan's foreign aid policy" dated 12 July 2010 in Electronic Journal of Contemporary Japanese Studies (ejcjs) [downloaded on 1 Jan 2016], available at http://www.japanesestudies.org.uk/articles/2010/FuruokaOishiKato.html.

[2] Kuboshima, Yuki, "The new trend: Japanese FDI to ASEAN" in British Chamber of Commerce Singapore [downloaded on 1 March 2016], available at http://www.britcham.org.sg/static-pages/o43-japanese-investment.

Historically, post-war Japan worked hard to create conducive conditions for workers and management to work with each other. Company unions facilitate a harmonious working relationship between management and workers since union representatives sit in the management board as well. Company unions helped Japan overcome the rocky and tumultuous relations between workers and management in the immediate post-war period when some militant union workers threatened to take over factories and run the enterprises autonomously by the workers themselves. With labour relations stabilised, salarymen in Japan were promised lifetime employment (LTE) and seniority-based promotion which provided job security for Japanese workers. Because of the successes of post-war economic recovery strategies and efforts, Japan went through a fast-growth phase in the 1960s that was known as the income-doubling plan when incomes effectively doubled for many Japanese working individuals and *sarariman* (salaryman or white-collared executives in the private sector). Japan's fast-growth performance from the 1960s onwards attracted attention from other East Asian economies keen to emulate the successful features of Japanese economic recovery.

The roots of Singapore's process of learning from Japan started in the 1970s. By the 1980s, Singapore promoted the "Learn from Japan" slogan in various industrial sectors successful features of Japanese management. Thang Leng Leng contextualised Singapore's origins of Learning from Japan movement in terms of a response to slowing economic growth in Singapore after the occurrence of the global oil crisis in 1973.[3] The crisis taught Japan and other East Asian economies the importance of developing hi-tech manufacturing industries that are energy efficient and resource-conserving. Singapore was engaged in low skills, manpower-intensive industries and in 1979, its government decided to transform itself into highly-skilled hi-tech workforce and industrial sectors based on the successful features of the Japanese economy and this reached a crescendo in the first half of the 1980s decade.[4]

---

[3] Thang, Leng Leng and S.K. Gan, "Deconstructing 'Japanisation': Reflections from the 'Learn from Japan' campaign in Singapore" dated June 2003 in *New Zealand Journal of Asian Studies* 5, 1, p. 91.
[4] *Ibid.*

Singapore was keen to study certain aspects of Japanese business management, including human resource (HR) training. There are several characteristics of HR training in Japan. First, the importance of *senpai kohai* (senior–junior) relationships — that some training is imparted through on-the-job observation of one's seniors and cannot be comprehensively written down in manuals and in return for the junior's dedication and faith in one's senior colleagues within the company, the senior exercises benevolence and care to nurture the juniors. Therefore, training in this context has an element of human relations (*ningen kankei*), an important aspect of a consensus-seeking and high context culture. Second, Japanese firms like to rotate personnel so that there is cross-training of staff in different skills and also offers opportunities for engineers and technical personnel to learn more about sales and marketing and *vice versa*. This may ensure a high level of knowledge competency, including contents-based domain knowledge.

Third, Japanese firms like standard operating manuals and tend to be meticulous when it comes to procedures and rules. Therefore, training in those procedures ensures employees follow the manuals when they are deployed to perform different functions within a department or company and there is continuity in such procedures when staff are rotated or changed. Certain aspects of this training culture are already incorporated into Singapore's productivity drive based on local conditions. An area that can be the source of further exchanges may be Japan's retail and service quality and training, as both economies are gradually transitioning from a manufacturing-based economy to include a service-oriented economy (especially for Singapore). Singapore can adapt some successful features based on its local conditions, such as the high level of service quality training, knowledge competency in retail sectors, high levels of craftsmanship amongst artisans while recognising the colourful cosmopolitan diversity of heterogeneous cultures in multi-ethnic, multi-racial and multi-religious Singapore.

Besides work ethics, Japanese companies also introduced contemporary concepts of shopping malls to Singapore. The icon of Japanese retailing in Singapore in the 1970s is Yaohan shopping centre. It was the pioneer in one-stop shopping mall concept (catered to both kids' and adults' needs in provision of goods) to cater to Singapore's rising middle class and their changing tastes for retail products starting from its first branch in 1974 in a joint venture (JV) with Development Bank of Singapore (DBS).[5] The 1974 Yaohan flagship store used up a cool S$13 million budget to build and quickly became the largest department store in Singapore with three storeys patronised by some 955,000 people weekly which showed Yaohan's ability to attract customers.[6] The Yaohan model of retailing was replicated throughout Singapore by other super-markets and shopping centres. I personally belonged to the generation of young Singaporeans at that time who patronised Yaohan, purchased cooked food from its fried chicken stall and also started buying my Star Wars toy collection through acquisitions at Yaohan. The bakery at Yaohan was another highlight for me since it served different kinds of Japanese breads like *anpan* (red bean bread) or *melon pan* (honeydew melon flavoured buns). I remembered the chance to observe bakers and cooks at work behind transparent windows at Yaohan. Yaohan also made retail history as the first mall to use the card-based non-cash payments made through the Network of Electronic Transfers Singapore (NETS) system and the Yaohan management eventually set up branches at Ang Mo Kio and Toa Payoh to reach into the Singaporean heartlands as Singaporean became wealthier and willing to spend.[7] Thus, the Yaohan experience penetrated the public housing estate heartlands of Singapore.

Other than the retail sector, the general economy was also tuned into Japan's developmental ideas and concept. By the 1980s, Japan had become an economic superpower and bookstores were filled with pub-lications like Ezra Vogel's *Japan as No. 1*. Japan also set up training facili-ties in Singapore to impart successful features of Japanese management to her Singaporean counterparts. The Economic Development Board (EDB) of Singapore took charge of enhancing the quality of Singapore's workforce and set up skill training institutions with other foreign part-ners to service the HR needs of global technological industries and thus, the Japan–Singapore Training Centre (JSTC), German–Singapore

---

[5] Goh, Kenneth, "Yaohan (Singapore)" dated 29 Jan 2014 in Singapore Infopedia An electronic encyclopedia on Singapore's history, culture, people and events (Singapore: National Library Board), 2014 [downloaded on 1 Jan 2016], available at http://eresources.nlb.gov.sg/infopedia/articles/SIP_2014-01-29_182139. html.

[6] *Ibid.*

[7] *Ibid.*

Institute and French–Singapore Institute were set up.[8] At the officiating ceremony of the newly-established JSTC on 13 January 1981, then Minister for Trade and Industry Goh Chok Tong shared:

> Singapore is now actively restructuring its economy. Training of manpower to upgrade skills is an important element of our economic restructuring policy. But skills alone is not sufficient to guarantee success of the restructuring programme. It must be matched by dedication, discipline and team spirit in work. It is in this respect that cooperation with Japan has an added significance. Japan has become a world economic power despite her almost total lack of natural resources because her people work as one and place national and company interests before self-interests. The Japan–Singapore Training Centre will be an additional medium through which we can learn such work and social attitudes from Japan.[9]

It was during this period when learning from Japan became a catchphrase as Singapore searched for an economic model that would lead its economy along the path of high-tech manufacturing for making items like pagers, disks, chips, notebook computers, computer assembly lines, etc. The Japanese qualities of *gaman* (endurance). *ganbaru* (trying one's best), groupism, collective societal instincts and other cultural characteristics were promoted during this period. The educational and training institutions set up by both countries disseminated both academic courses as well as ideas on social aptitudes at the workplace.

From high-tech manufacturing sectors to equipment in the digital age, Japanese investments in Singapore continually moved up the value chain. By the 1990s, Japanese investments moving into Singapore were mostly found in the telecommunications and mass media industries.[10] In the second decade of the 21st century, companies in the talent management, headhunting, advertising/marketing/public relations firms, professional and services outfits in the business sector joined existing

---

[8] National Archives of Singapore (NAS), "Expansion of infrastructure in the next decade" dated 2009 in the NAS website [downloaded on 1 Jan 2016], available at http://www.nas.gov.sg/1stCab/7585/travel_exh_Sec4.html.
[9] *Ibid.*
[10] Kuboshima, Yuki, "The new trend: Japanese FDI to ASEAN" in British Chamber of Commerce Singapore [downloaded on 1 March 2016], available at http://www.britcham.org.sg/static-pages/o43-japanese-investment.

Japanese companies already here, boosting the number of Japanese subsidiaries in Singapore from 1,500 to at least of 2,000.[11] Shimizu and Hirakawa, writing for a *Routledge* series on history, probably provided one of the most succinct and efficient summation of Japan's economic relations with Singapore in the 1990s (their book was published in 1999):

> The Japanese share in Singapore's total imports rose from 11.1 per cent in 1965 to 16.9 per cent in 1975, 17.9 per cent in 1982, and 18.2 per cent in 1996. In the same years, her share in the country's total exports rose from 3.7 per cent to 8.7 per cent and 10.9 per cent, even though it then declined to 8.2 per cent. Also, since the late 1970s, Japan has been the second largest investor in the country's manufacturing sector, coming after the US...At the end of 1996, there were 3,018 Japanese firms in Singapore, of which 701 were in the manufacturing sector, and the rest were in the services, commerce and other sectors. It is therefore not surprising that in 1996 Singapore had a Japanese population of 25,355, which was the fifth largest in the world, and the largest in Asia outside Japan. The large majority of Japanese residents are company employees and their dependants, and this is reflected in the fact that Singapore boasts the largest Japanese primary school in the world outside Japan. In addition to the residents, there are numerous short-term Japanese visitors to the country. Their number rose sharply from 118,668 in 1975 to 287, 395 in 1980, 377, 686 in 1985, 971, 637 in 1990, and since 1992 it has exceeded one million a year. In 1997, the total number of foreign visitors to Singapore amounted to 7,197,963 of whom 1,094,047 (or 15.2 per cent of total) were Japanese.[12]

From the passage above, Singapore was a major importer of Japanese goods in the 1990s and Singapore's exports to Japan increased until a slight decline in the 1990s, probably due to the onset of Japanese post-bubble economy in that period of time. Besides trading activities, Japan was also the second largest investor in Singapore's Foreign Direct Investments (FDIs)-driven economy with 300 Japanese companies operating in Singapore and the majority of them (about 700) were found in the then high value-added manufacturing sector. Because of this development, the Japanese community continued to expand, forming a visible community in Singapore, resulting in the need to introduce

---

[11] *Ibid.*

[12] Shimizu, Hiroshi and Hirakawa Hitoshi, *Japan and Singapore in the World Economy* (NY and London: Routledge), 1999.

infrastructures and facilities like Japanese schools to serve the needs of the community. This number is supplemented by tourists and other short-term stayers and visitors coming to Singapore, making up almost 1/7th of Singapore's tourism arrival total in the 1990s.

In the 10th Japan–Singapore Symposium (JSS) started since 1994, scholars and thinkers gathered to discuss the state of Singapore–Japan relations before SJ50 (the establishment of Singapore–Japan ties' 50th anniversary) in 2016. Economics appeared to be an important element in this relationship, according to the event's keynote speech. Keynote Speaker Minister of State for Finance and Transport Josephine Teo noted that Japan had an accumulated direct investment in Singapore to the turn of US$50 billion and a top three investor alongside the US and European Union (EU).[13] Today, Singapore continues to regard Japan as a leading producer of cutting-edge technologies in the world. International Enterprise Singapore (IE Singapore) encourages Singaporean companies to reach out to the Japanese tech sector:

> Japan remains a global technology leader, allowing Singapore companies who forge technology partnerships with them to increase their capability and global competitiveness.[14]

Besides tech goods and manufacturing collaborations, Japan also offers a living lab for implementing and retailing technologies useful for the elderly because, by 2050, above 40% of the population will be 65 years old or older.[15] Besides products targeted at the silver elderly population, according to IE Singapore, there are also opportunities in the

---

[13] Teo, Josephine, "Keynote address by Minister of State for Finance and Transport Josephine Teo at the 10th anniversary of JSS 20 November 2014, 0910 hours at Orchard Hotel Singapore" in the Lee Kuan Yew School of Public Policy (LKYSPP) website [downloaded on 1 Jan 2016], available at http://www.google.com.sg/url?sa=t&rct=j&q=&esrc=s&source=web&cd=13&ved=0ahUKEwj3u7Tp0O7KAhUPcI4KHccBB1s4ChAWCCYwAg&url=http%3A%2F%2Flkyspp.nus.edu.sg%2Fips%2Fwp-content%2Fuploads%2Fsites.

[14] IE Singapore, "Why Japan?" in IE Singapore website [downloaded on 1 Feb 2016], available at http://www.iesingapore.gov.sg/Venture-Overseas/Browse-By-Market/Asia-Pacific/Japan/Country-Information.

[15] *Ibid.*

renewable energy sector as Japan's economy has competitive feed-in-tariffs (FIT) for renewable energy, a contributing reason for the Japanese renewable energy industry's economic growth trajectory to become the globe's third biggest solar power industry.[16]

Other than technological developers, at the state level, the two countries are creating frameworks conducive to push bilateral ties to a higher level. Bilateral negotiations between Singapore and Japan on an FTA known later as the Japan–Singapore Economic Agreement for a New Age Partnership (JSEPA) was held on 31 January 2001. Mr Lim Chin Beng, a private sector leader and former Singapore Ambassador to Japan represented the Singapore side for the negotiations. At the political executive level, former Prime Ministers Goh Chok Tong and Yoshiro Mori expressed political will at the highest level for the partnership agreement to succeed. The JSEPA became effective on 30 November 2007. Singapore exported more plastic, chemical and petroleum products to Japan while Japan exported more alcohol to Singapore.[17] Because of the JSEPA, Japan conceptualised Singapore as the research and development (R&D) platform for the Association of Southeast Asian Nations (ASEAN).[18] History was made in this way when Singapore became the first state with whom Japan signed an economic partnership in further advancement of free trade.

With every milestone and closer economic ties, Singapore now hosts many Japanese operational headquarters (OHQs). Singapore's low taxes, availability of human talents, open and transparent economy, rule of law, geographical location, lack of political upheavals, widespread use of English and little restrictions on capital flows are some of the attractive points found in the Singapore economy. A state fund worth S$6.1 billion to attract investments beyond just semiconductors was started in 2010 with a duration of six years and it motivated Japanese companies

---

[16] *Ibid.*

[17] Ministry of Foreign Affairs (MOFA) Japan, "Joint Statement of the Japanese and Singapore Ministers at the Ministerial Review Meeting on the Agreement Between Japan and the Republic of Singapore for a New-Age Economic Partnership" dated 11 December 2003 in the MOFA website [downloaded on 1 Jan 2016], available at http://www.mofa.go.jp/policy/economy/fta/singapore.html.

[18] *Ibid.*

like Hitachi and Mitsui Chemical to invest in higher value-added R&D activities.[19] Besides industrial and R&D value-adding, Singapore and Japan are also working closely together in the financial sector. The Bank of Japan, on behalf of the Minister of Finance of Japan, and the Monetary Authority of Singapore (MAS) concluded and inked the third Bilateral Swap Arrangement (BSA) on 21 May 2015 to swap their currencies *vis-a-vis* US dollars.[20] Singapore is able to swap Singapore dollars against US dollars to a maximum of US$3 billion and Japan can swap yen with USD upto US$1 billion.[21]

The next lap in economic destiny between the two countries lies in their common stakeholder interests in the success of the Trans-Pacific Partnership (TPP). The TPP is likely to bind both countries closer to their major ally, the United States. In the near future, we are likely to see a more equitable partnership between Singapore and Japan since the former has evolved from a learner economy adapting from Japanese management practices and economic features to a model from which Japanese could pick out the best practices for indigenisation. This is especially the case in the financial sector where Singapore has become a leading financial centre in the region, e.g. Singapore's leading status and golden standard features of free trade with other nations in the world, the operations of the world's second largest casino sector after Macau that is socially and ethically conscious and also built into a one-stop entertainment and family activity centre known as integrated resorts. Japan is known to have an interest in studying these integrated resorts. Singapore's ability to attract global foreign talents as a migrant melting pot, ethnically and racially heterogeneous society is also a case study for Japan's homogenous society seeking for solutions to cope with an ageing society that needs more manpower.

---

[19] Kuboshima, Yuki, "The new trend: Japanese FDI to ASEAN" in British Chamber of Commerce Singapore [downloaded on 1 March 2016], available at http://www.britcham.org.sg/static-pages/o43-japanese-investment.

[20] MAS, "Signing of the Third Bilateral Swap Agreement between Japan and Singapore" dated 21 May 2015 in the MAS website [downloaded on 4 March 2016], available at http://www.mas.gov.sg/news-and-publications/media-releases/2015/signing-of-the-third-bilateral-swap-agreement-between-japan-and-singapore.aspx.

[21] *Ibid.*

Given Singapore's fast economic development and Japan's interests in sharing new cutting-edge technologies (this volume has a chapter on Akihabara), creative collaborations are also likely candidates for intensifying economic exchanges in the near future. They may have in fact already started. MOSH!, Singapore's pioneer in immersive digital media playground, will open in February 2016 in Sentosa designed by several Japanese collaborators like digitisation company Coconoe and creative design firm 1→10.[22] MOSH! required a budget of US$1.8 million (S$2.5 million) for its materialisation as a family entertainment centre that maximises creativity and imagination in education and recreational activities. It features high-tech interactive digital and projection technologies to create a virtual world.[23] According to Hitomi Komuro, director of Creative Future Park who leads MOSH!, the project is:

> ...an apt cultural exchange as we bring the Japanese unique brand of creativity to Singapore...[for] the celebrations of the 50th anniversary of diplomatic relations between Singapore and Japan.[24]

Here, three trends appear discernible. Technological exchanges which is symbolised in the collaborative work in MOSH! appear to be a trend in current and near-future collaborations between the two countries. The statement highlights the unique quality of Japanese creative works and this appears to be MOSH!'s value-add to Singapore's creative scene, a Japanese interpretation of digital arts for a cosmopolitan city. MOSH! was also cited as a commemorative project for half a century of relations, indicating the importance of creative cultural exchanges as a cornerstone of bilateral ties.

Finally, with economic development came responsibilities and obligations for Singapore and Japan. Singapore and Japan have also dispensed their responsibility to the region under the Japan–Singapore Partnership Programme for the 21st Century (JSPP21) by funnelling

---

[22] Sile, Aza Wee, "SG50 sequel: Singapore, Japan to launch SJ50 to celebrate bilateral ties" dated 31 Dec 2015 in CNBC AsiaOne website [downloaded on 1 Jan 2016], available at http://business.asiaone.com/news/sg50-sequel-singapore-japan-launch-sj50-celebrate-bilateral-ties.

[23] *Ibid.*

[24] *Ibid.*

technical help to other developing economies.[25] At the state level and fostering co-operation between educational agencies, diplomatic institutions and not-for-profit foundations, Singapore and Japan have also been collaborating in capacity-building activities for other ASEAN countries. For example, Singapore's IP Academy organised a 5-day long training course on Intellectual Property (IP) for ASEAN members from 13 to 17 October 2014 and it was funded by Singapore Cooperation Programme of the Ministry of Foreign Affairs (MFA) Singapore and the Japan International Cooperation Agency (JICA) under the Japan–Singapore Partnership Programme for the 21st Century.[26] Singapore and Japan's Intellectual Property Rights (IPRs) knowledge was disseminated to the ASEAN member states' representatives. Feedback from the representatives of the member states were generally positive. Dindo Dumali, IPR Specialist working in the Information and Technology Transfer Bureau Philippines, made the following statement:

> I think the programme is very good, especially in terms of having a new perspective on how IP is viewed in different countries. Indeed, ASEAN countries, if united, will really be a force, and having such a programme like this is a big step towards that goal. I hope more collaborations like this will take place in the near future. Thank you for the great time as well as lessons learned![27]

The feedback indicated the value-added quality of including comparative angles in the syllabus on IPRs. The comment also showed some of the participants' desire to use the Singaporean–Japanese funds for

---

[25] GlobalSecurity.org, "Singapore — Foreign Relations" dated 16 Feb 2016 (updated) in the Global Security website [downloaded on 17 Feb 2016], available at http://www.globalsecurity.org/military/world/singapore/forrel.htm.

[26] IP Academy, "Singapore and Japan Conducted Joint Intellectual Property Programme for ASEAN" dated 2015 in the IP Academy website [downloaded on 15 Feb 2016], available at https://www.ipacademy.com.sg/ipa/announcements/singapore-and-japan-conducted-joint-intellectual-property-programme-for-asean.

[27] IP Academy, "Singapore and Japan conducted Joint Intellectual Property Programme for ASEAN" dated 2015 in the IP Academy website [downloaded on 15 Feb 2016], available at https://www.ipacademy.com.sg/ipa/announcements/singapore-and-japan-conducted-joint-intellectual-property-programme-for-asean.

reaching the goals of ASEAN unity, something increasingly important in the construction of the ASEAN Economic Community (AEC).

Educational initiatives embedded in the bilateral co-operation between the two countries sometimes involve third parties like the International Organisations (IOs) as well. The IMF–Singapore Regional Training Institute (STI), based in Singapore and funded by the governments of Singapore and Japan, is the International Monetary Fund's (IMF) Asia-Pac training centre for instructions on macroeconomics, finance, law and statistic courses to an audience of civil servants and bureaucrats from 37 countries.[28] Offering courses 14 days in duration for ranking bureaucrats and civil servants, the STI is a beneficiary of the Singapore Cooperation Program and the Japan Subaccount for IMF that provides capacity building to other states and it annually trains more than 800 government personnel through courses as well as 100 officials through participation in national or regional courses outside Singapore.[29] Historically, from 1998 onwards, the STI trained more than 10,000 officials,[30] an achievement and feat in terms of a senior officials training system.

In sum, Singapore and Japan are likely to intensify their respective roles as nodes within the East Asian economies that can provide economic developmental training to other economies in the region, promote free trade by institutionalising structures and regulations to break down barriers, stimulate technological cooperation to disseminate technological knowhow to the Southeast Asian region in the latter's industrialisation process, enhance connectivity between economies in the region by encouraging production networking first set up by Japan in the past few decades. Both countries are likely to promote a form of loose, open, market-driven regionalisation that foster greater economic interdependence between different economies in East Asia. Singaporean

---

[28] STI, "Welcome to the IMF — Singapore Regional Training Institute" dated 2006 in the STI website [downloaded on 1 Jan 2016], available at http://www.imfsti.org/.
[29] STI, "Welcome to the IMF — Singapore Regional Training Institute" dated 2006 in the STI website [downloaded on 1 Jan 2016], available at http://www.imfsti.org/.
[30] *Ibid.*

is likely to value add to that process by being the neutral economic platform for all major economies to work together. To get an individual glimpse of how future Singaporeans view Japan's economy, business management methodologies and the prospects of learning from Japan, the next chapter takes the form of an experiential writing by a young Singaporean who made a visit to Japan on a study trip specifically designed to immerse in Japan's corporate culture, understand Japanese business practices and interact with Japanese business executives. It is not designed to be comprehensive but raises some points that may possibly shed some thoughts about future economic and business cooperation from the standpoint and perspective of a young Singaporean. This is followed by another experiential writing by an employee of a Japanese retail outlet based in Singapore. Another young Singaporean writes about her impressions of working in a Japanese retail outlet based in Singapore. She provides a standpoint perspective of Japanese service quality and also interesting observations on how Singaporean and Japanese employees interact with each other in a mixed setting with both nationals present in the same workplace. This chapter rounds up the collection of writings related to Japanese economy and business management.

4

A Survey of Japanese Management in Singapore

Kong Tuan Yuen*

Preface

Singapore separated from Malaysia and became an independent country in 1965. Singapore realised that it lacked natural resources to jump-start economic growth, so the Singaporean government provided a lot of economic incentives to attract foreign investments to support industrialisation and economic development, and then built up Jurong Industrial Park in 1968. Taking the advantage of lower labour costs and well-established seaports constructed in the British colonial period (1819–1963), Singapore grew to become one of the major electronic and petrochemical manufacturing countries in the world in the 1970s.

Japan established formal diplomatic relationship with Singapore from 1966, one year after Singapore became an independent country. In the

---

*Dr Kong used to work at a Japanese multinational company/enterprise (MNC) in Malaysia which moved from Singapore in 1988, to conduct business management, financial and planning analysis for four years. During his service with the MNC, he was sent to Japan to learn about Toyota's production system and manufacturing automation. He also conducted research on several case studies about Japanese manufacturing companies to compare the business management style.

1970s, the high value of the Japanese yen and the increasing labour costs led the Japanese companies to relocate their businesses outside Japan. Most of them selected Southeast Asian countries as the first destination, especially Singapore. The Japanese companies quickly became the largest foreign investor and trading partner in Singapore by the 1970–1980s.

Established Japanese electronics companies such as Hitachi, Panasonic and petrochemical companies, like Mitsui Chemical for example, followed after one another to move their partial production line from Japan to Singapore. Japanese companies contributed a quarter of Singapore's GDP in this period.[1] From 1990s onwards, Japanese companies also established or extended their businesses to telecommunications, home appliances and the semiconductor sector in Singapore.

For example, the production line of television sets (Hitachi, Toshiba and Mitsubishi), radio and radio cassette recorders (Daihatsu, Matsushita Electric and Sanyo) and hi-fidelity audio (JVC, Foster Electric and Trio Kenwood) were built up in Singapore during this period.[2] Apart from consumer electronics, industrial electronics was another major component of Japanese investment in Singapore this period. Fujitsu developed public switching equipment; NEC facilitated the manufacture of software devices; Toshiba set up elevator system production; Mineba manufactured the office printers.

In these decades, there was a lot of technology transfer from Japan to local companies and universities. For instance, moulding and cutting techniques for manufacturing the body coverings of electrical devices such as radio were transferred to local companies. It was worthy to note that Japanese companies not only brought such manufacturing and production technology to Singapore, but they also trained and educated the workers in Japanese management culture. At that point of time, some in the West believed work ethics is what has driven the "miracle" of Japanese economy.

---

[1] Cronin, Richard, *Japan, the U.S., and Prospects for the Asia Pacific Century* (Singapore: Institute of Southeast Asian Studies), 1992.
[2] Basu, R. Dipak and Victoria Miroshnik, *Japanese Foreign Investments, 1970–1998: Perspectives and Analyses* (New York: M. E. Sharpe Inc), 2000.

Toyota Production System (TPS)

TPS, known as Toyota way, was first introduced worldwide to eliminate the "overburden" (*muri*), inconsistency (*mura*) and waste (*muda*) in the production processes for increasing the production efficiency. It has been extended to seven wastes elimination processes which included overproduction, waiting, transporting, inappropriate processing, unnecessary inventory, excess motion and defects.

Waste in terms of overproduction always happen in manufacturing a product when it does not have proper plan and targeted customer. The consequence of overproduction will result in the waste of raw materials and labour costs, then a loss in revenues. Waiting is defined as the waste of time in a manufacturing process to make a product. For example, manufacturing a screw has seven processes, in total needing two hours to finish making it. But it could be delayed more than that if there are no proper arrangements because some processes need to wait in line for the one before it to be completed. "Transporting" is defined as moving one thing from a location to another. It could lead to wastage if the every step in the manufacturing process is located in different factories. The high level of inventory storage always causes unnecessary waste when the finished good becomes dead stock. Some products can be made in a five-step processes, but it takes seven-steps processes. This kind of waste has been called excess motion. And finally the defect product is the ultimate waste item. The value-addedness in every part of the process that goes into making the defected products such as labour time will amount to nothing because it cannot be sold.

Another three concepts of production management has been introduced based on the seven wastes elimination processes: Just in Time (JIT), *Jidoka* (Automation) and *Heijuka* (Standardisation). JIT is a concept to produce anything when it is just needed at that time. No excess supply, so when the demand is there, the production run initiates and the supplier provides just enough raw materials and the factory uses just enough manpower to make the product. No waste results. For this purpose, production automation and standardisation should be observed to avoid the waste in waiting, excess motion and so on.

The TPS concept has been implemented in Singapore's manufacturing industry nationwide. For example, The SSI SCHAEFER Singapore, ranked as the world's largest material handling system supplier for eight consecutive years, had helped Borneo Motor Singapore design a warehousing system based on the TPS concept and its extended storage techniques in order to relocate the Borneo Motors Central Parts Depot (CPD) to Senkee Logistics Hub. The TPS-based design is a multifunctional warehouse which maximises productivity and minimises logistics cost needed to fulfil the customers' orders.

Lean Production

After the development of TPS, a number of production management and techniques were explored to push forward the knowledge of production efficiency. They are integrated into the Lean Production system. The first important concepts that almost all the manufacturing companies implement are 5S and 3T. 5S comprises sort (*seiri*), set in order (*seiso*), shine (*seiton*), standardise (*seiketsu*) and sustain (*shitsuke*). This is a method many workers follow in the Japanese workplace. For example, everything in the sort room should be sorted and set in order. The place needs to be cleaned up routinely and this kind of job could be standardised and maintained every time and everywhere constantly. Paired with 5S, 3T is specified to decide what items (*Tie Hin*), where (*Tie*) and how much (*Tie Riyo*) are needed to insert certain things in specified areas. For instance, in a toolbox, what kind of screwdriver needs to be standby, placed in what layer and how many pieces are needed to be there. It is useful for everyone to know these standardised information, is easy to access and saves time when locating a particular tool. Consequently, some Singapore-based Japanese companies that provide logistics services and engineering solutions have added 5S training and introductory games in the employee's orientation programme.

Single Minute Exchange of Die (SMED) is another method that has been widely applied in the production flow management. Every production flow could be divided into several internal and external activities which have similar wastage potential, respectively. For example, die change-over is categorised as an internal activity which means the production line should be stopped. Engineers should try and implement new measures to externalise the die change-over, and then the production could be kept running. Meanwhile, they will try to shorten the die change-over time, so the total time impact of this procedure on the production line is limited.

The Kanban system is highlighted to assist the promotion of JIT. The term "Kanban" means a signboard or panel which show how much materials each section of the production line needed within the entire process. The Kanban system is an inventory control system for each component of the production line to provide signals to the supply chain. Kanban cards are always applied in the production process to tell the upper stream process the items and volumes of materials needed. Thus, Kanban system is also known as a demand-driven system, the volume of products needed to be manufactured is made known through the Kanban cards from the first process that involves the supply chain onwards. The material inventory controller also orders the required materials from external suppliers based on the information indicated on the Kanban cards. No wastage will be created unless there are some natural defects. There are several training centres in Singapore such as LeanKanban University that provided the certification for Kanban practitioners for understanding Kanban techniques and modifying the processes to limit the impact to the current production situation in areas like reallocating staff or manpower.

Poka-yoke system (error-proofing) is also implemented under the TPS and expanded in the lean production system. Simply speaking, Poka-yoke emphasises the need to insert some manufacturing techniques or processes to avoid human errors in the production process. For example, stainless steel for manufacturing printer components need to undergo plating for anti-rust qualities with the procedure taking up two hours, engineer will set a timer in the process to alert the operators following standard procedure. Poka-yoke system is followed not only to avoid the past mistakes made in production, but also tries to shape the human behaviour under a controlled environment that minimises defects.

Value stream mapping is applied to analyse the value of the product model from the start to the end of the production process when it is sold to the end customer. From this map, flow management is implemented to assess the target, problem and solution of each step of the process, and find out the value-adding time and non-value-adding time. Of course, the non-value-adding time is the time wastage that needs to be eliminated. Value stream mapping is the process to draw out the whole flow of product manufacturing and single out the unnecessary parts that potentially waste time, production space or even create more defects.

In Singapore, the "Lean" concept has gradually become an essential component for the industrial development and operations, equipping personnel such as the Lean production engineer in the production organisation to maximise the productivity. By searching the Jobstreet. com, lean production positions or related jobs posted by Singapore manufacturing companies can easily be found. For example, a multinational enterprise of the global data storage solution frequently hire Lean production engineers who have good experiences in applying lean manufacturing tools, value stream mapping and other lean knowledge. Another Singapore-based global leader of integrated marine and offshore engineering solution put out an ad for a risk management manager who is familiar with lean improvement tools. Among the job vacancies that I spotted, process improvement and quality controller has become a very popular position in the current manufacturing industry.

Total Quality Management (TQM)

TQM is another concept similar to TPS and Lean, but focused more on quality management issues. Most management studies believe that the term TQM originated from Armand V. Feigenbaum's book *Total Quality Control* and Kaoru Ishikawa's *What Is Total Quality Control? The Japanese Way*. The fundamental concept behind TQM is establishing company culture, management and organisation through quality control method in order to satisfy customer products and services needs. It is continuous process with an accent on constant improvement as a keyword to increase the quality standards of a company's manufacturing and production activities.

The Japanese word *Kaizen* means continuous improvement, frequently implemented in manufacturing companies. *Kaizen* does not only focus on skills upgrading, but also on machine equipment and management level improvements. There is a 4M checklist to motivate *Kaizen* activity, centred on the key concepts of man, machine, material and method. "Man" improvement indicates the operator-line skill, department communication skill, executive and manager management skill, CEO annual factory planning and business management skill and so on. "Machine" improvement concerns efforts to increase the productivity, for example modifying the speed of cutting or stamping to improve the industrial production output per minute. Quality maintenance in output such as changing tool and compliments is also one of the topics often highlighted in machine equipment upgrading and improvements. Material improvement focuses on the kinds of materials used in the production, their costs and reasons for the choice of materials. The quality of the material, including the criteria of hardness, density and anti-rustiness, is always checked for possible constant improvements in their performance and properties. Last but not the least, "method" improvement and upgrading suggests the need to apply the effective and productive procedures or processes to complete an assigned task. In the production line, reducing the costs needed and time taken for a particular manufacturing process is important for business profitability. In Japanese management, having employees follow instructions closely and organising routine communication meetings are important management procedures. Japanese companies in Singapore often organised *Kaizen* competitions within and between companies to share and learn the constant improvement activities with each other. Some of them also sent their employees to their own mother companies in Japan to acquire new skills for improvement and knowledge upgrading.

From the sustainability report of a Japanese multinational that I worked for in 2015, they made a lot of efforts on organising Kaizen activities. This company conducted E-Kaizen competitions among their subsidiaries around the world. The E-Kaizen teams which come from various parts of the world, termed as the "Japan bloc", "China bloc", "Southeast Asia bloc" and "Europe/America bloc", are selected to take part in the Worldwide Team Presentations Conference for President Award. The Award raises the awareness of the need for continuous improvement.[3] Fuji Xerox Singapore, a leader in printer services and solutions,

---

[3] <Sustainability Report 2015> Epson Group. Accessed on http://global.epson.com/SR/report/2015/pdf/epson_sr2015_all_e.pdf.

also conducts yearly competitive benchmarking surveys to ensure their quality products in the printer market. They organised a minimum of six cross-departmental *Kaizen* teams to evaluate the result from the survey and determine the direction towards further improvement.

Apart from Kaizen, PDCA is another method frequently used in TQM to encourage improvements and upgrading. PDCA is a cyclical procedure comprising four processes, which includes plan, do, check and action. It can be used in any kinds of processes or management techniques. For instance, typically in implementation, the CEO formulates a mid-term plan and requests all the departments to stick to this general direction to design their own annual plans for the company. After the annual plan is approved, it would be implemented (the "do" component of PDCA) accordingly. The department will carry out monthly or quarterly checks to confirm whether the planning is followed closely and achievable at different stages. If the plan does not go smoothly, then the management would take action to tweak the target or modify the original plan. Hypothetically, for example, when the CEO of a Japanese multinational set a target to reduce the production cost by 10% in a particular year. After carrying out further studies, it became achievable when procurement department was willing to give up the original plan to use Japan-manufactured materials and switched to China-manufactured materials. In turn, the procurement department would formulate a modified plan to implement the new instructions for materials procurement, for example, changing 75% of their materials source from place of origin within half a year. The management then tracks the progress made after this same half year period. In reality, the target would not be reached if the Chinese sub-contractor cannot provide the required volume of products made according to the quality standards prescribed or if the Chinese sub-contractor suddenly raises the price of the ordered materials. In such cases, if unexpected obstacles surface, the manager would modify the original plan or negotiate with their Chinese sub-contractor again in order to achieve the original plan and schedule with minimal disruptions to the procurement budget. After their plan is implemented, the PDCA cycle would be revisited again to make continuous improvements.

Continuing with this example derived from my experience, in term of TQM's implementation techniques, the Seven Basic Tools of Quality

Control (QC) was introduced for tracking and controlling the quality in the process. It was a useful graphically-based reader-friendly technique for troubleshooting problems including Cause–Effect diagram (also known as a fishbone or Ishikawa diagram), Check Sheet, Control Chart, Histogram, Pareto Chart, Scatter Diagram, Stratification (flow chart). Another Seven New Tools created recently include Affinity Diagram, Relation Diagram (why–why analysis), Tree Diagram, Arrow Diagram, Process Decision Program Chart and Matrix Data Analysis. Both the basic tools and the new tools are developed to help employees visualise the problem solving and troubleshooting processes to continuously improve the quality of products and services and fulfil the customer needs and requirements.

Others

Besides these management concepts which are derived and further developed from the TPS, Lean Production System and TQM, there are some other form of non-processes-based knowledge derived from Japanese companies' business philosophies, especially in terms of managing human relationships. The senior–junior relationship is one of the most important components in Japanese business management. When a newcomer enters a Japanese enterprise, they are placed in a junior role for a couple years in order to learn about the unique aspects of the company culture and study the experiences of senior employees, even if they have paper qualifications in terms of higher education degrees.

In Japan, loyalty to the company is very crucial for newcomers. Normally, when you select a company after graduating from a college or university, it means you will work there for a substantial period of time. Inversely, the entrepreneurs are responsible for their employee's welfare for life. This feature of Japanese corporate culture was transplanted to Singapore and implemented for a substantial period of time amongst Japanese companies. However, Singapore is an open society and a host for various multinational enterprises from different countries and cultures, employee mobility and job-hopping to other companies with better conditions is the norm. No matter how the overall economic situation changed, a substantial number of Japanese employees working in the same company for 25 years are not uncommon.

Some companies also turned to the "Horenso" concept to improve business communication among the employees to avoid the information flow obstruction or misunderstanding. *Horenso* is a Japanese word, an acronym combined from three words that means "report", "contact" and "consult". This concept requires every subordinate to report to their superior when there are some irregular events or special findings in the manufacturing process. The superior needs to call and hold a meeting with related parties to share this information or to discuss with their top management. Finally, the management needs to make crucial decisions and then consult with their subordinates to implement the new instructions to cope with irregularities. These processes can be implemented in any place and at any time and sometimes it is also initiated by superior or management-level employees if they spot something amiss.

Conclusion

Japanese multinational companies are some of the earliest countries to invest in Singapore. Due to the economic successes of Japanese firms in the 1980s and 1990s, some Singaporean firms adopted Japanese management practices and absorbed their knowledge and techniques to implement in their own businesses. Actually, Japanese business management is not only popular in Singapore, but is also studied in other western countries such as the US during that period, e.g. Toyota's ideas about *kaizen*. Compared to the West, there are some aspects of Singaporean work and corporate culture that resemble closer to Japanese culture, those elements are then expanded and implemented selectively in local companies.

Japanese management is also taught in college and universities, through prescribed business management textbooks and the MBA case studies. Some management training centre also adopt the Japanese management materials to teach participants, for example, why lean production is useful and implemented in some companies. For example, The Singapore Productivity Association (SPA) as an affiliated body of the then National Productivity Board [now known as Standards, Productivity and Innovation Board (SPRING Singapore)], often organises overseas study missions based on Continuous improvement — TPS to pick up productivity concepts and its techniques.

Nowadays, in the globalisation era, Singapore companies will apply various management techniques to meet their own manufacturing and management processes needs. The TPS, Lean production, TQM and other techniques can be applied appropriately according to management needs. Selected elements of Japanese business management techniques are still major areas of study, research, training and implementations in Singaporean local companies.

5

Japan's Corporate Sector: Perspectives from a University Student

Aomi Poh Ming Ying

In January 2016, UniSIM organised an Overseas Study Mission (OSM) to Japan, during which UniSIM students had the opportunity to visit several large Japanese corporations and emerging enterprises. Companies visited included Oriental Motors, Honda Motors and Panasonic. It was my first time visiting Japanese companies, and through these on-site visits, I was able to achieve a deeper understanding of them. To give a brief biographical background, I am half Japanese, and currently live in Singapore. Also, I have previously been to Japan on personal trips and cultural exchange programmes. Formerly, I studied Japanese in the MOE Language Centre during my secondary school and Junior College schooling period. Thus, I do have some prior knowledge of Japanese culture.

Before the OSM, each student was asked to identify a theme we were interested in and to prepare questions to ask the representatives of the various companies. At the end of the trip, in our groups, we had to present our learning points and observations to the group. My group tackled three main topics which are internal management, challenges and crisis and management and decisions. There were six members in my group and we worked in pairs on one of the three main topics. I was put in charge of the restructuring portion. During the OSM, there were various interesting points that I observed. These included Japanese culture in general and their unique working culture. It was personally intriguing to observe how Japan's working culture differs from western countries. Through these visits, I observed changes in Japan's traditions and their attempt to adapt to the modern corporate environment and become more globalised.

Throughout the trip, I observed some general Japanese working culture etiquette. Firstly, when we entered a company's premises, we had to remove our winter coats. Not doing so may come across as rude because wearing your coat in the building may imply that the heating is not strong enough. Also, dispensing name cards is very important in Japanese corporate culture. The name card is handed out using both hands, with the words facing in the direction of the receiver. Similarly, the receiver receives the name card with both hands as a sign of respect. Punctuality is very important, especially for formal meetings. Being punctual is the most basic form of respect towards the other party. It is important to be sensitive and aware of the other party's feelings, and to take the appropriate actions.

The collective behaviour of Japanese people is something prevalent in Japanese society, and in the corporate sector. Japanese people normally identify themselves as a group rather than as an individual. Also, more emphasis is placed on harmony, which is also known as *wa*. For there to be minimal friction in a group, the concept of *wa* is applied. The concept of *wa* dates back to the seventh century, when Japan was primarily an agricultural country. During that time, as Japan was a mountainous country with minimal natural resources and land for living and farming, people had to cooperate with each other to survive.[1] The idea of *wa* is closely related to the concept of *Honne* and *Tatemae*, which means true opinion and public façade. To elaborate further, *Honne* means to speak one's true feelings, while *Tatemae* means to put on a public façade to maintain politeness so that one does not come across as offensive and aggressive. It is expected for people to hide their true

---

[1] Inc., POV, "The concept of wa | Kokoyakyu | POV | PBS" dated 2016 in *POV | American Documentary Inc.*, available at http://www.pbs.org/pov/kokoyakyu/the-concept-of-war/.

feelings on many occasions to come across as being polite.[2] *Honne* and *Tatemae* are examples of Japanese cultural practices that result in a harmonious society. *Tatemae* is normally practiced in most circumstances, while the concept of *Honne* is used only in a close relationship.

I asked some of the company representatives the following question: "What are some strategies that can be used or have been used to boost morale to increase productivity of your employees". The answers I received surprised me as I was expecting companies to incentivise their employees through material and financial benefits. However, they mainly mentioned that they do not specifically incentivise their employees in this way. The employees are constantly reminded of the company's goals and missions and all employees work together as a whole towards the sole objective, which is the betterment of the company. This differs greatly from western companies, where individualism is encouraged and the idea of placing the group's interests before one's own is not very common.[3] Another example is the design of name cards. On the name card, the company's name is usually in the largest font size, and it typically identifies the cardholder as an employee of the company and not as an individual.

Although collectiveness and the concept of *wa* are part of Japanese culture, I opine that the companies may be placing much emphasis on these by boosting communication among employees. Through the dialogues with the company representatives, I have noticed that their communication methods result in aligned values that enhance collectiveness and boost motivation. Oriental Motors, a medium-sized enterprise, maintains its corporate identity internationally by regularly having meetings with leaders in Japan and visits to factories. This is especially important for overseas factories as when Japanese leaders visit the factories, they impart their culture, values and technology. Similarly in Honda Motors, Japanese officers are dispatched to overseas factories to impart culture and technology.

---

[2] Spacey, John, "Harmony in Japanese culture," dated 2016 in *Japan Talk*, available at http://www.japan-talk.com/jt/new/harmony-in-japanese-culture.

[3] Japan in Perspective, "Japanese collectivism vs western individualism — Japan in perspective" dated 2014, available at http://www.japaninperspective.com/japanese-collectivism-vs-western-individualism/.

Another key point is that the Japanese people display a very strong sense of loyalty towards the company they are working for. This loyalty is encapsulated in the term *karoushi*. *Karoushi* is when one dies from overworking, and they literally die their work desk. Loyalty is also closely linked to the *Ganbaru and Gaman spirit*, where employees put in their best at work and do not give up easily. The main reason behind the *Ganbaru and Gaman spirit* is to ensure that they do not burden their fellow peers and pull the whole team down. The *Ganbaru spirit* can be said to be one of the defining features of the Japanese workplace.[4] Japan is a country where employees work long hours as compared to their counterparts. Approximately 22% of Japanese work more than 49 hours in a week as compared to 16% of Americans, 11% of French and Germans.[5] Also, it is common for annual leave not to be fully consumed as Japanese employees feel guilty for taking leave to rest and recharge, when their fellow colleagues are still working. To have a deeper understanding of employee loyalty towards their company, I asked Alix Partners, a restructuring company, what incentives they used to prevent employees from leaving the company when their company is undergoing restructuring. They replied by saying that they are transparent about the company's current situation, and that most employees remain loyal and do not leave the company once they understand the situation of the company. The spirit of loyalty displayed by the Japanese was extraordinary as they chose to stay in the company and help to rebuild the company, rather than to leave the company and find a new job. Also, through the trip I have learnt that it was common for one to work in the same company till retirement in Japan, and that changing jobs is frowned upon. An individual normally will not change job of their own accord, as it would come across as disloyal. This would make it difficult to be hired in the next company as companies look for loyalty in their employees. Although the lifetime employment system is declining, the practice of individuals remaining in one job for life was widespread in Japan after World War II. This

---

[4] Transitionsabroad.com, "Working in Japan: The Japanese workplace" dated 2016, available at http://www.transitionsabroad.com/listings/work/articles/working-in-japan-the-japanese-workplace.shtml.

[5] McCurry, Justin, "Clocking off: Japan calls time on long-hours work culture" dated 2015 in *The Guardian*, available at http://www.theguardian.com/world/2015/feb/22/japan-long-hours-work-culture-overwork-paid-holiday-law.

means that employees are guaranteed a position in the company till they retire. With a secure job, this results in strong corporate loyalty, team proficiency and high motivation. This fosters a family-like environment in the company, thus employees are inclined to put in their best for the betterment of the company.[6] Also, there was a unique human resource strategy where employees are rotated around different departments. For instance, employees in the engineering department may be assigned to the sales department. I was initially puzzled by this tactic and thought it was counterproductive. I later learnt that it was a method to breed loyalty in the employees, as employees would understand how different departments function better.[7] For instance, when an engineer is assigned to the marketing department, and has more knowledge of the product, he or she may be able to market the product better than someone from the marketing department.

Japan has always been known for its creativeness, innovation and good quality. For instance, "DAISO", a two dollar shop based in Japan, which is known for its simple yet innovative and affordable products now have various franchises in Singapore. Similarly, many of the conglomerates showcased their advanced technology and innovations and left a long-lasting impression, most notably Panasonic and Honda Motors. As part of a tour of Panasonic business solutions, we were shown their smart home — the "Wonder Life-BOX". The "Wonder Life-BOX" is a smart home, which gives us a view into the future as conceived by Panasonic. The concept revolves around "an enriched lifestyle you will admire — Self-designing Life and Comfortable Life". We were given a live demonstration of the "Wonder Life-BOX" and we were thoroughly fascinated by it. In the Wonder Life-BOX, there is a

---

[6] Alston, John, and Isao Takei, "Japanese business culture and practices: A guide to twenty-first century business" dated 2016, available at https://books.google.com.sg/books?id=6lJTqe_IwdsC&pg=PA81&lpg=PA81&dq=japan+lifetime+employment+system+leads+to+loyalty&source=bl&ots=l8i9GAmJ6J&sig=Zpso6j6I_krxtoK6uxggbMBKy6w&hl=en&sa=X&ved=0ahUKEwjJmqrhvYvLAhXFRI4KHekEDNYQ6AEIPjAE#v=onepage&q=japan%20lifetime%20employment%20system%20leads%20to%20loyalty&f=false p. 81.

[7] Brasor, Philip, "Debating the merits of lifetime employment" | dated 2016 *The Japan Times*, available at http://www.japantimes.co.jp/news/2014/11/01/national/media-national/debating-merits-lifetime-employment/#.VssN4Y9OIwx.

program known as the "Partner". The "Partner" is an intelligent program and has the ability to control the appliances in the house at will when the homeowner requests it. One of the examples from the live demonstration shown to us by the staff was when she needed hot water and had to boil it. She first placed the kettle under the water tap, and asked the "Partner" for water. The tap turned on, filling the kettle to the right amount. Following that, she placed the kettle on the kitchen table, and the area where the kettle was placed lit up, indicating that the water was being boiled. Another example was a mirror in the bedroom that can measure one's heart rate and blood pressure. The "Partner" will estimate the owner's mood and adjust the room lighting and background music accordingly. The intelligence of the "Partner" and the technology implemented in the "Wonder Life-BOX" was really advanced and being able to observe it through the live demonstration made it more meaningful. We also learnt that Panasonic had built a smart city in Fujisawa, Japan, to experiment with smart homes and smart cities.

At Honda Motors, we were shown a live demonstration of their newest robot, ASIMO. In the 1980s, the very first robot, the Eo was created, and after much research and development, ASIMO was developed in 2011. ASIMO is an abbreviation of "Honda's Advanced Step in Innovative Mobility".[8] ASIMO is an intelligent and responsive robot and has various functions, such as sign language, being multilingual and so on. Honda's motivation in developing ASIMO was to create a robot that could contribute towards society.[9] The technology in ASIMO was used to develop other products such as the Bodyweight Support Assist, Stride Management Assist and the U3-X Personal Mobility. The Stride Management Assist supports one's body weight and allows people with weakened leg muscles to walk.[10] This is especially applicable to Japanese society, which is a greying society. With the walking assist, it would allow the elderly to walk more easily and comfortably.

---

[8] Asimo.honda.com, "ASIMO by Honda | The world's most advanced humanoid robot" dated 2016, available at http://asimo.honda.com/.
[9] Gizmag.com, "Honda's new ASIMO robot is all grown up" dated 2016, available at http://www.gizmag.com/new-honda-asimo-robot/32977/.
[10] Corporate.honda.com, "Honda — walk assist and mobility devices" dated 2016, available at http://corporate.honda.com/innovation/walk-assist/.

From the on-site visits to the Japanese companies, I noticed that Japanese companies are trying to compete in the global market, expanding their business into new overseas markets. There is also an increasing number of foreigners working in Japan, especially in big companies like Ricoh, Panasonic, Honda and Sumitomo Mitsui Banking Corporation. I asked some companies about their future prospects, policies relating to hiring foreigners and the challenges they faced in hiring foreigners. Honda Motors' representative, Ms Matsuura said that the company is becoming more flexible and open about it as they aim to be a more globalised company by increasing the percentage of foreigners. Currently, the "Japanese first" ideology is not as strong as compared to the past. She explained that in the past, in overseas branches, the head of the branch was normally Japanese. However, currently the head of the Canada Office is a Canadian. The rationale is that it is better to have a local as the head of the office as locals understand the country and the culture there better.

Sumitomo Mitsui Banking Corporation mentioned that the company is aiming to hire more foreigners. They have implemented a policy in which the best staff are recruited locally, thus resulting in most of the General Managers being non-Japanese. There is an increasing number of foreigners, currently 6 out of 20 are non-Japanese as compared to the past where 3 out of 20 were foreigners. Another company, Alix Partners explained why the percentage of foreigners in Japanese firms is still not significant. Firstly, foreigners are not given equal opportunities to rise to the top as there is a glass ceiling. Secondly, it is a prerequisite to be fluent in Japanese, and as a result many companies prefer to hire Japanese. Lastly, as companies prefer employees to stay with them in the long run, they are afraid many foreigners will only work for a short period before returning to their home country. Although most companies are becoming more open and globalised, the change is slow due to the fabric of Japanese society. This may be due to the specific characteristics unique to Japanese culture such as the *uchi* and *soto*, the reading of the air, as well as the concepts of *tatemae* and *honne*. Due to their unique culture, it is difficult for foreigners to fully understand and apply it to blend into Japanese society. Although change is slow, Japan is moving with the times.

Other than the increase in foreigners in Japanese companies, the demographics of Japanese companies are changing. Companies are caring more for the well-being of their employees, especially women. In Japan, most women resign and become housewives when they get married and have children. The most common reason is that it is difficult to take care of their children and work at the same time.[11] Although existing social problems such as traditional mindsets and lack of child care centres (*taikijido mondai*) discourage women from re-entering the workforce, there has been an increasing number of women re-entering in the workforce. Government intervention has met with limited success. However, companies are trying to encourage women to work longer and have become more understanding towards women. In a dialogue with Mr Onoda, who used to work in Sojitz, I learnt that Japanese society is consciously changing to allow more women into the workforce. Some companies are implementing policies to ensure the environment is a comfortable place for women to work in. Mr Patrick, from Marubeni, addressed this question and mentioned that there is an increased understanding towards women. It is becoming easier for women and men to take leave to care for their children. The gender roles are not as distinct as they once were and that it has become increasingly common for males to care of their children. Also, there is an increasing focus on work–life balance as compared to the past. Mr Patrick elaborated further by mentioning that currently it has become socially acceptable to request for leave on a Saturday to be spent with one's family. In the past, this would normally be frowned upon. He also mentioned that to consciously ensure that there are women employees, there is a certain quota for women employees for each department when hiring new employees. Although there are some fundamental societal issues which discourage women from working, such as the lack of childcare centres, major stakeholders such as the government and companies are attempting to alleviate the issue, to create a society to allow women to continue working.

Other than women, Japanese companies are committed in ensuring a comfortable environment for their employees. Ricoh adopted the open concept workplace, where people in the sales department have free seating. Also, to cater to the needs of the employees, there were various spaces dedicated for individuals and for project team discussions.

---

[11] Fukuda "社会貢献•高齢者福祉", dated 2016, available at http://www.jkri.or.jp/PDF/2010/Rep108hukushi.pdf. (First Paragraph)

For instance, there were open discussion rooms so that their progress can be checked more easily. For employees who need privacy, they have enclosed discussion rooms as well. The personal cubicles are mainly used by the General Managers who carry out evaluations of their subordinates.

Japan's culture results in a group-centric society. The concept of harmony, their collectiveness, loyalty and the *ganbaru* spirit results in a group-oriented country which is highly commendable. Employees stay motivated by working together to achieve the company's aim, and even when the company is undergoing restructuring, employees stay on and work towards overcoming hardships. Employees put in their best for the companies they are working for. This is also reflected in their language, in which 社会人 (*shakaijin*) is used to address someone who has started working, and contributing back to society. Its literal meaning is "a person in society". This shows the emphasis on contributing back to society. This trip provided many such learning points and was truly an eye opener for me.

6

Hello, Mr Isetan: Recollection of Childhood Wonders

Janice Kam

Singapore's reputation as a multiracial and multicultural nation-state is well-documented and not undeserved, and its efforts in maintaining that diversity are an integral part of its socio-political life. Alongside the syncretisms that have arose from celebrating and managing the diverse ancestries of its peoples and its struggle to find and sustain a national identity, lies the composite nature of Singapore's society, institutions and socio-cultural life, magnified by its status as a modern, urban, cosmopolitan society and the rapid waves of globalization that have lapped the island state. Singapore's British roots are well-known, it was a British colony for more than a century — with a parliamentary system of government, an education system based mainly on British assessment formats, and the use of English in almost every aspect of social, cultural and economic life. However, even the most casual survey of Singapore's physical and cultural landscapes cannot deny the impact that Japan has had, and continues to have, on Singaporean life. In particular, Japan has, to a large degree, been woven into the fabric of our daily consumption, from food to haircuts to electronics. Familiar associations dot the landscape, physical and mental images that speak to the near ubiquitous position Japan has in Singaporean life.

This essay is a very subjective account of my personal experience of Japan-in-Singapore and a record of my memories and sundry observations from my childhood. No doubt certain experiences mentioned below will resonate, while others may be unfamiliar, even to those of my generation. My childhood in the Singapore of the 1970s and 1980s was a time which saw active Japanese economic expansion overseas, with Singapore as one of the beneficiaries of Japanese investment. The role Japan has played in the development of Singapore, and the ubiquity of Japanese companies in Singapore is a commonplace fact of life. In turn, as Singaporeans have grown increasingly prosperous and cosmopolitan in their tastes over the past five decades, the proximity of Japan, familiarity with the more visible aspects of Japanese culture, and the awareness that we have only scratched its surface, have drawn Singaporeans to Japan to experience in person what they could only have experienced through intermediaries in less prosperous times.

As a child, my mental geography of Singapore was a bifurcated one beyond the immediate environs of my neighbourhood. One road led towards Chinatown, while the other led towards Orchard Road. For me, the Isetan building on Havelock Road was a notable detour on the way to Chinatown. Its roundness without tickled my imagination — a fully round building, much like those seen in two-dimensional cartoons, distinct from more customary angular shapes. Within Isetan, however, the interiors resolved into the familiar outlines of a department store, where I derived many happy hours touching toys and trying on clothing in the children's department.

As for the other fork on my mental landscape, trips to Orchard Road, no matter how often or how regularly scheduled, were always a treat. The rows of shophouses stood out, Cold Storage, the western-style supermarket, prominent among them, while farther down the road, the shophouses gave way to the concrete monumentality of Plaza Singapore, symbol of urbanization and a transforming and modernizing cityscape. But Plaza Singapura was always more than just a large building. For me, its high walls shielded from sight, but never from mind, spaces such as Yaohan and Yamaha, and the attendant associations with food, family, music, learning, fun and friends. To a young child, Plaza Singapura might have been fortress-like, anchoring one end of Orchard Road, if not for the fact that this fortress was easily breached by its many entrances, and by my habit, acquired young, of going to Plaza Singapura, shopping at Yaohan and attending music classes at Yamaha, a habit typically reinforced by the week.

Like the age-old problem of the chicken and egg, it is difficult to recall which came first for me — Yaohan or Yamaha. Perhaps, to my childish mind, the two were ineluctably conjoined, with their physical shell — Plaza Singapura — a bold and looming background presence, as in a graphic print. To me, Yaohan meant the delicatessen and the children's department (like Isetan in the case of the latter), on two separate floors. Perhaps others might find more pleasure in recalling the supermarket, or the sheer variety of goods, from foodstuffs, to clothing, to appliances, that Yaohan gathered under one roof like an air-conditioned bazaar,[1] but my special thrill came from watching the controlled bustle of the delicatessen or from walking past toys and little girls' paraphernalia.

Wending one's way through the children's sections of department stores like Yaohan and Isetan in the late 1970s to the 1980s, filled with the stuff of a little girl's life, was an exercise in comparison, competition and desire. At that time, Hello Kitty was coming into her own as a cultural phenomenon in Singapore, accompanied by other Sanrio stars, not the least My Melody and Little Twin Stars.[2] They were also seen regularly at children's and toy fairs, displayed and promoted to girls just my age. To me, Sanrio toys were a forbidden temptation, banned from the home by my parents for their expense and frivolity, but my heart longed to grasp the figurines and play with them, and I had classmates who would satisfy that yearning. One, in particular, not only owned many of the figurines, but also a rather magnificent doll's house which she brought to school, and deigned, like a little princess, to share with us, though she, of course, remained undisputed ruler of our little play world.

---

[1] "Plaza Singapura" (extracted 4 April 2016), available at: http://eresources.nlb.gov.sg/infopedia/articles/SIP_2014-01-29_182204.html.
[2] Benjamin Ng Wai-Ming, "The Hello Kitty Craze in Singapore: A Cultural and Comparative Perspective," dated 2001 in *Asian Profile* 29, 6, pp. 6–7.

It seems to me to be the height of irony that my mother herself fell victim to the wiles of Hello Kitty several years later, when MacDonald's, with permission from Sanrio, offered several different sets of Hello Kitty and Daniel dolls along with purchase of their meals.[3] An entire tribe entranced by Hello Kitty stood in line for hours in order to wrangle their set of dolls, my mother among them. By that time, of course, Hello Kitty had become an international figure and symbol of cute, quite surpassing her origins as an anthropomorphic girl with cat features drawn on a purse.[4] To this day, she remains possibly the most iconic of anthropomorphic characters, her versatility brought to bear on all sorts of goods and consumers.[5] Though my younger self might vehemently disagree, I must confess to a sneaking fondness for Nendo's 2015 rendering of Radiograph Kitty, visualizing, as noted, "an x-ray image revealing Kitty's skeleton, shedding light to her mysterious internals," and imagining the structural underpinnings of the famous girl-as-cat visage.[6] In some ways, Japanese creations have provided the definitive criteria for assessing "cuteness" in the products we purchase and use.

Apart from toys and girlish accessories, the Yaohan delicatessen of my childhood retains a place in my heart, even though its physical counterpart has long disappeared. Apparently, the Yaohan delicatessen was known for introducing the an-pan to Singaporeans.[7] Yet so ubiquitous is this bun in a bakery's repertoire that its association with Yaohan quite escapes me by this point in time, savoury snacks on sticks holding instead pride of place in my memories. As an aside, many years later,

---

[3] *Ibid.* pp. 1–12.

[4] *Ibid.* p. 9.

[5] See the use of Hello Kitty as a two-dimensional cultural Japanese ambassador in the SJ50 Memorandum Tourism Logo (extracted 4 April 2016), available at: http://www.jnto.org.sg/assets/files/pdf/20160119_MOC%20Press%20Release.pdf.

[6] For an image and the designers' description, see http://www.nendo.jp/en/works/hello-kitty-by-nendo-2/

[7] "Yaohan" (extracted 4 April 2016), available at: http://eresources.nlb.gov.sg/infopedia/articles/SIP_2014-01-29_182139.html. Later, of course, higher-end retailers appeared in Singapore, in particular, Takashimaya, anchored at Ngee Ann City, in the heart of Orchard Road. See also "Takashimaya" (extracted 4 April 2016), available at: http://eresources.nlb.gov.sg/infopedia/articles/SIP_2013-11-29_163901.html?s=takashimaya.

when I learnt that *pan* is the Japanese word for bread, my only reaction was to think, "But of course, the an-pan!"

It was another red-bean filled dessert that evokes the strong place association — *obanyaki*, round and crispy at the edges, first a personal favourite at Yaohan, then at Sogo. I would await the completion of a fresh batch with glee as I watched the pancakes brown and crisp. Though those early associations remain strong for me, the *obanyaki* has nowadays lost some of its exclusive association with Japanese snacks and has been localized with a variety of fillings. Instead, the fish-shaped *taiyaki* seems to taken the position *obanyaki* once had.

For other snacks, there was Daimaru at Liang Court, though these had different connotations for me. I hardly ever visited the confectionery aisle at Daimaru — instead, I took part in a seasonal sweet exchange with a childhood friend. During important occasions such as Christmas and the New Year, she would present me with a bag of Daimaru goodies, with stiff, childish etiquette and politely worded inquires after my parents. In turn, I would respond similarly, with homemade confectionaries. Such were our expressions of friendship over snacks both Japanese and local, and our early lessons in social interaction.

Staying on the topic of food, entire meals and Japanese restaurants came later. At some point, sushi was exotic, and sashimi doubly so, and something like inari sushi, or futomaki would have been the extent of my first encounters. I was not among the first rush of Singaporeans to experience Japanese cuisine in the 1970s — those restaurants were exclusive and expensive. My experiences began a decade later when Japanese restaurants became mass market phenomena and chains began establishing themselves in the various shopping malls.[8] Even then, it took the dinner invitations of friends for us to get our feet wet, and to realize that new culinary horizons had opened up in front of us, not just new dishes, but also new ingredients. For instance, salmon became a regular part of our diet, a choice further borne out by emerging research at that time in the efficacy of omega-3 oils.

---

[8] For instance, Hoshigaoka, originally at Apollo Hotel, opened at Centrepoint in the 1980s. See "Hoshigaoka: Our History" (extracted 6 June 2016), available at: http://hoshigaoka.com.sg/our-history.

At the time of writing, Japanese cuisine in Singapore has become even more variegated. My recent meals include *sashimi* and *sushi* dinners and grilled Miyazaki beef buffets. Over the past few decades, Japanese cuisine and Japan-inspired cuisine has changed the diets of many Singaporeans, not as exotic or strange fare but as part of a familiar smorgasbord of choices, from the humblest hawker stall offering *teriyaki* salmon and *chawanmushi* to the most traditional multi-course *kaiseki* meals by Kyoto chefs transplanted to Singapore. We see the proliferation of specialized eateries — ramen shops, *izakaya*, grill and *shabu-shabu* outfits — and culinary collections in food emporiums, and are beneficiaries of the leap into the food courts and hawker centres. It is difficult to recall that there ever was a time where access to Japanese cuisine, or Japanese-inspired cuisine, at every price point and degree of authenticity, was not part of our daily culinary choices.

As mentioned above, Yaohan and Yamaha are twinned in my mind, and it is impossible to recall one without the other. Yamaha can be considered a music and service pioneer in Singapore.[9] It had been offering music lessons in Singapore for only a decade when I expressed an interest in music in the late 1970s, but it was, by then, sufficiently well-established such that it was the obvious choice for my parents. With Yamaha came the Suzuki Method, and the practice of starting group lessons before embarking on individual instruction.[10] My parents and, it seems likely, the parents of my group-mates, thought this arrangement ideal. There was no particular formula for the right age to begin music lessons — though the younger the better — but at an age when genuine interest could not be easily distinguished from mere whim,

---

[9] See "Japanese Enter New Field in Singapore" *Straits Times*, dated 23 November 1966, p. 12 (extracted from NewspaperSG, 4 April 2016) In the article, the Yamaha music scheme first began in 1954, in "America, Mexico, Germany and Bangkok", before arriving in Singapore. Its stated aims were to "promote music consciousness among the younger generation" along with sales of musical instruments, and its impact was to "indirectly help to swell the number seeking specialized tuition in music."

[10] The program began in 1968. See "Fun to be key note in music lessons" *Straits Times*, dated 21 August 1968, p. 4 (extracted from NewpaperSG 4 April 2016) with small classes of 10 or less, of an hour's duration, and with an emphasis on musical games.

participation in group lessons, configured as play and accompanied by a parent, provided a good testing-ground before committing to several years of formal individual classes and the expense of a piano in the home, from Yamaha, of course, that learning the piano, even as a hobby, required. Once my interest was established, Yamaha proved to be a springboard to the larger music-learning and music-making community of children and youths in Singapore — there were groups to play music with, concerts to attend, and friends to support at competitions. What would have been the solitary experience of a single keyboard was instead transformed into a congenial meeting of interests.

In short, Yamaha was not only my musical incubator — the friendships formed in group classes between the students and between their parents continued through the years, albeit edged, Singaporean style, with a finish of competition and one-upmanship. Play before and after class, running through the labyrinthine corridors of Yamaha while the adults gossiped, sharing meals at the cafeteria across the music school after class, shopping and window-shopping at Yaohan, such was the substance of childhood weekends. Till this day, Yamaha, still at Plaza Singapura, still evokes memories of youthful pleasures.

As I grew older, my encounter with Japan changed in various ways. Beyond my own internal ambit, I also became cognizant of what Japan meant to those around me. Friends, neighbours and family acquaintances had immediate and distant family members in Japan, some there for study and short-term work, while others had settled in Japan and were building families. Some brought Japanese spouses home to Singapore. Others neither studied nor worked in Japan, but engaged with Japan and Japanese culture as a long-term endeavour, punctuated with travel.

As my friends grew into jobs, better incomes and higher standards of consumption, their conversations and, later, their Facebook pages filled with photos of holidays taken in Japan, occasionally accompanied by an anecdote or an encounter. Some took Japanese language classes, which in part enabled their travel. Japanese travel magazines found in Kinokuniya were eagerly scoured for travel itineraries, for aids to the imagination and for pleasure. Visits to Kinokuniya, which has become a fixture on the Singaporean book scene, and partially localized and multi-cultural in its business approach and stocking, were associated with "Japan-related research". In conversation and on social media, I was regaled with tales of travel in Japan. As my friends matured as travellers, visits to Tokyo and Osaka and other major cities were exchanged for smaller locales, for repeated rediscoveries of some favourite area. Where conventional travel no longer sufficed, I heard of the beauties of the *onsen*, set in landscapes of the varying seasons, for leisure, for aesthetics and for personal beauty. I saw photos of *ryokan* and accounts of interactions in *minshuku*, accompanied by *kaiseki* dinners. I vicariously followed a hike along Basho's trail, poetry quoted at me along the way. I drank varieties of alcohol, unavailable in Singapore, ferried back from travel. In short, with increasing income and more cosmopolitan tastes, my Singaporean peers travelled to bring what was previously seen at a distance, the immobile, physical reality of the Japanese islands and their appurtenances, closer to home, and to experience both Japan's long-standing traditions and her rapid changes.

My first trip to Japan at the age of 15 was under Japanese auspices. By the late 1970s, Japan saw its relationship with ASEAN as necessarily extending beyond economic ties and launched several cultural and education initiatives to deepen Japanese outreach efforts to Southeast Asia.[11] I was a participant in a science program, where students from the South East Asian countries met in Tokyo for a technology and cultural study tour. Among my best memories of the trip are the homestay with Japanese families, mine in a Tokyo suburb, my admiration for the Filipino students who were working on easily applied solutions to environmental problems at home, a trip to Disneyland as part of a day off, and the tea ceremony. I would enjoy a repeat of the tea ceremony a decade later, in the United States, though perhaps not an unlikely occurrence, given that the Hakone Gardens in Saratoga in California exists as a symbol of US–Japan friendship. A friend so loved the taste of the bitter green tea used in the ceremony that he said, when asked if we had

---

[11] Makoto Yamanaka, "ASEAN-Japan Cultural Relations: A Japanese Perspective" (Singapore, 24 July 2009) *Embassy of Japan in Singapore*, available at: http://www.sg.emb-japan.go.jp/bi_ISEASpeech_09.htm. See also "Japan-ASEAN Friendship and Cooperation: Shared Vision, Shared Identity, Shared Future" *Mission of Japan to ASEAN*, available at: http://www.asean.emb-japan.go.jp/documents/20150402%20pamphlet.pdf for a recent overview.

questions, "Mo ippai kusadai," probably committing a social and cultural solecism, though amusing our hostess.

My own long-held dream of travel in Japan has been directed at the rails of Japan, inspired by an episode of *Japan Hour* many, many years ago featuring the delights of the railway bento of the diverse regions, a quick meal that strays away from fast-food conventions — homogeneous, cosmopolitan, universal — instead offering the traveller a radical hint of the local, the homegrown, and the familiar-unfamiliar, for want of a better word. Given how powerfully *Japan Hour* has inspired my personal fascination with the diversity of railway stations, it has doubtless inspired other viewers, and it is perhaps no surprise that the programme is still currently ongoing on Channel NewsAsia, delving ever more deeply into the diversity of Japan's various regions.

So far, I have invoked my experience and memory of my consumption habits, probably held in common with the habits of other middle-class Singaporean. Yet, we often forget that our consumption is enabled not only by trade and entertainment, but also by the decades-long foreign direct investments Japanese firms have made in Singapore, in the retail and non-retail sectors. As a child, however, I neither knew nor noticed that these stores and services were part of the internationalization efforts of Japanese firms expanding from domestic markets or that this expansion went far beyond retail and services, and created intra-region strategic, financial and trade networks. I did not comprehend the domestic factors that took Japanese companies out of Japan, nor the welcoming taxation or import regimes that drew them into the region. Nor did I know of the logistical chains that moved raw materials from source to manufacture, and then from factory to store, within and between regions.[12] I did not think of construction sites with the names of Japanese companies in large letters as nexus of finance, technological

---

[12] See Hiroshi Shimizu, *Japanese Firms in Contemporary Singapore* (Singapore: NUS Press), 2008, for a comprehensive study of the range and activities of Japanese firms in Singapore in the post-war period. See also Keri Davies and Fergus Ferguson, "The International Activities of Japanese Retailers," *The Service Industries Journal*, dated 1995, 15, 4, pp. 97–117, and Yung-Fang Chen and Brenda Sternquist, "Differences between International and Domestic Japanese Retailers," pp. 118–133, in the same issue, for analyses of the reasons

and managerial knowhow, urban planning and cooperation between Japanese and Singaporean partners. They were merely temporary inconveniences leading to potential finished buildings or transportation networks. To me, Isetan was the interesting round building nearby where we shopped, Kikkoman was something we used in the kitchen because the name was a guarantee of quality and good taste. When our first, European television broke, a Sony TV was the chosen replacement. Made in Japan (or made by a Japanese company) was a statement and a guarantor.

Singaporean society, especially its middle class, is very open to experience and consumption. We pride ourselves on our multi-culturalism and see that as an indicator of our development, sophistication and cosmopolitanism. By the same token, and through the decades-long accommodation to Japanese firms in Singapore, we are also receptive to and welcoming of various aspects of Japan. From pop culture, to regional differences, to high culture, to the creative industries, the diversity of Japanese culture and cultural expressions both traditional and innovative appeal to different demographics in Singapore, while the depth of Japan's heritage appeals to an increasing urbanized and cosmopolitan environment, supported by her decades-long presence in Singapore and her already significant impact on the tastes and consumption habits of many Singaporeans.

Japanese companies ventured abroad and the various strategies they used to enter different markets.

7

Introduction to the Japanese Food and Business Sector: A Foodie's Perspective

Soh Hui Shi

If one were to ask any Singaporean on the streets what their impression of Japanese cuisine was, it would be no surprise to receive a positive one. As younger Singaporeans become increasingly well versed in Japanese culture and are exposed to Japanese cuisine, it is no surprise that the superb quality of Japanese service attitudes and food have resonated with most Singaporeans. Growing up, I was always envious of others patronising Japanese eating places: beautiful shop decorations, realistic food models that can be easily mistaken as edible products and the comfortable ambience make Japanese eating places irresistible. With quality ambience, service and the high quality of food, it guarantees a positive dining experience in Japanese eateries.

To understand the consumer's affinity with Japanese food and the quality service it provides, I was keen to examine Japanese Food and Beverage (F&B) business models and derive valuable lessons that may be applicable to the F&B industry in Singapore. My analysis in this chapter is based on my own general observations, my experiences working in a Japanese retail establishment and my reading of the literature on this subject.

Like many Singaporeans, I was impressed by Japanese humility and genuine customer service attitudes and, at the same time, I became a fan of Japanese desserts and sweets. This led to my decision to work in a Japanese café when I was trying to find a part-time job two years ago. I was attracted to its beautiful food displays manufactured as authentic as possible to entice customers, and the cosy atmosphere in the café. It was a fruitful learning experience as I was able to work with a number of Japanese customers and had many opportunities to learn about Japanese culinary culture.

Japanese Culture and Philosophy
Related to Customer Service in F&B Establishments

One prominent aspect of the Japanese retail business models lies in its excellent customer service culture. From my working experience in a Japanese retail outlet, irrespective of F&B, retail or hotel services, there is often a high level of customer satisfaction as their service is centred on a strong personal touch tailored to customer needs. In Japan, this is widely known as *Omotenashi*, which means to "entertain guests whole-heartedly", a reflection of selfless hospitality. Japanese hospitality is regarded as an important aspect of Japanese pride. In their opinion, the ability to anticipate customers' needs and provide a good experience for their guests serves as the greatest source of reward to them.[1] At the same time, their delivery of quality services ensures that they are able to attract most customers, subsequently improving business. In recent years, some Japanese companies have started to lay a heavy emphasis on the concept of *Omotenashi* as a marketing effort to surpass dominant western companies. For example, it is common for Japanese companies such as Uniqlo and Muji to send employees working in foreign branches to the Japanese headquarters so that they continue to provide high quality customer service adapted from Japan. In light of the 2020 Olympics

---

[1] Spivock, Jeffrey, "Omotenashi: The secret of Japanese service — Sparksheet" dated 29 Sep 2015 [downloaded on 19 Feb 2016], available at http://sparksheet.com/omotenashi-secret-of-japanese-service/.

to be staged in Tokyo, Japanese companies offering hospitality services will also be awarded *Omotenashi* grades as a benchmark of their level of sophistication in customer service.[2]

Their businesses also pay particular attention to ambience, which they believe is integral to maximising the comfort for customers. This explains the colour section and aesthetically-pleasing restaurant designs accompanied by specially selected gentle background music. These factors help to guarantee customer satisfaction and ensure customers come back again.[3]

Lastly, with regard to the quality of food, what is unique about Japanese cuisine lies in its philosophy of what defines a good food. There is a belief that all five senses are integral for one to be able to enjoy their meal. While other cultures tend to only focus on taste and smell to define good food, Japanese cuisine also places a strong emphasis on food presentation and the use of aesthetically appealing cutlery which adds much enjoyment to one's dining experience. One's sense of touch also plays an important factor, where apart from the texture of the food, the cutleries used are also integral to the dining experience, where they believe that one's level of comfort in holding the utensils should be maximised (the science of ergonomics). Lastly, the audio ambience that diners enjoy also plays an important role in the dining experience. This is exemplified by the higher-end Japanese eateries that ensure a quiet and serene environment for customers to enjoy their meals.[4]

---

[2] The Japan Times, "Ministry to develop certification system for 'omotenashi' hospitality" dated 12 March 2016 in *The Japan Times*. [downloaded on 8 Feb 2016], available at http://www.japantimes.co.jp/news/2016/03/12/national/ministry-develop-certification-system-omotenashi-hospitality/#.VuY4QJx97IV.
[3] Brennan, Bridget, "'Can I help you?' Three ways the Japanese do customer service better" dated 23 Apr 2012 in *Forbes*, website [download on 28 Feb 2016], available at http://www.forbes.com/sites/bridgetbrennan/2012/04/23/three-habits-of-japanese-merchants-that-could-save-u-s-retailing/#6cda8054dcfa.
[4] Savory Japan, "The power of five: Five pillars of Japanese culinary tradition dated 2010 [downloaded on Feb 2016], available at http://www.savoryjapan.com/learn/culture/power.of.five.html.

Japanese-Originated F&B Businesses in Singapore

There are a number of Japanese-originated food and beverage businesses in Singapore, ranging from *ramen* restaurants, *teppanyaki* stalls, *sushi* places, cafes and even fast-food chains such as the well known Yoshinoya and Mos Burgers. The main reason for why they are so widely popular in Singapore can be attributed to Japanese foods and contributes to the strong following of Japanese popular culture among Singapore youth. While these businesses strive to provide quality service, ambience and food as found in its original outlets in Japan, most agree that many service quality practices and items on local food menus have been altered to fit the Singaporean palette. One prime example is the range of *sushi* outlets available in Singapore. While the Japanese are used to placing *wasabi* in individual *sushi* that consists of *sashimi*, Singapore *sushi* is not served with *wasabi* by default and instead it is provided separately as Singaporeans have varying degrees of preference for *wasabi* in their *sushi*. Popular localised varieties of spicy cheese *maki* and curry *sushi* are also commonly found in *sushi* restaurants.[5]

In terms of *sushi* availability, the past few years have seen a rising trend of Japanese minimarts and supermarkets being established in Singapore. These outlets typically offer a range of Japanese products such as popular Japanese snacks and cooking ingredients, appealing to customers with their attractive packaging and unique flavours. For example, assorted snacks such as Pocky, Pretz and Kit Kat are often available in special flavours of Matcha, Pizza and even Wasabi to name but a few. Just a few months before writing this chapter, the first Japanese Emporium in Singapore — *Emorium Shokuhin* in Marina Square — commenced operations, offering a wide variety of food items from a Japanese gourmet grocer, live seafood market and a variety of dining options.[6] These markets offer an option for shoppers to consume culinary dishes made from authentic fresh Japanese ingredients.

---

[5] Ng, Wai-Ming, (2001, June 1), "Popularization and localization of sushi in Singapore: An ethnographic survey" dated 1 June 2001 [downloaded on 29 Feb 2016], available at http://www.nzasia.org.nz/downloads/NZJAS-June01/Sushi.pdf.

[6] Quek, Eunice "Mega Japanese food emporium opens in Singapore" dated 27 Sep 2015 in *Straits Times*. website [downloaded on 20 Feb 2016], available at http://www.straits times.com/lifestyle/food/mega-japanese-food-emporium-opens-in-singapore.

My Experience

I would now like to share some of my own experiences from my interactions with fellow Japanese colleagues and some observations derived from work experiences.

Lessons Learnt from Work

Working in a food establishment run by Japanese management, you are always expected to do your very best to provide customers with service that match standards found in Japan. Strict enforcement of staff attitudes in customer service, along with cleanliness, plating and creation of foods are emphasised, and sub-standard service and quality are not tolerated. As such, cultural and attitude differences between Singaporean and Japanese working styles have led to both parties understanding more about each other's practices and applying lessons learnt from each other's interactions at the workplace.

For example, some Japanese colleagues were initially horrified upon witnessing Singaporean staff willing to forego food quality and plating standards to achieve maximum efficiency in serving customers during peak periods. This caused some tension between the local and Japanese staff members at times as both parties felt their methods of serving customers were justified. However, after experiencing the hectic demands of the fast pace of living in Singapore and their penchant for maximum efficiency, Japanese staff working in my retail outlet in Singapore also personally witnessed tendencies and expectations by Singaporean customers who are less patient and demand to be served as quickly as possible. On the other hand, the Singaporean team members witnessed high levels of customer satisfaction generated as a result of Japanese emphasis on consistent quality in standards when it comes to food production and plating, consequently attracting a sizable number of regular return customers. As such, both parties in my work environment have learnt to compromise and adapt to appropriate practices to meet the rapid response demands of Singaporean customers while ensuring quality of food is not compromised.

From my experience, the Japanese employees also value and emphasise the importance of following precise instructions when it comes to completing certain tasks while Singaporeans have a more flexible approach in their approach to accomplishing tasks. For example, my Japanese colleagues are particular about the shape and appearance of the bread produced at work, such that they painstakingly memorise and remember correctly prescribed dimensions of all the breads. The same applies when it comes to the amount of ingredients used in their desserts. Before the breads are baked or proofed, they would take the extra effort to measure the breads such that it would be of the desired size. Similarly, they would also weigh the desserts while plating in order to ensure that their final products always look consistently similar. On the flip side of the coin, however, the Singaporean staff do not feel that consistency in amount of ingredients served to customers each time is the topmost priority — instead, the speed at which the food is being produced is more important. My main lesson from such incidents is that even though the local staff may pride themselves on being able to complete certain tasks by means of "shortcuts", the quality our company's products may be compromised in the long run due to the failure to adhere to certain standards of consistency. Therefore, the level of meticulousness in the way we complete our tasks may enable us to reap higher rewards in the long run.

Punctuality is also very strictly enforced upon all staff and latecomers are strictly rebuked for being selfish and irresponsible. As such, while the local staff tend to arrive on time for work and are forgiving of others who may be a few minutes late, the Japanese always make it a point to arrive at work at least 15 minutes early so that they can properly prepare themselves physically and mentally before they begin work.

As a whole, while some Singaporeans in my workplace may interpret the Japanese way of staunchly following the rules as being inflexible and unnecessary, especially since Singaporeans are focused on the ends rather than the means. However, as we reflect on the consistent standards maintained by authentic Japanese cuisine, we will realise that their extra efforts placed on achieving high quality standards may be worth it when there are satisfied customers.

Another key lesson from working in a Japanese F&B establishment is the high level of respect that the Japanese display to all workers in the team — be they superiors, customers or even their subordinates. This is reflected in their unwavering ability to treat customers with respect and courtesy even when customers are rude. Their respect to customers can also be witnessed through their extra care taken in not disturbing customers at work by keep conversations at minimal volume. Any substandard service and food is viewed as being disrespectful to customers in their opinions since customers are willing to fork out a particular sum of money to dine in the establishment. Furthermore, the way in which subordinates and superiors great each other with the honorific "-san", implying familiarity and respect for the other party is evidence of respect toward others.

Learning More About Japanese Colleagues

From my interaction with the Japanese working in Singapore, most of whom are female colleagues, they typically come to Singapore due to spouses' relocation to work in Singapore for business or research purposes. There are also others who came to Singapore to learn the English language as they believe that acquiring good English communication skills will increase future career prospects.

Generally, the Japanese residents in Singapore, including the ones that I am acquainted with, are delighted with the wide range of Singaporean cuisine. They enjoy Singaporean delicacies such as our ubiquitous *roti prata*, *rojak* and fried rice. However, just like the culture shock that Singaporeans experience upon learning that the Japanese consume raw chicken or horse meat, some of our cuisine also surprises them in ways they have not anticipated. For example, some Japanese are surprised to find out that "chicken rice" in the Singaporean context is very different from what they had imagined the dish to be. In the Japanese context, "chicken rice" consists of a plate of rice and chicken fried together with ketchup, vastly different from the Singaporean Hainanese version. This led to confusion by some of them over the actual concept of the Singaporean chicken rice. They also need to adapt to our spicy palate. While they do enjoy dishes such as *laksa* and curry, the level of spiciness must be cut down so that they can properly enjoy the dish. They also have the tendency to cut down on the amount of chilli in their Malay dishes like *nasi lemak* since the normal amount of chilli is regarded as too spicy for them.

Future Aspirations

The partnership between Singapore and Japan has certainly come a very long way since Singapore achieved its independence in 1965. In light of the celebration of the 50 years-relationship between Singapore and Japan, such as the upcoming Super Japan festival that will be held in Esplanade,[7] I am sure it is an event many Singaporeans will participate in to learn more about Japanese popular and traditional cultures. It will also be ideal for such organised activities to encourage the Japanese community in Singapore to interact with locals more extensively. Through this, it will foster a stronger understanding of each other's unique cultures and traditions.

---

[7] Esplanade "Esplanade launches a new cultural festival — super Japan — Japanese festival of arts dated 2016 [downloaded on 29 Feb 2016], available at https://www. esplanade.com/~/media/files/press-room/2016/pr-super-japan-2016.pdf?mw=1 920&hash=EE543CAF0E674548B73601B7C1C396905599234D.

8

Social Exchanges

The previous chapters discussed Singapore and Japan's bilateral political and economic exchanges. The two platforms, particularly economic exchanges, are traditional prisms in which the mass media and state view official ties. But an important aspect of relations between the two countries is neither state-led nor market-driven, instead people-to-people exchange is interest-driven and motivated by more altruistic goals compared to political-institutional and commercial ties. Two societies can only reach long-term understanding if their peoples are engaged culturally, linguistically and morally. These qualities are expressed through volunteerism, personal motivation to pick up the language of communication and acts of compassion and mutual help. This chapter is an account of some recent and past examples of exchanges between the two peoples of Singapore and Japan.

Just like the bilateral economic exchanges, Singapore has been learning from the best practices in Japan in terms of social management systems and educational training. In the field of education for example, for years, the Singapore government working with the Japanese Ministry of Education, Cultural, Sport, Science and Technology to dispense the Monbukagakusho scholarships to Singaporeans aspiring to study in the top universities in Japan. It has been an important channel for Singaporean students to learn about Japanese society, business management and its technologies, foster relations between the two and channelling best practices and ideas back to Singapore for implementation. The Japanese social system has been intensely studied by her Singaporean counterparts.

History of the Koban

Singapore also adapted the Japanese *koban* system and institutionalised it as the Neighbourhood Police Post (NPP) in Singapore. The *koban* system which provided a law enforcement function and administrative support at the local level was also useful for providing public security and one-stop administrative services in Singapore's densely-populated public housing estate and private residential area. The crux of the motivation behind the establishment of the NPP was a strategic rethinking of the role of the policeman in Singapore. Initially, from colonial period to the early 1980s, the policeman was a law enforcement officer, an office holder who is seen to implement the force of law on wrongdoers. This may have inspired some fear and distance from members of the public who want to stay out of trouble. But such public attitudes were not suitable for Singapore which had by then developed public housing estates with high population density and highly unitised habitats. With well-developed grassroot organisations like the Community Centre management, Community Clubs, Residents' Committees (RCs) and others, NPPs were small nimble units that can tap into the grassroot communities' resources for crime resolution purposes. Decentralised nimble units can also reach deeper into the population at large within a certain area for crime prevention purposes.

NPP were more suitable with the proliferation of mini community policing working closely together with residents to resolve issues from petty crimes to national disasters. At the same time, the policeman had also become an administrator as law and order improved in Singapore over the years. The police force was no longer a combat unit dealing with lawlessness and large organised gangs or political protestors. They also began to serve important administrative functions. Therefore, the NPP served also as convenient little units for one-stop administrative functions such as change of addresses on the Singapore identity card. I first made this argument in the paper and the idea of policing priorities in a densely-populated public housing estate area was corroborated by a resource paper written by Jarmal Singh, Deputy Director Operations, Police Headquarters, Singapore Police Force (SPF), Republic of Singapore and his paper is also reviewed in this chapter and listed out in full in the bibliography.

Historical background behind the NPP

The NPP was established in 1983. The idea was a re-orientation strategy in 1983 to focus more on patrolling and rely less on vehicular mobility to increase police appearance within the community, not just to solve crimes but to deter them.[1] The Japanese *koban* was its initial model and overall case study for neighbourhood community watch. In 2008, there were approximately 6,000 Kobans (literally translated as "Police Boxes") and approximately 7,000 "Chuzaishos" or literally translated as "Residential Police Boxes".[2] The SPF noted the following characteristics of the *koban*:

> Each Koban is manned by only a few officers, and the Japanese policemen on duty are trained to be approachable and friendly so that community-members see them as protectors, mediators and partners, as opposed to intimidating crime-busters.[3]

The above explanations of the *koban* highlight several features. First, they are small in scale, usually involving a handful of people and this is the same case for the NPP which are manned by a handful of policemen. Second, the officers on duty are friendly to the public and acceptable. There are attempts to provide the right coaching to them to be nice and courteous. This is in a bid to be seen as guardians of peace rather than enforcers of the law or tough cops. In other words, the *koban* is more than a law enforcement agency. The *koban*s provide the

---

[1] Singh, Jarmal, "Community policing in the context of Singapore" undated in the United Nations Asia and Far East institute for the Prevention of Crime and the Treatment of Offenders (UNAFEI) website [downloaded on 1 March 2016], available at http://www.unafei.or.jp/english/pdf/PDF_rms/no56/56-11.pdf, p. 126.

[2] Yamanaka, Makoto, "Opening ceremony of the international seminar on 'The Community Policing Strategies Evolving from the Koban System of Japan and the NPC System of Singapore' Speech by Makoto Yamanaka, Ambassador of Japan to Singapore, 17 August 2009 Amara Hotel, Singapore" dated 17 Aug 2009 in the Embassy of Japan Singapore website [downloaded on 1 Jan 2016], available at http://www.sg.emb-japan.go.jp/bi_KOBNSpeech_09.htm.

[3] Loh, Kenny, "Celebrating 30 years of community policing" dated 14 Dec 2012 [downloaded on 1 March 2016], available at https://www.hometeam.sg/m/article.aspx?news_sid=20121214ptKQOxhG89bE.

one-stop fundamental administrative services of a police station, maintains neighbourhood watch, reacts to crises, provides guidance/ directions and works with the community to earn their respect and trust to solve crimes.[4]

Singapore's historical experimentation with community-based policing started in April 1981 when the then Deputy Prime Minister (DPM) Goh Keng Swee penned the *Goh Report* for the renewal of the SPF and change directions in policing. The model they studied and adapted was from interactions with Japanese experts from the National Research Institute of Police Science. Retired Commissioner of Police Tee Tua Ba recalled this period:

> In the Koban system, the village constable was known to everybody. The strength was the community. Japanese patrol officers were known as Mr Omawarisan (Mr Walkabout). He walks around, so he knows everyone.[5]

NPP introduced a systematic foot and bicycle patrol mechanism and the first institutionalisation of the NPP was in the former Toa Payoh Police Division's pioneering Khe Bong constituency on 3 June 1983.[6] Retired Assistant Commissioner (AC) Tan Ngo Chew, former Officer-in-Charge of the Division and awardee of the Japanese government's Order of the Rising Sun, Gold Rays with Rosette, went to Japan, indigenised useful features of the *koban* in Singapore and mobilised his subordinates to become the Neighbourhood Police Post Officers (NPPOs).[7] A primary objective in designing initial training was to

---

[4]Yamanaka, Makoto, "Opening ceremony of the international seminar on "The Community Policing Strategies Evolving from the Koban System of Japan and the NPC System of Singapore" Speech by Makoto Yamanaka, Ambassador of Japan to Singapore, 17 August 2009 Amara Hotel, Singapore" dated 17 Aug 2009 in the Embassy of Japan Singapore website [downloaded on 1 Jan 2016], available at http://www.sg.emb-japan.go.jp/bi_KOBNSpeech_09.htm.
[5]Loh, Kenny, "Celebrating 30 years of community policing" dated 14 Dec 2012 [downloaded on 1 March 2016], available at https://www.hometeam.sg/m/ article.aspx?news_sid=20121214ptKQOxhG89bE.
[6]*Ibid.*
[7]Loh, Kenny, "Celebrating 30 years of community policing" dated 14 Dec 2012 [downloaded on 1 March 2016], available at https://www.hometeam.sg/m/article. aspx?news_sid=20121214ptKQOxhG89bE.

change the images of the cop from being authoritative to easily accessible and augment bonding between members of the public and police officers.[8] This encouraged individuals to work with the police on community issues. Starting from eight experimental observation NPPs in various constituency, by 1993, the envisaged 91 NPPs that dotted the island were ready operationally (each covered an area of about 35,000 residents) and from the Japanese experience, 80% of the members of the public gave useful tips to the *koban* to go after crime suspects which is a testimony to the *koban*'s success.[9]

Singapore and Japan collaborated on the Koban Seminar arising from the Japan–Singapore Partnership Programme for the 21st century (JSPP21) circa 1994 that evolved into the JSPP21 in 1997 and both countries have since moved on to capacity building activities for other developing economies and supply technical assistance programmes to them.[10] Within 19 courses on offer in 2009, community-policing technical courses are most sustainable and the longest lasting and most positive results with implications for Singapore–Japan relationship.[11] The Koban Seminar facilitates both *koban* and NPP to exchange information, experience and for officers to network and be partners. From 1995 to 2009, approximately 320 officials went through the exchange sessions.[12]

Besides adaptation of institutional units like *koban* (which later morphed into the NPP in Singapore), learning from Japan also took on other forms like the intangible dissemination of knowledge, including

---

[8] *Ibid.*

[9] Singh, Jarmal, "Community policing in the context of Singapore" undated in the United Nations Asia and Far East institute for the Prevention of Crime and the Treatment of Offenders (UNAFEI) Resource Material Series No. 56 website [downloaded on 1 March 2016], available at http://www.unafei.or.jp/english/pdf/PDF_rms/no56/56-11.pdf, pp. 126–127, 129.

[10] Yamanaka, Makoto, "Opening ceremony of the international seminar on "The Community Policing Strategies Evolving from the Koban System of Japan and the NPC System of Singapore" Speech by Makoto Yamanaka, Ambassador of Japan to Singapore, 17 August 2009 Amara Hotel, Singapore" dated 17 Aug 2009 in the Embassy of Japan Singapore website [downloaded on 1 Jan 2016], available at http://www.sg.emb-japan.go.jp/bi_KOBNSpeech_09.htm.

[11] *Ibid.*

[12] *Ibid.*

training future Japan experts. The Department of Japanese Studies at the National University of Singapore is a centre for learning about Japan, producing graduates "with a deeper understanding of Japan, and a thorough appreciation of Japanese social and cultural values as well as Japanese institutions and practices".[13] The duty of cultivating Japan experts academically at the tertiary level fell upon this department. The area studies approach provided Japanese studies graduates with an all-rounded approach in understanding Japan through international relations, sociology, anthropology, literature, history, philosophy, etc. The graduates are highly deployable in the business sector in Japanese companies and also serve as a people's bridge between Japan and Singapore.

Besides local community neighbourhood watch and tertiary education, Singaporeans also try to observe and adapt from other aspects of the Japanese system and its culture. Singaporeans are sometimes curious about their Japanese counterparts' dedication to their profession, work and crafts. And Japanese dedication range from the most mundane jobs like taxi drivers who turn up for work every day dressed in suit, cap and gloves to skilled occupations that requires a high level of skills competency like a top *sushi* chef who can make accurate lacerated cuts after decades of practice on a fresh fish or saw a *tuna* without damaging muscle texture. Even for white-collared executives, some of them work so hard that they apparently die on the job (*karoushi*). There had been many explanations for such dedication to one's job proposed by academic analysts. They range from a collectivist homogenous society encouraging the idea of reaching a common goal or destiny for the society as a whole (sociology) to concepts of shame and fear of being criticised for not contributing to collective goals in a groupist culture (anthropology) to Confucian work ethics and remnants of the code of Bushido that emphasises dedication to craft (philosophy) to traditions of a peasant society which required every individual in the village to contribute their best for rice cultivation (social history) or a combination of all these explanations (area studies). Given that such factors are uniquely historical, cultural, societal and both constructed as well as

---

[13] Thang, Leng Leng and S.K. Gan, "Deconstructing 'Japanisation': Reflections from the 'Learn from Japan' Campaign in Singapore" dated June 2003 in *New Zealand Journal of Asian Studies* 5, 1, 2003, p. 96.

naturally-occurring, it may be difficult to implement Japanese societal traits in other societies without modifications, although elements of which had been distilled and indigenised in the four tiger economies in East Asia, including Singapore, adapted and fitted to local conditions. Elements of Singapore's productivity drive in the 1980s and 1990s reflect this aspect.

Other than the state and issues of economic productivity, Non-Governmental Organisations (NGOs) and Non-Profit Organisations (NPOs) have also been active in promoting bilateral exchanges. NGOs also play a crucial part in Singapore–Japan ties. The Japanese Cultural Society (JCS), for example, was established in 1963 and it was registered by the Registrar of Societies on 26 August 1964. Perhaps one of the activities closely associated with JCS is its language programme. The pioneering Society founders and its rank and file had the robust view that language acquisition is part and parcel of understanding the culture of Japan and therefore, in March 1966, a "language study committee" was formed for organising and teaching Japanese language, starting with initial first three classes with the help of the Japan Embassy.[14] The language activities expanded gradually. From 1973 to 1980, a single Japanese language specialist was despatched by the Ministry of Foreign Affairs Japan (MOFA) to be attached to JCS alongside three more experts from Japan Foundation and eventually JCS attained the status of the largest establishment for the teaching of Japanese language to Singaporeans and Singapore-based individuals in the city state with 2,000 students annually.[15] The JCS language institution was institutionalised as the JCS Japanese Language School and its status officialised and registered with the Ministry of Education (MOE) in Singapore in October 1982 operated and supervised by a Board of School Committee.[16]

Besides Japan Cultural Society (JCS) which is really run by local Singaporeans, another organisation, the Japanese Association, is equally important in the Japanese expatriate community's integration into life in Singapore. The Japanese Association is located at 120 Adam

---

[14]JCS, "JCS history" dated 2013 in JCS website [downloaded on 1 Jan 2016], available at http://jcss.org.sg/jcs-history.
[15]*Ibid.*
[16]*Ibid.*

Figure 1: A photograph of the Japanese Association, Singapore's main entrance that I took on 11 March 2016.

Road (Figure 1). At the point of this writing, my latest visit to the Japanese Association was to attend the fifth anniversary of the Great East Japan Earthquake's occurrence. The Association serves as a clubhouse and community centre for Japanese residing in Singapore to keep in touch with each other. According to The Japanese Association's official website, the Association was founded a century ago in 1915 and reconstituted in 1957 and the objective of the Association was to form a mutual help group, looking out for each other's well-being, setting up schools, overseeing the Japanese cemetery and promoting global exchanges.[17] The current 8,000 square metres (utilisable space located in a 5,600 square metre property) club facilities inaugurated by the then DPM BG (NS) Lee Hsien Loong (Singapore's Prime Minister (PM) at the point of writing) on 23 May 1998 is a modernist design structure fused with traditional Japanese aesthetics and it hosts 5,512 ordinary members (Japanese citizens who can vote in the Association) and Associate

---

[17] The Japanese Association, Singapore, "About the Japanese Association, Singapore" dated 2016 in The Japanese Association website [downloaded on 10 Feb 2016], available at http://www.jas.org.sg/aboutus/about_en.html.

members (as of 23 February 2016).[18] The Association also publishes a newsletter titled *The Southern Cross* which is chocked full of information about Singapore and provides important information for the Japanese expatriate community in Singapore as well as others who can read Japanese language. Past issues of *The Southern Cross* have been compiled into bumper volumes to preserve the posterity of knowledge accumulated by Association writers and contributors over the years.

Besides language education-related issues and social networking functions, the non-governmental sector's exchanges are equally vigorous in other areas. In March 2011, a devastating earthquake that hit Japan triggered a triple disaster that included an earthquake, tsunami and nuclear meltdown, in that order. The disaster was subsequently officially designated as The Great East Japan Earthquake or nicknamed "311" for short. The whole world pitched in to contribute to the rescue and recovery efforts, with the US launching the extensive Operation Tomodachi in these efforts. Singapore's contributions to the affected areas during and after the disaster was also significant and notable. In the aftermath of the quake, Singaporeans contributed funds to the Singapore Red Cross (SRC) to build four recovery centres in the quake-affected areas. Because of the contributions of the international community and Japan's relentless efforts, three years after the quake, the Japanese PM Mr Shinzo Abe noted that agriculture was returning back to normalcy, fishing ports resumed seafood supply and public housing emerged to house those affected.

In Japan's recent past, disasters have helped to rally the Japanese society together with closer bonding. For example, the 1995 Great Hanshin Earthquake changed Japan in many ways, raising the profiles of NGOs who chipped in to help with the rescue and recovery efforts and the authorities strengthened existing building regulation to cope with future earthquakes. Statistically, the national census indicated that the affected towns in Tohoku's Miyagi Prefecture did not experience a hollowing-out of population. While there are slight dips in population figures, this is counterbalanced by a rejuvenating inflow of people who are volunteering in the area, contributing to reconstruction and working as construction industry personnel. Multiple stakeholders are chipping in

---

[18] *Ibid.*

to archive and celebrate the recovery efforts while remembering the tragic event in a sombre manner. Besides planners, spiritually, the victims need remembrance, archived memories and closures as well. The event has spawned culturally creative works based on memories and the Japanese sense of aesthetics. Producers of the iconic *anime* series *Evangelion* is putting together an animation to detail and record the recovery efforts of 311 victims. Through animation, powerful messages can be sent but unlike real images, they are not as jarring and can enhance the audiences' acceptability of such messages without excessive emotive stress that real images may bring about.

Besides creative producers, women's contribution in disaster relief have also been highlighted. At the Third UN World Conference on Disaster Risk Reduction (14–18 March 2015) held in Sendai Japan, PM Shinzo Abe took the opportunity to highlight female leadership in disaster relief efforts. Some of their achievements in the Great East Japan Earthquake was to raise the need for the provision of milk powder to children, their counselling persuasion to prevent people from contemplating suicide as a psychological fallout from the quake and manpower contribution to police teams that are made up mostly of women. Another stakeholder in northeast Japan's recovery are the consumers. Japanese consumers banded together to purchase the region's products to contribute to its economic recovery. Entrepreneurs are also moving to the region to figure out ways to leverage on the region's assets and strength to come up with new businesses to rejuvenate the region. They help to transition the motivations behind the acquisition of such goods from emotive instincts of helping out victims to cognitive rationale in buying such products because they have good quality and appealing designs. The Tohoku or northeastern areas have premium lumber, textiles and high quality artisanal craftsmanship that its crafts and manufacturing industries can tap on.

Besides aesthetic, emotive and cognitive recovery, Tohoku is also undergoing physical landscape changes with the impending end of the temporary pre-fabrication housing that were set up for victims of 311. The national government is donating such housing to the northeastern prefectures where private sector entities can then use them to set up medical/nursing and storage facilities. This plan saves resources, prevents wastage and are also pragmatic to meet practical needs on the ground. Over 50,000 units were built and some of them will be converted for the above-mentioned purposes. Medical, nursing and storage needs will exist as continuing needs way after immediate recovery efforts have tapered off (the number of evacuees have decreased dramatically in the post-disaster efforts). The 311 efforts have been a combination of private and public sector, state–civil society cooperation in a society known for its consensus-seeking ways. For a disaster of this magnitude, there remain some challenges for the authorities to tackle in its aftermath.

The Japanese government organised a centralised agency, The Reconstruction Agency, to tackle these challenges. According to the Japanese government's Reconstruction Agency, Fukushima radiation has dissipated naturally and levelled off to a certain extent and this is partially also due to decontamination efforts by the authorities. The authorities are also focusing their efforts to enhance food safety by testing for radiation and so far, in 2014, the Reconstruction Agency has confirmed that radiation levels in food is less than the standard value, including its seafood products. Such a development should boost the fishing industry's prospects. What help it receives from the international community, Japan returns them in kind. Japan's role in a field of disaster can be derived from preventive expertise as well as lessons from actual experience. This is especially so, with respect to Emergency Assistance, Japan have dispatched "Japan Disaster Relief Team" overseas many times, including China's Sichuan earthquake and Indonesia's tsunami. Singapore may be a small state but it utilised its resources within the limits of its capacity to contribute to the recovery efforts too. Singapore's contributions to the affected areas during and after the disaster was also significant and notable. In the aftermath of the quake, Singaporeans contributed funds to the SRC to build four recovery centres in the quake-affected areas. Toyama Nursery School in the quake-affected area was also re-opened with Singaporean resources and in commemoration of this effort, the school is given the informal name of "Lion Park" in honour of the "Lion City" (English translation of Singapore's old name Singapura).

Five years after the Great East Japan Earthquake, students at Republic Polytechnic (RP) hosted a photo exhibition to commemorate the event and some of them were visibly crying dut to the tragic consequences of the natural disaster. The Polytechnic had close affiliation with the disaster recovery process because the SRC joined forces with RP to dispatch nine students from the mass communications department and two lecturers from Singapore to Japan from 4 to 13 June 2015 and the photo exhibition named "The Strength of the Human Spirit" at Ion Orchard was an account of that trip as part of the 50th anniversary of relations between Japan and Singapore officiated by the Singapore Minister of Foreign Affairs Vivian Balakrishnan.[19] When the Singapore team was there, the kids of Toyama Nursery School put on a show for the RP students and presented them with folded paper hats and the team went to look at locations financed by Singaporeans through S$35.7 million funds canvassed through charity.[20]

A commemorative event held on 11 March 2016, elegantly coined as the "Blossoms of Hope of Strength, Support & Friendship" at the Japanese Association was put together to show gratitude to Singaporeans who have helped and contributed to the recovery and reconstruction of the area affected by the Great East Japan Earthquake. A PowerPoint slide showed the cherry blossom Sakura flowers that typically symbolises resilience and fragility of life as the blossoms bloom under adversity of weather conditions but only for a short period of time. The event was well attended by civil defence officials, including those who took part in the recovery phase, members of the diplomatic corps and business community as well as RP students who volunteered with the SRC at the site and published a book titled "The Strength of the Human Spirit" as a photo-narrative of their efforts on the Fifth Anniversary of the Great East Japan Earthquake. A choir was also assembled by the Japanese Association for a touching performance executed in this event. The occasion was sombre yet joyous in the face of rescue and recovery. The dinner event was accompanied by a small exhibition at the Japanese Association and I visited the exhibition on the same day on 12 March 2016. The exhibition placard read: "The exhibition pays tribute to the strength and magnanimity of the human spirit — from the resilience of

---

[19] Awang, Nabilah, "Singapore students moved to tears in Japan" dated 3 March 2016 in *The New Paper* [downloaded on 3 March 2016], available at http://www.tnp.sg/news/singapore-news/singapore-students-moved-tears-japan.

[20] Awang, Nabilah, "Singapore students moved to tears in Japan" dated 3 March 2016 in *The New Paper* [downloaded on 3 March 2016], available at http://www.tnp.sg/news/singapore-news/singapore-students-moved-tears-japan.

the survivors to the compassion of the donor community. It also hon-
ours the friendship and close ties between the People of Singapore and
Japan." This bilateral display of friendship was apt for both countries
who are celebrating 50 years of ties in the same year. It also emphasises
the people-to-people exchanges between the two countries.

At the exhibition, there were also photos of this bilateral cooperation,
for e.g. the SRC personnel with the (*Gaimusho*) MOFA and Shichigahama
local government staff at the Shichigama Toyama Nursery School officiating ceremony with VIPs, SBC Council Members, Mr Chew Hai Chwee
and Mayor Mr Yoshio Watanabe. The SRC Secretary General/Chief
Executive Officer (CEO) Mr Benjamin William and Council Member Mr
Chew Hai Chwee were also present. Devastated by the quake and re-
opened with bilateral cooperation, the nursery was affectionately
renamed "The Lion Park" after Singapore which means "Lion City" in
Malay. Besides this nursery, Minister of State for Foreign Affairs and
Minister for the Environment and Water Resources Masagos Zulkifli,
Chairperson of SRC Tee Tua Ba and Rikuzentakata Mayor Futoshi Toba
officiated the rebuilding of a grand hall in the city on 17 March 2012. One
of its holding areas was also named as the 380-capacity "Singapore
Hall", again to recognise people-to-people exchanges. In the same city,
another structure was completed on 16 March 2015 and stood in place
of the old facility devastated by the quake and it holds the record of
being the biggest SRC financed project thus far at a cost of S$11.1 million
with a land area of 2,000 square metres and 20,000 people capacity. This
time, the hall is constructed on high elevated grounds with conference
rooms and display areas armed with technological links to the fire and
law enforcement departments, therefore it is able to serve as a future
disaster recovery facility. According to the exhibition captions, it has a
power generator with the capacity to provide 72 hours of electricity.

The third facility featured in the exhibition was the Taro Support
Centre at the transitional residential facility in the city itself constructed
by the SRC for community activities. According to the exhibition captions, sited in Miyako City, the S$41.05 million project hosts 1,700 indi-
viduals (30% of whom were the elderly) on a monthly basis and has 10
caregivers to take care of the residents with events organised to keep
them busy, entertained and motivated. There are also rehabilitation
facilities. Contributions by the SRC was not only restricted to

post-disaster relief. Even in the immediate aftermath of the disaster, the SRC was already mobilised and it activated the "Restoring Family Links (RFL)" system to locate the family members, loved ones for Singaporeans and Japanese affected by the quake. On a long-term basis, the SRC also organised campaigns to donate to the Japan Disaster Relief Fund at the Red Cross House.

The platforms for people-to-people social exchanges discussed above like JCS, Red Cross, polytechnic volunteers, the *koban* institutions represented exchanges between Singaporeans who have an interest in Japan and things Japanese as well as Singaporeans who are keen to study the language from native Japanese or interact with Japanese people based in Singapore. Through such exchanges, it is inevitable that local Singaporeans as well as long-term residents in Singapore will develop their own impressions of the expatriate Japanese community residing in Singapore. For example, Taos Whittaker, a January 2015 session student at Tokyo's Sophia University wrote about her impressions of the expatriate Japanese community in Singapore which was published in the Asian Century Institute:

These 27,525 Japanese expats, recorded in 2013, consist mostly of corporate employees and their families, along with many Singaporean citizens of Japanese ancestry. Writing from personal experiences of living in Singapore for 11 years, an essence of Japan can be easily found within the small Island... My dentist of 11 years, including his dentistry company, is almost completely Japanese. Various doctors, who have helped me with the occasional but not plentiful illnesses I've had through my childhood, were Japanese. When I built my first desktop computer, the shop owners who helped me were Japanese...I've even had a high school recommended art teacher, who barely spoke any English, help me in creating my portfolio during my university applications. Even despite the language barrier, she was actually the best art teacher I've ever had, which shouldn't be mentioned to the high school art teacher who recommended me to her...Japanese Retail chains, such as Takashimaya and Isetan, both very popular in Japan, share as similar popularity in Singapore. Both have outlets in the central shopping districts of Singapore, dominating some of the largest and most recognizable buildings, which is partially due to these Japanese outlets in the first place. Uniqlo, having multiple outlets around the world, have 22 in Singapore. Their fashion is commonly worn in

Singapore, due to the simple designs that can be appropriate for Singapore's harsh humidity. Japanese food chains in Singapore, such as Pepper Lunch and Mos Burger, also have gained large popularity within the country.[21]

In this personal narrative, one can spot three significant points related to Whittaker's impressions of the Japanese expatriate community in Singapore. Firstly, the contributions that the community made to Singapore is tremendous, judging from this personal narrative. It appears the expatriate community does not only consist of salarymen (white-collared executives) working in the high-tech manufacturing industry in Singapore but also retail service providers and professionals like dentists and doctors who provide essential services. Quantitatively, it is one of the largest expatriate communities visible in Singapore's cosmopolitan and multi-cultural social fabric. Secondly, the penetration of Japanese household and cultural products, according to this narrative, is extensive with choices of Japanese food and apparel products on offer. Finally, there is a fair amount of integration of individuals with Japanese heritage who have become actual Singaporeans and have integrated successfully into local society. The indigenisation of ethnic Japanese is interesting, but rarely mentioned in current literature on Singapore–Japan relations. The narrative also talked about Singaporeans' penchant for Japanese lifestyle products, foods and designs, all of which will be covered in greater details in the subsequent chapters.

Given the closeness in ties and friendship between the two countries and the comprehensiveness of such exchanges, one can extrapolate and expect relations between the two peoples to intensify. For two societies to have *sustainable* ties, they must be able to stand the tests of economic difficulties, political turbulences and geopolitical challenges. The two peoples' understanding of each other's societies help create a substratum of goodwill and generosity that helps to overcome environmental difficulties, unexpected externalities and shocks inherent in the

---

[21]Whittaker, Taos, "Japan's business and economic relations with Singapore" dated 21 March 2015 in Asian Century Institute website [downloaded on 1 Jan 2016], available at http://www.asiancenturyinstitute.com/international/857-japan-s-business-and-economic-relations-with-singapore2.

world system or economy. It is this reservoir of goodwill that act as a buffer to absorb shocks in the international system, be they economic or political in nature. This chapter discussed mainly institutional forms of people-to-people exchanges within the rubric of non-governmental, non-profit and volunteer organisations. Much of the exchanges mentioned in this chapter are ethically-conscious and purposeful, e.g. directed towards natural disaster recovery or law enforcement. They are also functional, like the world of the Japanese expatriate community in Singapore, i.e. salaryman who bring their families along to conduct productive business activities for their companies and firms. The next chapter will examine people-to-people exchanges from a leisure-based, recreational perspective, including personal tours taken by Singaporeans including myself to Japan to explore Japan by trekking, backpacking, taking road trips and train rides.

9

Singapore–Japan Exchange Programmes: Japan Encapsulated in a Singaporean View

Hilda Tan

I am a Singaporean first year university student currently studying Human Resource Management. I took on this writing to reflect upon my experiences with Japan's culture, symbolisms and lifestyle trends. As I look back on my recollection, it seems that "Japan" has been in my life in more ways than I expected it to. From initially being introduced to *anime* by my cousin at the age of 12, to learning Japanese and meeting Japanese students, to travelling to Japan, and even having the opportunity to visit hugely successful Japanese companies, it seems that I've experienced Japanese culture in more ways than one.

I've divided my experiences into three sections.

Introduction to Japanese Culture

My first experience with Japanese culture came through *anime* consumption. It made such a big impact and became such a major part of my life that I still remember the very first *anime* that I watched: Cardcaptor Sakura. Through the eyes of my young self, *anime* brought me to a whole other world. Vivid pictures, exciting storylines, magic and the very cute *kero-chan* was my favourite character. I enjoyed it thoroughly and stayed glued to the entire televised season. Even as I grew up, I never got bored with *anime*. It definitely stood out as something different in comparison with my usual diet of western cartoons, and brought about new interest in animation areas and genres that I was not exposed to before. That was the beginning of my experience and exposure to Japanese popular culture. After *anime* got me more curious about Japan's culture, I started gathering pictures and information about Japan in my spare time. The televised programme "Japan hour" was something I looked forward to each week as it displayed Japan's beauty, culture and tourism areas splendidly and graphically. Soon, it became my dream to be able to travel to Japan and experience its culture and beauty in real life. To my young self, Japan encompassed delicious food, the beautiful *sakura* season, enjoyable *onsen* soaking in the winter, fun school times and polite people. It was a cultural image of Japan accumulated from consumption, the popular media and other experiences.

Going Deeper: Language, Activities and Meeting People

A few years on when I joined Singapore Polytechnic as a student, with no prior intentions or plans, I made friends with people who were Japan "crazy" (Japanophiles). From Jpop, to *anime*, to its culture, my friends were totally immersed in Japan's popular culture. They were also the main reason why I decided to take up the Japanese language as a course subject. Till today, it has been a decision that I definitely do not regret. Though it took a lot of effort, these weekly classes soon became a memorable part of my school experience. Through these classes, I learned *hiragana, katakana* and the basics of Japanese language. Besides theory, I learnt the importance of honorific forms and the importance of punctuality and other values in the Japanese culture. I remember clearly the first meeting with my Japanese teacher. This might sound unconventional to most people, but everyone in the class was just so excited to meet a "real" Japanese person in the flesh. Maiko *sensei* was my first Japanese teacher and part of the reason why I had such a positive experience learning the Japanese language. Attending her classes for a year and a half made me truly understand the importance of various qualities that are important in Japanese culture. Though she firmly corrected us as a teacher during lesson time and ensured that we were being taught how to be respectful and polite, Maiko *sensei* never once shouted or reprimanded us. With a pleasant smile on her face and a gentle disposition, she taught us with patience and calmness.

Through these Japanese classes, I also became exposed to Japanese culture and the age old tradition of the Japanese tea ceremony (*chanoyu*). As our Japanese teachers volunteered in several other cultural activities, we were given plenty of opportunities to experience Japanese culture in the comfort of Singapore. I experienced my first Japanese festival in my first year of polytechnic studies. Known as *Natsumatsuri* or "summer festival" in English, the festival allowed me and my excited friends to experience some aspects of the Japanese culture up close. Enjoying live performances, food stalls and traditional games, my friends and I played the night away while continuously eating *okonomiyaki, takoyaki*, drinking Mitsuya ciders, playing *Yoyo-tsuri* (water balloon game) and even trying on *yukatas* (the summer version of *kimonos*). I experienced the Japanese cultural feel of summer for the first time in Singapore. What made the experience even more real, however, was seeing members of the Japanese community in Singapore, whose existence I was unaware of, coming together to re-create what they normally do for summer traditions back home. Though I was not physically in Japan, the whole atmosphere allowed me to imagine what it would be like to celebrate the summer festival in Japan.

In my second year of polytechnic studies, I decided to join an eight-week course that taught participants the basics rituals of the Japanese tea ceremony. This course once again allowed me to experience Japanese culture first-hand, though it was a different kind of experience from the classroom environment. The grace and poise of the tea ceremony was accurately demonstrated weekly by the tea ceremony teachers and my seniors who had already been learning the art form for a few years. Attracted initially to Japanese traditional culture through my love of sweets (*okashi*), I soon found out that the Japanese tea ceremony meant so much more in its philosophical aspects. We learnt that the origins of the tea ceremony started from the desire to provide a communal place where people from all walks of life were respected equally. And as the weeks went on, it was clear that each process of the tea ceremony clearly supported this; from the significant symbolism of having a small door that required everyone to bend down to get in, to the polite phrases the tea master and the participants used for interactions and exchanges, to the respect paid to the tea master's perfection of the art form. I loved how each tea master took his/her time with the process and the pride they had in their art to create a beautiful experience for anyone who participated in the ceremony. It wasn't long before I fell for the tea ceremony and its charms. I persisted with two rounds of lessons and even managed to help my tea ceremony *sensei* in an official tea event. Though I no longer practice the art of tea ceremony, this unique experience definitely gave me a glimpse into Japan's past and present.

Another wonderful experience began with joining the Singapore Polytechnics Exchange club with my friends. Participating in this club gave me the chance to interact with Japanese students while we brought them around Singapore as part of an exchange programme. This gave me the perfect chance to practice my Japanese language as well as to step out from our comfort zone. Awkward at first, I barely spoke. But with time, I plucked up the courage to speak to them. As basic as my Japanese language proficiency was, it turns out that the students were just as nervous and excited to meet us. Letting go of my fears of sounding stupid when I spoke Japanese soon helped me befriend the students. We chatted about our dreams, likes and dislikes, passions, hobbies and life's challenges. And though culturally different, I soon realised that these friends were just like us. I will always hold dear to the amazing bonds we forged over the course of a few days, the chance I had to meet some of the kindest people, and also the tears each one of us had as we parted ways at the end of the exchange. Looking back, the chance to interact with the students allowed me to further add another layer of reality to my perspective of Japan and its people.

Work Culture

Finally, I would like to share the experience of my most recent trip to Japan. As part of my school's programme, we were given the chance to take part in an Overseas Study Mission to Japan. Focusing on adaptability and change, the trip sought to examine efforts taken by some of Japan's most successful conglomerates in restructuring their business operations to cope with the changing Japanese economy and global conditions. This excited me as change management is an important topic for Human Resource Management students. As the Japanese are known to display amazing motivation, organisational loyalty, teamwork and the tenacity to continuously strive to design and produce innovative and high quality products, I was also excited to learn if there was a "secret" management formula behind the Japanese manufacturing process and whether it could be applied in Singapore's local context. Fortunately, I was able to pass the interview required to participate in the trip to Japan.

As part of our pre-trip preparations, the teacher-in-charge challenged us to think about a personal question that could become an object of focus for our trip. Excited to learn how companies formed this unique working culture, my first focus was on their best management practices. My next priority was to understand how Japan's leading corporations dealt with the challenges that came with a changing market and economy. Understanding restructuring efforts would most probably include the high possibility of retrenchment, I was curious how the management would deal with an issue that arises out of the restructuring process that can be construed as uncommon and even non-existent in Japanese working culture. With that in mind, I quickly crafted a question centred around internal management techniques and human relations management.

In my group, I worked with a teammate whose topic was similar to mine to expand our questions into several sub-topics. These included communication, productivity, teamwork, motivation, foreign talent and policies they had in relation to retaining and attracting employees.

I doubt I can do justice in explaining my whole experience in words, but this trip was honestly one of the best experiences I've ever had. Besides receiving amazing hospitality from our Japanese hosts and visiting major corporations like Panasonic, Honda Motor, Ricoh and SMBC, this trip also gave me a chance to enjoy and observe Japan's unique corporate and human relations culture.

Listening to and learning from Japanese managers with years of experience under their belt, has allowed me to expand my perspective on a variety of subjects such as work life, leadership responsibilities and best practices. As part of the trip, we often got to visit and see first-hand the company's newest product offerings, their work-line process and even office spaces.

Out of the many things I learnt, I would like to share a few lessons and observations I took away with me in relation to my own personal questions and curiosities about Japanese business management.

The first point is how extensive Japanese culture is in the working environment and how they do things in the office environment. To my understanding, Japan's culture is one that generally promotes the qualities of community togetherness, collectiveness, politeness. This has clearly translated into Japanese working culture as it was clear that many, if not all, of the Japanese companies we visit practiced the open office concept. With everyone sitting together in a main area, including heads of departments, open communication, information sharing and collectiveness is encouraged. Reflecting the country's culture, employees assist one another in teams to work towards a common goal. Though this concept of collective behaviour cannot be entirely emulated in its exact form in Singapore, I believe that some of the practices are potentially useful for us to adopt. One is having good business communication. This can make or break an organisation, especially in times of crisis, as it is the foundation of how well a company will be able to execute its plans. One of the companies we visited was a specialist in restructuring efforts. The speaker shared a point on how greater transparency in the company matters is not necessarily bad nor will it drive the employees away. An important lesson I learnt that day is that sometimes the best way to bring about a sense of urgency, is to be honest with employees so that they step up to the level that is required.

The next lesson I learnt was on the importance of motivation. The presence of equality and an adequate amount of competition is paramount as it creates a working environment where employees are constantly challenged to strive for a better outcome. In Japan's case, I have observed that their corporate culture plays a part in being a natural form of motivation for employees. Similar to the point above, I have observed that the Japanese culture of collectiveness, teamwork, community as well as one's *Ganbaru* spirit ("spirit to never give up, do the best they can") has shaped individuals to be personally motivated to do the best he/she can for the company. An interesting lesson we learnt from our teacher was how fresh graduates are recruited into the company and trained from the very beginning by a mentor. By learning the skills and trade from a mentor, employees not only assimilate faster into the company, new recruits also get to build new relationships with their colleagues. This in turn encourages organisational loyalty and also motivates employees to do well in their work to make their mentor proud of their efforts. My key lesson from the interaction session is that the management should never downplay the importance of mentorship or spending time on forming a corporate culture that encourages employees to do their best, as this drives employees in the long run.

One similarity the organisations in Japan had was that they continued to place importance on the well-being of the employee even as they competed for higher profit margins. Though this might be seen as unnecessary and a waste of resources to maintain processes and policies relating to an employee's well-being, this has reminded me that for employees to be able to work at their fullest capacity, companies need to first meet the employees' well-being and needs. From Ricoh's feedback system to ensure good communication flow, to AlixPartners' retrenchment services, to Marubeni's take on eliminating overtime practices, such efforts and policies are a good way for the organisation to build trust and organisational loyalty.

Another thing I wanted to touch on is Japan's innovative spirit. As a child, I remembered marvelling at my first ever Gameboy. Known for being an innovative and creative country, everyone was excited to play an actual Gameboy. Creative ideas are visible all around the city, from vending machines retailing many products, to machines used to order food. Nearer to the end of the trip, we even got to marvel at Panasonic's idea of smart cities. Experiencing a variety of technologies such as a talking assistant that will assist you to organise the house, to a mirror that will show its owner virtual images of how they look wearing different clothes and makeup, to the idea of the city running on electricity solely produced from solar energy. In this showroom, my teammates and I could not stop gaping at some of the coolest inventions and gadgets I've seen in my life. Japan's level of innovation never ceases to amaze me. It is also amazing how many of these creations benefit people in need. An amazing example we managed to see was a live demonstration of Honda's ASIMO's capabilities. Started in 2000, the development of this robot as a multi-functional mobile assistant was to help people who had trouble with physical mobility. Whether it is in the field of creative designs, innovating new products, or creative solutions in lifestyle products, or just randomly quirky inventions and gadgets, I admire the pride and amount of time and effort Japanese people put into their work.

Though there have been many other competing countries hot on the heels of Japan in terms of catching up with innovation and creativity, a new trend in encouraging start-ups, might be just the thing that Japan needs to maintain its economic standing in the world. With the successes of many start-ups in the last few years, more and more entrepreneurs are embarking on their own journeys to begin their own ventures. In our trip, we visited a successful start-up based in Akihabara. This start-up provides a platform for entrepreneurs or people who want to test, design and create products with high-tech equipment. By paying a simple membership fee, creators can use the equipment and space available at this creative loft to bring their ideas to life. Speaking to the representatives of the top management there, I clearly felt the passion and drive to create a successful platform that supported entrepreneurs with limited capital. Located amidst many start-ups located in Akihabara, the few levels of office space occupied by this start-up incubator and facilitator felt vibrant and colourful with lots of creators and inventors bustling with ideas everywhere in the company space. With creators and spaces exuding creativity and innovation in every room of the office building, it presented a very different experience compared with the multinational corporations (MNCs) we visited in my exchange.

In my personal view, one challenge facing Japanese business management that I picked up was the need for efficient decision making in Japan. As Japan's culture supports harmony, managers and leaders often take time in decision making as they garner support from different parts of the organisation for a collective decision. Though this is an advantage in keeping good relations between employees and conveying the macro picture of the organisation to the public at large, this quality also brings about issues, especially in an economy that is both fast-paced and ever-changing. Especially in bigger business organisations and conglomerates, the time taken to gather and disseminate information as well as obtaining the entire team's approval can lead to a devastating effect on the company's leading position in the market and its fickle consumers and fashion trends as well as dynamic global economic conditions. This is a challenge that a lot of Japanese companies are facing, though there are some companies that have been successful in overcoming these issues such as Uniqlo by making decisive strategic decisions in a timely manner.

In retrospect, my biggest lesson from this trip is that each system and policy has its own challenges and disadvantages. There is and will never be a right or perfect answer. What is most important is for us to always be open to learn from others and be constantly willing to adapt to the ever-changing environment that we live in today.

On the whole, I can conclude that Japan is still a country that I find amazing and very unique. Surely impacting us in more ways than I've written about, I definitely believe that the world and I will be able to continue to learn and benefit from their best practices while continuing to enjoy Japanese popular culture, tourism, traditions and hospitality.

10

Tourism and Travels: Notes from Fukuoka Travels

Tourism is an important form of people-to-people exchange. Unlike bilateral exchanges between state agencies or non-governmental organisations (NGOs) involved in a specific purpose (e.g. disaster relief) from both countries, it is not driven by altruistic reasons. In fact, a tourist's motivation for travelling can be very personal and self-centred. But, because it is self-motivated and enjoyable, it may actually end up as one of the most important ways to conduct unofficial diplomacy because of the self-motivating factor. In its commodified carnation, it can also be considered as an important contributor of tourist revenue to the overall economy. At an official ceremony witnessed by His Excellency Japanese Ambassador to Singapore, Mr Haruhisa Takeuchi, President JNTO Ryoichi Matsuyama, Chairman Singapore Tourism Board (STB) Chew Choon Seng and Deputy Secretary MFA Peter Tan, Chief Executive Lionel Yeo of the STB associated tourism with official bilateral relations and people-to-people exchanges in general:

> Over the last few decades, Japan and Singapore have strengthened our relations through multi-faceted collaborations and regular people-to-people exchanges. Relations between Singapore and Japan are in excellent shape, and we have shared a long history of tourism exchange.[1]

---

[1] Yeo, Lionel. "JNTO-STB MOC Signing — Message by Lionel Yeo, Chief Executive, Singapore Tourism Board" dated 18 January 2016 in the STB website [downloaded on 22 Jan 2016], available at https://www.stb.gov.sg/news-and-publications/lists/newsroom/dispform.aspx?ID=638.

There are three points of significance here. First, the bureaucracy is included amongst the actors in both countries promoting tourism and bilateral relations. Second, tourism is acknowledged as a form of unofficial people-to-people exchange, indicating its important role in fostering bilateral ties. Third, it is acknowledged by the state that such non-official ties have been longstanding. And this was the motivation for Singapore to propose a Tourism Memorandum of Cooperation (MOC) "to deepen our tourism collaboration and improve two-way tourist traffic" and to kick-start the activities for SJ50 throughout this anniversary year.[2] The ultimate beneficiary of such activities are tourists who can enjoy better deals, tourist-targeted activities and the economic gain for the state is in the form greater tourist revenues through promotional activities such as "Double the Miles" campaign for Japanese visitors to Singapore organised by the STB, Singapore Airlines and Changi Airport and "10 times Super Points" online sales promotion with Rakuten Travel.[3]

Travel promotions by the tourism authorities are relatively well-documented. In this chapter, I wanted to examine tourism from a more personal and experiential perspective through unstructured observation studies without the constraints of fixed schedules, institutional arrangements and restrictions. I wanted to discover Japan from a grassroots perspective as a traveller to local communities and off-the-beaten tracks to the suburban periphery of the Japanese whose cosmopolitan centre is Tokyo. I was keen to experience tourism in Japan's islands outside the main island of Honshu, therefore, I decided to tour and experience the charms of southern Japan in the island of Kyushu. As the largest city in Japan, Tokyo is inevitably the most well-known location of tourists from Singapore and other parts of the world. But there are also direct flights run by Singapore Airlines to other major Japanese cities like Fukuoka. The format for this chapter is one of a personal narrative, a standpoint perspective of Japan's local communities observed at the ground level. The accent is on the authenticity of experience, experiencing Japan that is non-manufactured, un-commodified and non-packaged. It was a personal trip to observe what makes up Japan, and how one Singaporean interpret Japan from ground up. The chapter can also be conceptualised as a photo-log or travelogue of a Singaporean's journey through authentic Japan in its peripheries, outside the core centre

---

[2] *Ibid.*
[3] *Ibid.*

of Tokyo. In this chapter, I specifically focus on Fukuoka in Kyushu and it includes Fukuoka City (the biggest in Kyushu) and Fukuoka Prefecture.

For observation studies, I took a trip through Japan's largest city in the South, Fukuoka. It's been a while since my previous road trip so I thought it would be opportune to take my last trip for 2015 in the island of Kyushu, in the rural countryside and suburbia of Fukuoka prefecture. It is a little-known fact even to the Japanese that outside the bustling city of Fukuoka lies endless miles of pristine green environment in the out-skirts of its prefecture. Having studied in upstate New York, I often encountered friends who are unable to distinguish the difference between Manhattan (New York City) and the apple-cultivating state of New York. Same issue when I was based in Hong Kong, my friends often thought I was in bustling Kowloon and Hong Kong Island when I was working in the mountainous greenery of New Territories. My personal trip to Fukuoka was designed to be Zen, serene and green. As I passed through the farmlands and rice paddies of Northern Fukuoka, I waved to farmers harvesting the winter vegetables under the cold but clear blue skies. I also stopped to look at the calming effect of rice paddies where stalks of rice waved gently in the cool breeze. Saga prefecture in Kyushu is one of the main rice bowls of Japan, producing high-quality Japonica rice for Japanese and overseas consumers. For Singaporeans, the texture of Saga rice is glutinous and sticky, shiny in appearance and sweet in taste.

As the road trip progressed, besides green farms and rice paddies, I weaved through the long mountain ranges of Kyushu Island. Mountainous in terrain, Japan has long undulating mountain ranges that seem to run on forever. In the cold wintry foggy weather, the ranges looked mysterious, foreboding and melancholic. Alpine flowers line the pavements in the elevated highlands, blooming even in the coldest of winter. Used to the tropical botanics of Singapore, I looked on with interest at the winter flowers located in the evergreen variety of local carpet grass.

There are other exotic plants blooming at this time of the year, including decorative cabbage and the unopened velvet buds of *sakura* flowers (cherry blossom). Whenever the sun shone over the ridge of the mountain range, local birds flocked to the green fields to search for insects, making "hay while the sun still shines" as the saying goes.

The winter season yielded Kyushu's well-known sweet and succulent Mandarin oranges, while Yuzu citrus fruits are harvested for making tea, sauces and dips. The refreshing smell of citrus fruits cleansed indoor spaces quickly and efficiently.

The countryside of Northern Fukuoka and its national parks were teeming with wildlife even in winter. The thick furred wildcats in the

region find spots like dried hay to hibernate during winter, catching small natural preys for survival. The elegant Japanese *kois* continue to swim gracefully in the pond water, several degrees warmer than the surface area. In order to preserve the environment, vending machines at the national parks sold *koi*-feeding pellets encased in biodegradable wafer that can also be used to feed the *kois*. No non-biodegradable plastic bags or containers were used in the process.

The countryside also yielded rustic rural architecture of Japan. I admired the classic pre-modern style elongated *oni* (demon) tiles on the rooftops and also rural houses sitting on rock mounds as

foundations overlooking the fields and curved glazed roof tiles that allow water to slide onto rain-holding sleeves and directed towards the ground.

As the terrain gets blocked by large canals and rivers, my road trip transited to trains for more convenient travel. With a hot drink in my hand, I warmed my hands and went up the train for a spectacular view of the countryside as the train carriage snaked through the rural areas and suburbia. The drink can fit snugly by the window ledge.

When my nomadic existence came to a sedentary stop, given the arrival of the wintry season, I could not resist having winter seasonal Japanese foods. They include local specialties like *fugu* or pufferfish *sashimi* cut so thin that the slices simply melted away in my palate and mouth. It is lightly dipped in the Yuzu light soy sauce and prepared by a certified chef as pufferfish emit neuro-toxins that must be removed by a professional. I also ate the *oden* stew, a hot soupy dish that warms up many Japanese during the winter season.

When I was on the move again, a convenient food to fill the stomach was handmade (hand cut and hand rolled *udon* noodles). The simplest *udon* dish was usually the best, hot piping *shoyu* (soy sauce) *udon* flavoured with *wagyu* beef slices.

To get a feel of continental Northeast Asian nomadic tradition, I tried *karubi*, a Mongolian-inspired barbeque grill that cooked finely-sliced *wagyu* Japanese beef and intestinal parts. Like a nomadic horseman, I chomped off pieces of local sweet potato simply baked over pit fire. They warmed me up quickly.

I also tried rice cake baked with *mentaiko* fish *roe*, another specialty of Fukuoka prefecture, a quintessential experience for anyone trying out local cuisines. I then ended my road trip in Northern Fukuoka with hand-prepared fish *roe sushi* combined with raw succulent *uni* or sea urchin meat. Other fresh seafood catches off the Northern Fukuoka coast off the Sea of Japan include raw Japanese baby Pacific abalone and preserved shrimp slices preserved in spicy fish *roe*. Preserved foods were important in the past for keeping foods edible throughout the wintry months.

I then embarked on the train journey again for the trip back to the vehicle as the express red trains and the blue metallic Sonic trains sped back to train stations in the boundaries of Northern Fukuoka. Like living things, the trains travelled through the extremely cold wintry December rains as human passengers remain grateful for the cushioned seats warmed up by central heaters.

Upon reaching the destination, I took time off to admire the setting sun in the cloudy and blue late evening skies before a full lunar moon with visible craters took its rightful place in the cosmic order. My road trip in Northern Fukuoka had come to a peaceful moonlit end.

Images from Urban Hiking through Fukuoka City and its Peripheries in Southern Japan (3 and 4 July 2015)

Besides the southern countryside, Singaporean tourists who have been to Fukuoka are more familiar with its urban landscape, including Hakata (the old name for an old city port in Fukuoka, the current main terminal train station is known as "Hakata station"). For this publication, I went on an urban hike in mid-2015. The total distance hiked over two days was 18 km on 3 and 4 July 2015.

Fukuoka is the sister city of Auckland, Oakland, wine-producing region of Bordeaux and Guangzhou.

Scene of downtown Fukuoka.

Downtown Fukuoka.

A human-powered taxi at downtown Fukuoka.

More of downtown Fukuoka.

A Yamakasa festival display at downtown Fukuoka.

Nature and Agriculture in Suburban Fukuoka

Flowers in bloom.

Rice paddy cultivation.

A furry-eared wildcat.

A suburban rice paddy field co-existing with residential and retail sites.

Food Culture in Fukuoka City

Fresh *sashimi*.

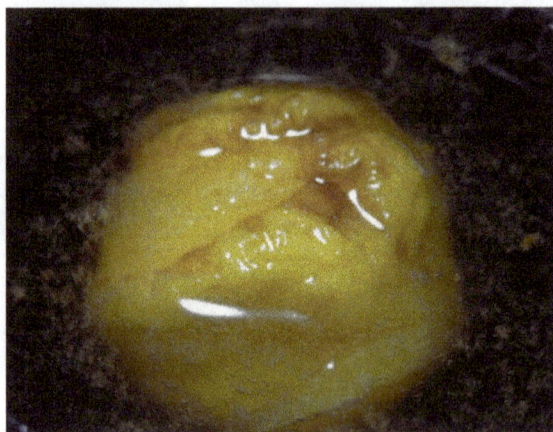

Plum season, time for plum juice.

Sweet fresh prawn *sashimi*.

Spicy fish *roe* rice with minty leave.

The iconic Ichiran Ramen from Kyushu. The entire building belongs to this *ramen* company.

Monastery food, the yellow-pickled *takuon*.

Yuzu citrus chilli.

Traditional Hakata dish: the *SuuMotsu*, hot-plated stir fried pig intestines.

Deep fried *gyoza*.

Railway Technology

Trains are a popular way to travel. This photo shows the Sonic series of trains.

The long distance rapid train service.

Different kinds of trains visible in Fukuoka Hakata station.

One of the latest Shinkansen model.

Traditional Culture

The city of Fukuoka is busy preparing for the annual Yamakasa festival. Copper printing plate design becomes part of street grill.

The traditional Hakata textile.

The landmark Kabuki theatre in Fukuoka that also features foreign musicals like *Les Miserables* in the current theatrical season.

Fukuoka also has an Asian art museum well-known in Japan that specialises in Asian collections.

The south is also historically one of the first areas to accept Catholicism, eventually becoming a bastion of Catholicism in Japan.

This shows designs from a popular *manga* comic series Sazaesan. The decoration is part of a float for the city of Fukuoka's most important annual festival Yamakasa.

Float shows *samurai* doing battle.

Festival float with the seven immortal deities.

Floats with Kabuki theatrical designs.

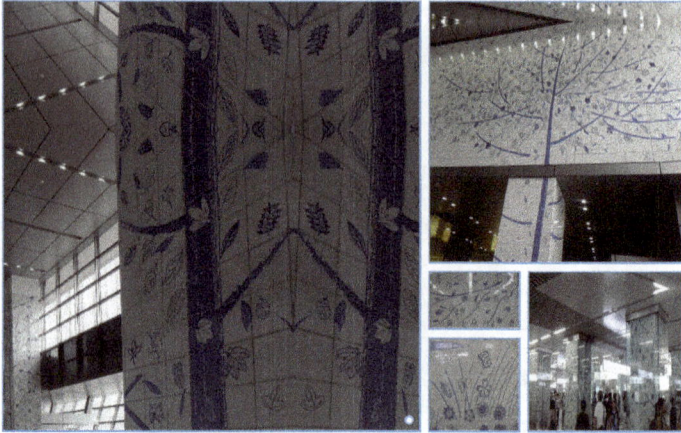

The south is famous for its porcelain especially from Arita, Japan's most well-known Japanese porcelain making region. Here volunteers from the city draw on porcelain tiles and their designs are fired in kilns before installation at Fukuoka's Hakata station.

The Yamakasa annual traditional festival.

Historical Images of Fukuoka

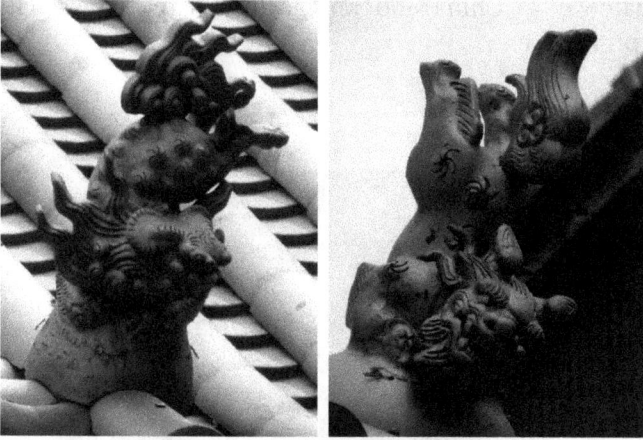

Roof ornaments of early Zen Temples in Kyushu Southern Japan. One of these temples were found by a trader from Sung China living in the Hakata (now Fukuoka area) in mid-13th century.

Traditional rooftop ornamental designs in Japan.

Fukuoka City is also well known for its history, culture, nature as well as its hospitality as the traditional gateway to the rest of East Asia as it is Japan's gateway to China and Korea, and as the largest city in the Fukuoka prefecture.

Urban Wildlife

The traditional Hakata dolls.

Japanese *kois* in a variety of colours.

Shrubs and flowers in bloom in the warm and rainy summer weather.

Summer blooms.

Pleasant open-topped river cruise along the rivers in Fukuoka which has an active night festival.

Still summer but autumn-like leaves juxtaposed with summer green shrubs.

Beautiful short bobtailed wild cat in Japan.

The large fearsome looking *karasu* crows rule the skies of urban Japan.

Ajisai flowers in bloom.

More red autumn-ish leaves juxtaposed against the summer green leaves.

Flowers in bloom.

The Zen Gardens at some of the earliest Zen temples in Japan. Circular lines are drawn in the white gravel to represent waves. Bamboo door leads to the teahouse for the Japanese tea ceremony.

A Japanese crane hunting for fish at the mouth of a river.

Flowers in bloom.

The earliest green tea plants from China were planted here, beginning tea cultivation in Japan.

The natural pine and bamboo decorations in the Shinto tradition.

History of Downtown Fukuoka

A major retail street now, but this area was once overrun by Mongol troops during the Mongol invasions of Japan. The Mongol ships were later destroyed by storms that came to be known as *kamikaze* or divine winds.

An old architectural heritage now preserved as a gallery.

Traditional stone bridge at the Tenmangu shrine. Tenmangu Shrine built after a famous scholar official stopped at this site and saw his own reflection in the river. This shrine is now traditionally worshipped by students who pray for good results in school exams.

A bronze lion guardian at the entrance of the shrine.

Wood carving panel with plum tree design.

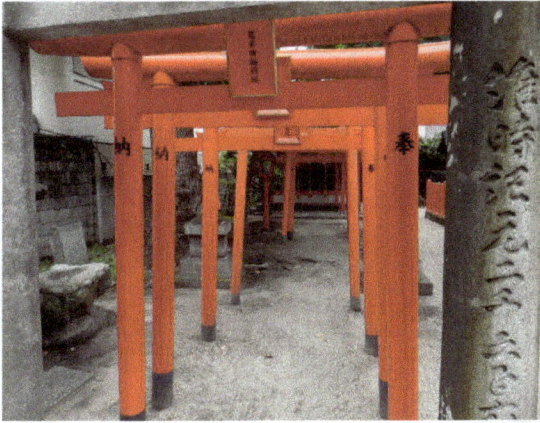

A series of red *tori* gates at the shrine.

Devotees drink from the spring mineral water and wash their hands before entering the shrine.

Indigenised Tang-Style Architecture

Founded at the start of the 9th century, the Tochoji temple is the oldest one in Fukuoka and behind the temple lie the tombs built for the feudal lords of the Fukuoka clan. The previous 10 photos depict the historical temple that was influenced by Tang style architecture but indigenised with strong Japanese features. Caption for this Tang-era temple reads: "Legend has it that this temple was founded in 806 by Kukai upon his return from Tang China. The principal object of worship here, a statue of a standing thousand armed Kannon, has been designated a national cultural asset."

The Zen Temples

Fukuoka features some of the oldest Zen temples in Japan. Green tea cultivation was transmitted to one of these temples and it began the history of green tea agriculture and consumption in Japan. Some of the temples served as embassies for foreign emissaries and traders. Below are some pictures of these old Zen Buddhist temples. Zen flourished in Japan after introduction from China and it became a powerful doctrine both in the religious sense and nationalism as it mobilised Japan to prepare for defence against the Mongol invasions in the 1200s. The next 12 photos show some of these Zen heritage temples.

The Showa-period (built in 1964) architectural design of the 100 m tall old Hakata tower.

Contrast the Showa-era tower with an old wooden tower at one of the oldest Zen temples in Japan.

The Great Hakata Wall

In the 1200s, the Mongols under Kublai Khan had already controlled China and set up the Yuan dynasty. Kublai's forces mobilised two great fleets, one Korean and the other from the central Chinese plains to invade Japan. To defend themselves against the formidable Mongol forces, Japanese feudal lords built a great wall in Hakata to defend themselves against the incoming Mongol forces. Parts of this great wall remain. Below are four pictures of the wall.

A major takeaway from my travels was my appreciation of Japanese culture, arts, traditions and designs, both contemporary and tradition. The element of authenticity cannot be satisfied unless the traveller or tourist is willing to read up and research on some fundamental aspects of Japanese culture in general. Efforts made in pre-departure research on cultural nuances and local customs encountered during travels in Japan can deepen people-to-people exchanges when Singaporeans and Japanese encounter each other in their travels. The next chapter in the volume discusses state of cultural exchanges between Singapore and Japan.

11

Cultural Exchanges between Singapore and Japan

In the previous chapter, I put forward a personal narrative based on observations derived from an experiential tour of Japan. A large component of this personal experience is cultural in nature. Social exchanges do not take place bereft of cultural influences. For the volume's chapters on cultural exchanges, I am adopting several approaches to examine the topical matter. First in this chapter, I will discuss impressions that Singaporeans have of Japan through travels, food experiences (particularly since food is almost a national pastime for Singaporeans), popular cultural performances, etc. I am including personal observation studies and impressions from my own travels to Japan as well as culinary experiences as a foodie. In the following chapter, I will discuss Japan's creative economy. This chapter is drawn from my publication on Japanese pop culture with the same publisher. It talks about my case study on Akihabara, the Mecca of Japanese pop culture in Japan in terms of both consumption and trend-spotting. This is then followed by a Singaporean *otaku*'s account of his experiences and encounters with Japanese popular culture. By including this three-pronged approach to examining Singapore–Japan cultural exchanges, I hope to provide a pluralistic diversity of glimpses into the bilateral exchanges but it does not pretend to be comprehensive. The actual exchanges are even more intense, indepth, multi-faceted, multi-layered and cosmopolitan than what is portrayed here.

In terms of artisanal art forms, Singaporean impressions of Japan tend to strike an equilibrium between traditionalism, creative breakthroughs and selective indigenisation. Japan's penchant for indigenisation of culture was described by Sam Tan, Singapore's Minister of State, Prime Minister's Office & Ministry of Culture, Community and Youth, at the opening of *The Beauty of Kogei: Art Crafts in Japan* in Japan Creative Centre (JCC) in May 2014 as:

> We all know that Japan is a country steeped in tradition and rich in innovation. In Japan, there are many things that they have done over thousands of years; every now and then, they will always inject fresh ideas and new creativity to refresh all these old traditions.[1]

In the quotation above, three impressions of Japanese creativity can be discerned. First, the ability of Japan to preserve and conserve traditional customs appears to be highlighted here. Many Singaporeans have images of Japan through its *kimonos, sushi,* artisanal goods, etc. The second point is the ability of Japan to reinvent itself. Singaporean consumers of Japanese products, including sweets, snacks and popular culture character goods are also exposed to Japanese ability to fuse the new with the old. Traditional designs are rehashed for contemporary tastes and lifestyle. The third indirect point made here is the awareness of Japanese ability to adapt to change, at least in the field of culture and design.

According to Narushige, Michishita, in the 1990s, food has become the centrepiece of bilateral cultural exchanges when *sushi, okonomiyaki* and Japanese pancakes were some of the items that resonated with

---

[1] Tan, Sam, "Taking bilateral relationship between Singapore and Japan to newer heights — Speech by Mr Sam Tan, Minister of State, Prime Minister's Office & Ministry of Culture, Community and Youth, at Opening of 'The Beauty of Kogei: Art Crafts in Japan', Japan Creative Centre" dated 31 May 2014 in the Ministry of Culture, Community and Youth website [downloaded on 1 Jan 2016], available at https://www.mccy.gov.sg/news/speeches/2014/May/Beauty_of_Kogei_exhibition.aspx.

consumers in Singapore.[2] I belonged to this first generation of Singaporeans who grew up in the 1990s with exposure to *sushi*, Japanese-designed goods, cute or *kawaii* products and sweets. Some Singaporean youngsters and teenagers in my generation shuttled between shopping in the older Yaohan shopping centre in Plaza Singapura and the newer and trendier Daimura shopping mall in Liang Court at River Valley. Such sentiments about the popularity of Japanese culture amongst Singaporeans are also echoed by the Japanese expatriate community residing in Singapore. Satsuki Ikegami, secretary general of the Singaporean chapter of the Japanese Association noted:

> I can feel that Singaporeans love Japanese culture very much, and know a lot about it... the popularity of Japanese culture in Singapore could be seen from the crowds of locals drawn to Japanese Association-organised events, such as the annual Summer Festival [in Ikegami's interview with CNBC].[3]

From this statement, it appears Japanese popular culture is making inroads into the lifestyles, habits and consumption patterns of Singaporeans. As early as 1988, Japanese artistes came to Singapore to celebrate Singapore's traditional festivals like the Lunar New Year (LNY) and promote Japanese popular culture. In the LNY celebrations in 2016, I visited the floating stage at Marina Bay for the River Hong Bao celebrations and came across the caption that mentioned J-pop singer Naoko Kawai performed in Singapore in 1988 against the backdrop of a large snowman prop flown to Singapore from Japan. SJ50 celebrations include the Japanese Food Festival in January 2016, a Japanese Festival by Esplanade in May 2016 and a film fest in July 2016.[4]

---

[2]Michishita, Narushige, "BY INVITATION Japan, Singapore, and 70 years of post-war ties" dated 11 Feb 2015 in *The Straits Times* [downloaded on 1 Jan 2016], available at http://www.straitstimes.com/opinion/japan-singapore-and-70-years-of-post-war-ties.

[3]Sile, Aza Wee, "SG50 sequel: Singapore, Japan to launch SJ50 to celebrate bilateral ties" dated 31 Dec 2015 in CNBC AsiaOne website [downloaded on 1 Jan 2016],availableathttp://business.asiaone.com/news/sg50-sequel-singapore-japan-launch-sj50-celebrate-bilateral-ties.

[4]Sile, Aza Wee, "SG50 sequel: Singapore, Japan to launch SJ50 to celebrate bilateral ties" dated 31 Dec 2015 in CNBC AsiaOne website [downloaded on 1 Jan 2016],availableathttp://business.asiaone.com/news/sg50-sequel-singapore-japan-launch-sj50-celebrate-bilateral-ties.

J-pop continues to be popular amongst some audiences in Singapore. On 16 February 2016, the Esplanade Theatre organised a press release and revealed that J-pop sensation Kyary Pamyu Pamyu will be working with Butoh veteran Sankai Juku, Singaporean and Japanese theatre director Chong Tze Chien and Shigeki Nakano, respectively in the new cultural initiative Super Japan — Japanese Festival of Arts.[5] The programme from 13 to 22 May 2016 will showcase 25 paying and 60 non-fee paying items and both Kyary Pamyu Pamyu as well as Hiromitsu Agatsuma (*shamisen* master) are highlights of this festival.[6] The festival itself is rotational thematically, with a country or cultural focus every three years and this time round, Japan is emphasised and it can facilitate exchanges between the artists and Singaporean audiences.[7] Kyary Pamyu Pamyu is a pop star, fashion icon and visual artist who is sometimes nicknamed Japan's Lady Gaga currently on her fifth anniversary globetrotting tour and is probably an optimal choice to front this event.[8] Kyary Pamyu Pamyu is well known in Japan as the queen of pop and an icon in the *kawaii* or cuteness movement. With her outlandish dressing, high pitched stylised singing and choreographed dance moves as well as colourful costume, Kyary Pamyu Pamyu enjoys the support of some Singaporean fans steeped in the *kawaii* (cuteness) culture.

---

[5]The Esplanade Co. Ltd. Press Release, "Esplanade Launches a New Cultural Festival — Super Japan — Japanese Festival of Arts" dated 16 Feb 2016 in the Esplanate.com website [downloaded on 17 Feb 2016], available at https://www.esplanade.com/~/media/files/press-room/2016/pr-super-japan-2016.pdf?mw=1920&hash=EE543CAF0E674548B73601B7C1C396905599234D, p. 1.

[6]The Esplanade Co. Ltd. Press Release, "Esplanade Launches a New Cultural Festival — Super Japan — Japanese Festival of Arts" dated 16 Feb 2016 in the Esplanate.com website [downloaded on 17 Feb 2016], available at https://www.esplanade.com/~/media/files/press-room/2016/pr-super-japan-2016.pdf?mw=1920&hash=EE543CAF0E674548B73601B7C1C396905599234D, p. 2.

[7]The Esplanade Co. Ltd. Press Release, "Esplanade launches a new cultural festival — Super Japan — Japanese festival of arts" dated 16 Feb 2016 in the Esplanate.com website [downloaded on 17 Feb 2016], available at https://www.esplanade.com/~/media/files/press-room/2016/pr-super-japan-2016.pdf?mw=1920&hash=EE543CAF0E674548B73601B7C1C396905599234D, p. 2.

[8]*Ibid.*

All Hail the Queen of J-Pop

The Esplanade promises to be a cultural centre of celebration in the run-up to the 50th anniversary of diplomatic ties between Singapore and Japan. Interestingly, one of the highlights in the programme is the arrival of the doyen of J-pop (Japanese popular culture) with the artiste name Kyrary Pamyu Pamyu (actual name: Kiriko Takemura). Takemura started off as a "Harajuku girl". This is a term given to youths who used to hang out at this fashionable district in Tokyo which spotted a mish-mash of foreign products (much of which originated from the US like hard rock and hip hop items) and local innovations. It is a cultural zone in which different genres of global pop fashion (burlesque, street fashion, hip hop, rock, etc.) interface with Japanese cultural sensitivities and are hybridised into completely new products and fashion trends (*lolitha*, *kawaii*, etc.). The district was so well known that international pop superstar Gwen Stefani dedicated one of her songs to this cultural phenomenon titled simply as "Harajuku Girls". International superstars have also been spotted shopping at this district. A prominent example is Lady Gaga who apparently liked shopping *incognito* (sometimes not so inconspicuous) at Harajuku fashion labels such as "Dog", an exclusive cyberpunk and street fashion store.

It was in this district that Kyary honed her skills in fashion imaging and eventually rose to become a model for the *kawaii* cuteness movement after she was spotted on the streets of Harajuku by talent scouts. One thing led to another and she was invited to join the clubbing scene as a DJ at the iconic teenage dance event Takenoko.

At Takenoko, she met her future production team led by Yasutaka Nakata (who is based in Harajuku) and this led to her first pop album in 2011. The Harajuku fashion scene with *lolitha* and gothic costumes that contributed to the phenomenon of cosplay (participants masquerading themselves in fancy costumes and taking on the persona of the *anime* or *manga* characters) was combined with Japanese dance music, becoming a new J-pop sensation appealing to fans in East Asia.

It gestated in East Asia but soon the hybridised cultural form spread to the West and found popularity in Europe and North America. That heralded the global age of Kyary Pamyu Pamyu's music. The characteristic dance tunes, high pitched voice, zany lyrics and a sense of irreverence appeared to appeal universally across borders. Some fans have even found the appeal of Kyary's works in lying in its deliberate seemingly nonsensical and grammatically-inaccurate lyrics and even mildly annoying and irritating singing styles and pitches.

This unconventionality and sense of irreverence may represent a sense of angst and rebelliousness of her fans living in a structured world. It is also a way of rejecting social norms by taking on textually nonsensical lyrics to push beyond the judgmental gazes of social expectations imposed by mainstream society. Mainstream values create insecurities in the psyche of young people and Kyary's music plays on such insecurities by making them cool through deliberate mistakes in her music. But even fashion trends and teenage rebelliousness have their own shelf life and fans can become bored quite easily when a particular J-pop format is milked excessively. Creative destruction is necessarily the mother of invention. One of Kyary's uncanny skills is the ability to create multiple images of herself, ranging from punk rock to psychedelic fashion icon. The portrayal of multiple identities keeps fans guessing about her fashion inclinations and her sense of aesthetics. But one fashion genre characterises the pop star more than others. Kyary Pamyu Pamyu is also known as the Queen of the "kawaii" or "cuteness" movement.

Kyary is not the originator of the *kawaii* movement in Japan which is associated more with the globally conspicuous evergreen cultural product of Hello Kitty, a cute stuffed toy designed in the image of a cat with no mouth and short limbs, to convey a sense of non-threatening helplessness that denotes cuteness. Kyary's innovation in this cuteness movement is the integration of grotesque and soft gothic images and made them acceptable to mainstream fans by contouring and mitigating their grittier and risqué nature with *kawaii*-ness. Her colourful costumes and props, for example, may integrate gothic bones and skulls or dark nocturnal creatures such as bats or even monster (*yokai*) icons.

Constant change and innovation marking Kyary's music, the attempts to do something different and unique from others and hybridisation of different ideas including those from the East and West seem to characterise Singapore's own nation-building approach and its next lap of development as well. It also symbolises Japan's status as the first country to modernise in East Asia by modernising and indigenising new ideas. Perhaps, Kyary Pamyu Pamyu embodies the innovative cultures of both countries and this is something apt for commemorating their 50th anniversary of diplomatic ties through popular culture. Later on in this publication, a Singaporean *otaku* fan will articulate his opinions of Japanese popular culture in a later chapter in this volume.

Besides J-pop fans, there is also a community of *anime* and *manga* character figurine collectors in Singapore. This community throng the likes of toy shops in Vivo City, Bugis Junction, China Square for the latest offerings in Japan-made toys. They co-exist with other toy-collecting communities such as those collecting Star Wars toys, Marvel/DC products or Trekkies' models. Sometimes, some of them meet at China Square during the weekends to look through the Japanese toy models on sale and bargain for good prices on the latest *manga/anime* figurines. This community was formerly based in Clarke Quay but they moved to China Square when Clarke Quay was converted into a drinking, night entertainment and clubbing district. Even the Sunday Clarke Quay flea market was moved to China Square. Many of these figurines are pricey as they come from the Akihabara district of Tokyo where *otakus* or Japanese popular culture fans all over the world gather. The next chapter examines Akihabara in detail.

To understand the Japanese toy collectors in Singapore, I became a collector of toys myself and attended weekend toy flea marts and visited the specialty toy stores regularly for one year from February 2015 to February 2016. The Japanese toy collecting community can be divided into sub-groups. They include the mainstream collectors who stick to collecting characters in popular cartoons such as One Piece, Gundam and Ghost in the Shell. There are the *kawaii* cute character collectors who focus on the likes of Hello Kitty and other Sanrio collectors, Doraemon, Licca dolls, etc. This community attracts mostly women although I have seen men collect cute Japanese toys as well. The third group consists of hard-core *otaku* collectors who look at very specific genres like gothic dolls, vocaloids like Hatsune Miku, Japan-made full articulation Star Wars models, etc. Interestingly, some collectors go for Japanese-made Star Wars toys because the figurines have full articulation in their limbs and are well-designed. Some of these figurines belong to the fusion variety where authentic Star Wars designs, for example, are fused with traditional *samurai* designs to create hybridised characters. The fourth group are the nostalgic crowd, going for old collectible toys such as antique tins toys made in the Occupied Japan period (1945–1952) or the 1960s–1980s retro toys with early versions of Godzilla, Ultraman and Kamen Rider figurines. This group is probably the most well-endowed fandom group since antique toys generally cost much more than new toys. The last group of toy lovers are the model kits assemblers — people who believe in constructing their own toys through supplied parts and then painting and decorating them creatively. They are a hands-on crowd.

Toys and Japanese popular culture are often appreciated for their high quality, creative designs and aesthetics display values. Good designs and quality merchandise have come to characterise Japanese lifestyle products. Since the 1990s, some Singaporeans have found Japanese goods, services and lifestyle attractive. In fact, bilateral exchanges in design, popular culture and creative craftsmanship intensified as early as from at least 2014 onwards, proximate to the time of the scheduled SG50 or SJ50 events. At that time, official cultural exchanges related to Japanese artisanal quality were visible when Japanese Prime Minister (PM) Mr Abe visited Singapore and attended a Japanese art exhibition "The Beauty of Kogei" in May 2014. Japanese craftsmanship of pens and stationary embodying traditional art forms were on display here, warranting minis-terial-level mention and visits.

Quality products and presentation styles apply to the Japanese food culture as well. A survey in 2014 organised by Borders Asia Market Insight and AsiaX discovered that Japanese food cuisine is the most popular for-eign culinary choice according to the Singaporean palate.[9] With regards to culinary culture, I personally discovered the exquisite nature of Japanese food when I attended a national reception in Singapore that featured Japanese food products and culinary cuisines from different regions of Japan. Japanese food (*nihonryouri*) needs no introduction but

---

[9]Michishita, Narushige, "BY INVITATION Japan, Singapore, and 70 years of post-war ties" dated 11 Feb 2015 in *The Straits Times* [downloaded on 1 Jan 2016], available at http://www.straitstimes.com/opinion/japan-singapore-and-70-years-of-post-war-ties.

Japanese food served in an official capacity is not an everyday affair. I had the privilege of experiencing Japanese culinary culture recently in an official reception by the Japanese government celebrating a public occasion. Japanese food in the fusion tradition is well paired off with Italian finger food on picks with a combination of bread and smoked salmon. The idea is to confuse the palate with different tastes before trying out the minimalist approach of Japanese food. Other guests with the sweet tooth preferred to tease their palates with confectionary before moving onto the *nihonryouri* offerings. Puffs, tarts and cakes soaked in rum with a dash of gold-leaved berries become a favourite amongst the guest.

To create the mood for consuming Japanese food and to add pomp to the circumstance, the setting is very important. The perfectionist Ikebana arrangement decorated a lacquered horse carriage model and add a touch of royalty to the occasion, while the use of local flowers in this arrangement binds the Singaporean sense of aesthetics with its Japanese counterpart. Placed on a red carpet and a folding screen, the simple understated beauty of this arrangement tease the visual senses with colours framed by streaks of intertwined red and white stems. In the same room, the gold-leaved folding screen reminds me of the famed Kyoto Temple Kinkakuji, a golden coloured Zen temple that appears to be floating in a pond surrounded by Japanese dwarf maples or *momiji* that turns red during the autumn season. It mitigates the grand ballroom and its impressive chandelier in an understated way, contouring excessive ostentatious displays with simple monochromatic gold screen without designs embossed on it. It lends Kyoto Zen-like decorum to the occasion without being opulent.

Any Japanese culinary tasting session cannot be complete without serving *sushi*. The Red Seabeam or *Tai* in Japanese during winter season is at its fatty best. Succulent and sweet, they were hand-pressed by *sushi* experts with a dash or *wasabi* and rice and then dipped lightly in soy sauce for that light flavour to fish meat that comes with a rich texture. Two schools of thought arose with regards to the use of soy sauce, the traditional orthodox way is to flip the *sushi* and dip only the *Tai* portion of the *sushi* lightly into the soy sauce while an unconventional and sometimes considered as inaccurate methodology is to dip the rice portion of the *sushi* into the sauce. I do not judge, to each his own, as long as their palate can enjoy the cuisine.

Eating *sushi* has become so ubiquitous that locally made *sushi* are now served at catering services' regular menus, alongside local food items like *mee goreng*. In other words, *sushi* is de-exoticised as a Japanese food item and integrated into Singaporeans' cosmopolitan food map and served alongside local delights. *Sushi* has been integrated and incorporated into the local menu.

Tai is historically known as the King of the Fishes in Japan, enjoying high prestige amongst *sushi* connoisseurs. The reception served Tai Sea Beam from the Aichi Prefecture which organises a famous annual ritual or *matsuri* festival to celebrate the availability of the fish. The most attractive part of consuming Tai Sea Beams is its texture, possessing a chewy yet complex fibrous tissues that contrast with the smooth layered feel of salmon. It requires more efforts to chew and thereby releases more taste from additional chewing to the mouth.

The crown jewel of the culinary experience is probably the delectable *wagyu* which melts in one's mouth because of the high fats contents. Eaten medium-rare with a dash of sea salt, the thinly sliced *wagyu* is best at its simplest and most unadulterated taste. I queued up 20 minutes for this dish, along with other dignitaries to the party. The wait was well worth it as it generated curiosity in the senses and the palate.

Cognitively and emotively, the suspense drove my anticipation to taste Japan's finest beef product. The visual image of the marbled *wagyu* beef as a block while the guests were in the queue kept the visual senses busy as it tries to perceive the taste of the beef cognitively before the palate can taste it. The poster introducing this Iwate *wagyu* simply reads "elegant taste on a clear day". It depicts a cattle grazing the green fields of Northeast Japan underneath a clear sky.

The reception is then concluded with French desserts and pastries. Once again, the sweetness of the sugared delights wraps up the *wagyu* session as the occasion concludes on a sweet note. The fruity tarts also neutralises the rich oily taste of the *wagyu* beef and the uncomplicated juicy succulent flesh of the fruit bits contrasts with soft marbled texture of the beef.

Overall, the Japanese dishes harmonised well with continental European fares to provide a cosmopolitan feel to the occasion. Together with the delicious local fare like Mee Goreng, the fusion approach to a national ball leaves a distinct impression on its guests. Fine Japanese foods are no longer confined only to special occasions and grand ball-rooms. Some aspects of it have integrated into Singaporeans' daily lives. For example, the Japanese *sake* is now widely available in Singapore, especially in Japanese restaurants and beverage outlets. In restaurants, they are often served in ornate pottery or glassware.

In deconstructing what is native and what is others, Singaporeans have proved to be adept in hybridising non-local foods including Japanese food items. In a curious case of multiple hybridisations, Singaporeans have taken a liking to Japanese interpretations of Italian culinary culture like pizza, spaghetti and pasta, enjoying these cuisines as a form of East–West fusion dishes. Food is probably the most funda-mental and basic cultural approach to Japanese lifestyle products.

Japanese Lifestyle goods. The accent on design, functionality and Zen minimalistic aesthetic have appealed to some Singaporeans. Japanese lifestyle appears to appeal to Singaporeans as well. According to the same poll, Japan is the third choice after Australia and New Zealand where Singaporeans would like to reside.[10] As a frequent visitor to Japan, it is possible to understand some of the appealing features found in

---

[10]Michishita, Narushige, "BY INVITATION Japan, Singapore, and 70 years of post-war ties" dated 11 Feb 2015 in *The Straits Times* [downloaded on 1 Jan 2016], available at http://www.straitstimes.com/opinion/japan-singapore-and-70-years-of-post-war-ties.

Japanese design is also visible in the Singaporean landscape. For example, the spinal design in Nanyang Technological University was conceptualised by famous Japanese architect Kenzo Tange and his associates.

The city skyline of Singapore captures the towering silhouette of the Raffles Place buildings designed by Kenzo Tange, Japanese architect, located in the financial heart of Singapore.

Japan for Singaporeans. They include orderly and well-mannered behavioural norms and social relations. Many around the world were impressed by the orderly queues that formed at the supermarkets after the occurrence of the devastating Great East Japan Earthquake. These

The picture shows Kenzo Tange's works amongst a cluster of skyscrapers in Shenton Way, Singapore's financial district. This view is taken from Marina Bay on an amphibious vehicle.

A shot of the South Spine in Nanyang Technological University (NTU) and the carpark nearby.

images were telecasted worldwide for the global audience. Japan's penchant for design and quality is also well known in East Asia. Some of these design masterpieces including the highly-visible buildings designed by Japanese architects have become permanent features of Singapore's landscapes.

Figure 6: The two Raffles Place Building designed by Japanese architect Kenzo Tange, they are now iconic landmarks in Singapore's financial district.

Place for Consumption

Japanese designs and lifestyle goods are well-known for their quality and design. This section of the chapter discusses the locations where such goods are consumed. These consumption centres have effectively become specialised hangouts and shopping areas for the Japanese expatriate community, Japanese lifestyle goods lovers and not forgetting Japanese foodies. The advantage of shopping in areas like Yaohan, Liang Court, Sogo at City Hall, Little Ginza, Meidi-ya at Liang Court and Takashimaya at Orchard Road is that they provide the one-stop experiences for procuring different genres of Japanese products. There are substantial numbers of consumers of Japanese popular cultural products from the ubiquitous Hello Kitty dolls to very niche highly specialised *otaku* products like Evangelion. The locations however are not static and are dynamic in nature. Japanese malls are trendy for a certain period and then decline due to natural market forces and also performances of their mother companies in Japan. Yaohan, Daimaru and Sogo are shopping experiences of the past as they have ebbed and declined according to Singaporean shopping habits. But Takashimaya at Orchard and Meidi-Ya in Liang Court remain strong evergreen flagship stores that carry Japanese brands, food products and lifestyle goods.

When I was growing up in the 1970s, the place to go for consuming Japanese products was Yaohan in Plaza Singapura at the tail end of Orchard Road bordering Dhoby Ghaut (refer to the section on Yaohan in the chapter on Singapore–Japan economic ties). In the 1980s, Daimaru in Liang Court became the place to visit for such products. Simultaneous with the shopping experience in Daimaru, another quaint location where Japanese expatriates hung out was "Little Ginza" in West Coast of Singapore. Similarly, "Little Ginza" (actual name "Ginza Plaza" with rentable space of 160,000 sq ft) became relegated to the past when it was refurbished by the Far East Organization working with DP Architects in 2007–2008 through a S$26 million upgrading process and a name change to West Coast Plaza and it was given a new nickname "An Oasis in the West".[11] The reasons for the decline of Little Ginza as a spot for Japanese lifestyle goods consumption by the Japanese expatriate community is explained in the following *Business Times* article:

> Vivienne Tan, president of Far East Retail Consultancy, said changing demographics in the West were a key factor in the decision to refurbish the mall. 'As its original name suggests, Ginza Plaza used to cater to the Japanese expatriate community that lived in the area,' Mrs Tan said. 'But now we're seeing a good number of other nationalities moving in. There is also a growing private residential population,' she said.[12]

Analysing this business report, the following points are relevant. Beyond drawing only Japanese expatriates, by 2008, West Coast Plaza became a location for Western Singapore residents who have higher disposable incomes living in a disproportionate number of private homes at that time (relative to other parts of Singapore), multinational expatriates crowds, discerning tertiary student shoppers who study within 3 km of the mall and a high-income professional crowds employed in the One-North hi-tech incubator cluster.[13] It was no longer the exclusive haunt of the Japanese expatriate community. With the

---

[11] Business Times, "Ginza Plaza to get $26m facelift" dated 20 November 2007 in the *Singapore Property News* Singapore Property Press website [downloaded on 1March2016], available at https://sgpropertypress.wordpress.com/2007/11/20/ginza-plaza-to-get-26m-facelift/.

[12] *Ibid.*

[13] *Ibid.*

decline of Yaohan, Daimaru, Sogo and Little Ginza, Liang Court is currently considered as the place to go when one wants to consume Japanese cultural products. With an array of Japanese restaurants, retailers, bookshop and even *ramen* outlets, Liang Court offers the one-stop experience for Singaporean and Japanese expatriate shoppers keen on consuming Japanese lifestyle products. Liang Court even has its own Japanese barber, clinic and traditional tea school operated by Urasenke tea school. Another evergreen location for Japanese goods consumption is found in Orchard Road. Perhaps, a milestone event in the supply of Japanese lifestyle goods for Singaporean consumption occurred when Takashimaya moved into Ngee Ann City in the heart of Orchard Road and became its anchor tenant. Since then, Takashimaya is the place to shop, particularly for high-end products and Japanese goods.

Liang Court, now widely considered as one of the places to go to consume Japanese products and foods.

After Daimaru moved out of its premises in Liang Court, Meidi-ya the Japanese supermarket moved in as a 24 hour outlet. It remains at the same location today although no longer operating 24 hours. Opened from 10 am to 10 pm, Singapore's Meidi-Ya Supermarket (the second overseas shop after the first one got into business in Amsterdam, Holland) aspires to deliver fresh foods to Singapore residents that originates from Japan, non-Japanese products, Singaporean food items and cooked food *bento* (Japanese for lunch boxes).[14] Its signature products first made available in 1911 include "My Jam" processed from the freshest fruit ingredients that are strong in protein, fibre and vitamins ingredients with no cholesterol, its in-house peanut butter with marshmallow bits and smooth texture and a range of colour-filled "My Syrup" presented with traditional tastes and made from fine ingredients.[15]

Besides the above-named places, at different points of time, Far East Plaza and Bugis Junction featured Harajuku-like and Shinjuku-ish retail outlets although only remnants of those outlets are left today. They cater to fans of Japanese fashion trends like the Kawaii or cuteness movement. Today, Japanese retail outlets and restaurants are highly decentralised and they have proliferated throughout the island in neighbourhood malls and in local food court. In other words, a larger number of Singaporeans can enjoy them now. Japanese consumption is known to be ethically conscious. Japan is an avid practitioner of ethical behaviour with a strong recycling system that meticulously divide up the trash into neat categories for collection. In the retail sector, for example, when Daimaru and Sogo existed, paper bags were often provided for shoppers instead of non-biodegradable plastic bags.

Traditionalism

Besides Singaporean appreciation for contemporary Japanese popular cultural and lifestyle goods, Singaporeans are also receptive towards some aspects of traditional Japanese culture. Regional sports events become an avenue for Japan to share its culture with Singapore and other ASEAN countries. Japanese *koi* carps and gardens have also become important fixtures in the Singaporean physical, commercial and residential landscape. Some of my photographic observation studies are detailed below. They are some very visible displays of traditional

---

[14] Meidi-Ya, "Singapore MEIDI-YA Supermarket" dated 2016 at the Meidi-Ya website [downloaded on 1 March 2016], available at http://www.meidi-ya.com.sg/en/about.asp.

[15] *Ibid.*

The photo shows a splash of colour on *kois* reared in the temple pond of a Tenmangu shrine in downtown Fukuoka.

Japanese popular culture but the most permanent symbol and perhaps unchanging features of Japanese traditions is the large Japanese garden found in Lakeside Jurong. While traditional Japanese cultural performances may be limited in temporal durations and visual arts and performing troupes may come and go, the Garden is a mainstay of visible Japanese cultural influence on the landscape of Singapore, in the Jurong area which was historically the site of Singapore's industrialisation birthplace and an area that was reclaimed from the swamps. Regional sports events like the 28th Southeast Asian (SEA) Games hosted by Singapore in 2015 became an opportunity for Japanese cultural performances like Taiko shown above. Judo was a featured event in these games.

A material evidence of the enduring nature of Singaporean interest in traditional Japanese culture is in the form of the largest Japanese garden in Jurong near Lakeside Mass Rapid Transit (MRT) station. The garden is both a traditional cultural symbol as well as a representation of friendship between the Japanese and Singaporean peoples. It was cultivated under the nurturing care of expert gardeners and dedicated park officials. An old foundation stone at the garden reads:

Seiwaen — This garden is a symbol of friendship and co-operation between the peoples of Singapore and Japan and has been made possible through: The government of Japan who made available the services of Professor Kinsaku Nakane: Professor Kinsaku Nakane who designed and personally supervised the construction of the garden and his tree associates for their dedication and hardwork...

At the point of this writing, the garden is undergoing renovation and refurbishments. Before the renovations, the caption to the Torii gate of the garden read:

No Cup Gate. The name of this gate comes from the famous Zen story, "A Cup of Tea". Nan-in, a Japanese master during the Meiji era, (1869–1912), hosted a university professor who came to inquire about Zen. Nan-in served tea. He poured his visitor's cup full and then kept on pouring. The professor watched the overflow until he could no longer restrain himself and exclaimed. "It is over full. No more will go in!" "Like this cup", Nan-in said. "You are full of your own opinions and speculations, how can I show you Zen unless you first empty your cup?"

The gate's name urges visitors to experience the Singapore Japanese Garden without any preconceptions, notions and ideas about Japanese culture. Zen Buddhist practice emphasises the virtues of nothingness. Its uncomplicated life philosophy is reflected in the Garden's simplistic landscape, uncluttered, clean contouring lines and serene environs.

In this chapter, the elements of popular cultural and lifestyle goods consumption as well as appreciation for Japanese traditional culture were discussed. They are by no means comprehensive discussions but serve to survey some aspects of the embeddedness of Japanese culture

Torii Shinto entrance to the Japanese garden in Jurong.

The red wooden traditional Japanese bridge stretches from one bank of a pond to another side of the bank.

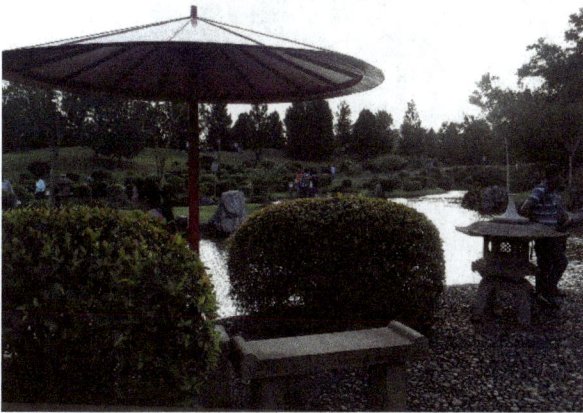

An outdoor umbrella with red handle, typically used to host Japanese tea ceremony. Traditional Japanese designs for stone lanterns and benches are visible in the photo.

Zen-like rock gardens with pruned ornamental plants and *bonsai* trees.

The long corridor by the side of an enclosed space with Japanese cast iron lanterns and water chimes made out of recycled materials.

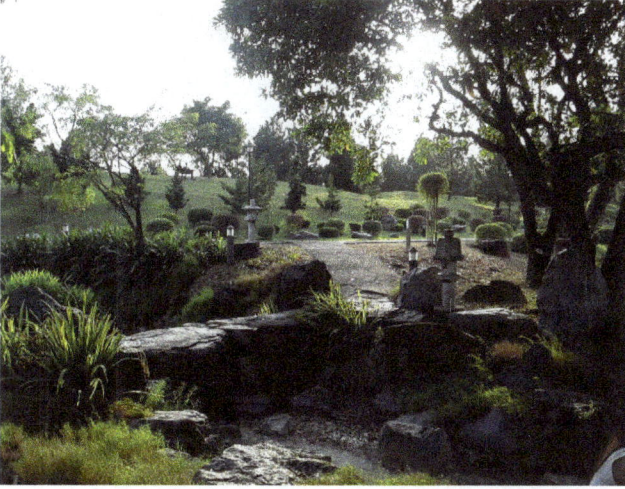

A panoramic view of the garden with visible rock formations.

Two more curved traditional red Japanese bridges spanning a large pond within the Japanese garden.

A large activity hall space within the Japanese garden. When I was there, many foreign workers based in Singapore as well as local residents were relaxing in its wide open space which provides cool shelter from the hot afternoon sun in Singapore.

in the local landscape. The two chapters on social exchanges through tours and travels as well as cultural exchanges focus on how contemporary Japanese culture is manufactured and produced in Japan before it is exported to Singapore. The commodification of culture is not possible without a complex cultural ecological system to produce such goods for the Singaporean and global consumers. The chapter immediately following this examines popular cultural consumption in Akihabara, a district in Tokyo that has been the trendsetter for Japanese popular culture since the 1990s. This chapter is followed by my latest observation studies in my travels to Akihabara and other Japanese popular cultural sites in Tokyo. With this eclectic collection of popular cultural perspectives, I hope to present a nuanced and complex picture of Japanese popular cultural consumption in Singapore or in Tokyo by Singaporeans.

12

Centring Akihabara: The Positionality of Tokyo's Pop-Cultural Nucleus in Cool Japan Industries and Globalised Fandom Consumption

Introduction

To understand the process of producing Japanese popular culture, I raise several questions in this Chapter. First, historically, how did relationships within the iron triangle of production companies (producers), fans (consumers) and the state (regulators) evolve to the current contemporary system of sales, distribution and production? Second, what sort of influence does it have on regional audiences, do the products resonate with a regional audience through collective consumption, contents-based depictions of normative values and network-based peer pressure? Third, how does consumption emanate soft power — through the encouragement of consumption in regionally rising middle classes and/or production networks in the region. These three questions will be discussed and analysed in this chapter and they will be contextualised in the case study of Akihabara, Japan's premium Japanese popular cultural centre.

I have benefitted from reading Jakob Nobuoka's persuasive article on Japanese Cultural Economy focusing on Akihabara as one of its case studies. His central arguments and thesis statement include how media mix (one image or narrative used in many categories of media including *anime, manga,* digital game, etc.). The capability to send contents-based narrative through various forms of media and technologies is the basis for Japan's creative industry competitiveness.[1] Agreeing with Nobuoka for most parts of this theoretical discussion of the cultural economy, I adopt his definition of the term as "the system of production, distribution, consumption and management of goods that primarily have a symbolic value which serves the preference to express culture."[2]

Historical Background

A signboard put up by the local authorities at the main retail street of Akihabara narrated the late pre-modern history of the district:

> This neighborhood was once called Kanda-Tashirocho. It is said that the name derives from the fact that in the late 18th century, land that had been used by a retainer of the Shogun was offered as alternative land for people who had been displaced from a nearby town to make way for a firebreak.

From a firebreak, the district has since evolved from a trading outpost to a train station trading stop in the modern period and then a second-hand radio repair workshop district in the early post-war period operated by demobilised technicians and engineer military men. In the contemporary era, Akihabara the district is known to *otakus* affectionately as "Akiba" and the consumers that shop there are the "Akiba kids". From the 1960s onwards, Akihabara's history reflected Japan's industrial development in manufacturing high-tech electronics and retailing the latest electronic gadget lines. This is how the signboard put up by the

---

[1] Nobuoka, Jakob, *Geographies of the Japanese Cultural Economy Innovation and Creative Consumption* (Sweden: Uppsala University Geografiska Regionstudier NR 83), 2010, pp. 18–19.

[2] Nobuoka, Jakob, *Geographies of the Japanese Cultural Economy Innovation and Creative Consumption* (Sweden: Uppsala University Geografiska Regionstudier NR 83), 2010, p. 29.

authorities near the Akihabara station on the side of the Denkimachi exit narrated the history of the district:

> The name of this neighborhood comes from a bridge Maebashi that crosses the Kanda River. Even before World War II, this area was home to many wholesalers and retailers in electric goods and today has become, under the name of Akihabara, one of the world's most famous shopping areas for electronic goods.

The signboard itself may be outdated, given that Akihabara is no longer a premium district for electronic goods shopping but a location increasingly infused with retailers in popular cultural products. The large electronics retail businesses have declined due to severe competition in the 1980s and 1990s, leaving only a select few large players behind. The other factor that accounted for the electronics retail sector decline is the suburbanisation of Japanese cities, resulting in the appearance of large chain branch stores that serve the needs of the middle-classes residing in the suburban areas.

In the 1970s and 1980s, it was an electronic retailing district that was transformed into the centre of *otaku* culture in the 1990s. In the 1980s, according to Marcias and Machiyama, Akihabara experienced a brisk sales period from retailing "illegal electronic devices like mini cameras, radio scanners, eavesdropping devices and bootleg software", becoming a "hacker boom" and a "nerds" historical phase until digital encryption in the 1990s halted its advancement.[3] By the first decade of the 21st century, Akihabara was firmly known as a place for *otakus*, a paradise whereby specialised comic books for self-identified communities (*doujinshi*) could acquire and consume their products throughout the year. Tora no Ana is an Akihabara-based chain store that sells products which are specialised for *otakus* and not easily understood or acceptable by the general public (e.g. sexual themes, homosexual fantasies, etc.).[4] The

---

[3] Macias, Patrick and Tomohiro Machiyama, *Cruising the Anime City* (Berkeley, CA: Stone Bridge Press), 2004, p. 81.
[4] Macias, Patrick and Tomohiro Machiyama, *Cruising the Anime City* (Berkeley, CA: Stone Bridge Press), 2004, pp. 22–23.

The photograph shows one of the last surviving corners of Akihabara that still retails electronic components and wires in the traditional open stall (*yatai*) format. It is unclear if this corner can even survive the ongoing gentrification process in the lead-up to the Tokyo Olympics in 2020.

The clutter of wires at the last surviving corner of Akihabara that sells such products in open stalls. Wires used to dominate the retail industry here during Japan's fast-growth economic period.

A retro-looking gaudy in-your-face advertisement by electronics dealers/retailers recommending their latest products. These images are reminiscent of Akihabara in the 1980s and 1990s.

Today, you can still find large electronics retailers in Akihabara like Laox interspersed with the Japanese popular culture retailers. These are the survivors of the electronics retailing shakeup in the 1990s.

Electronics retailing continues to be a shared component of Akihabara's business activity, especially in the annual Akihabara Electric Town Summer Campaign in 2014. When I did this fieldwork as part of a study tour in summertime 2014 in Akihabara, Doraemon was the official mascot for the summer campaign. This is a picture of a banner that hangs on public street lamps out in the main street of Akihabara.

initial success of retailers like Tora no Ana inspired other niched popular cultural outfits to follow and this resulted in formation of clusters of competitive as well as complementary fellow retailers selling the same genre of products, making Akihabara a convenient one-stop location for popular cultural goods.

In the first decade of the 21st century, Nomura Research Institute, Ltd. published an authoritative study which estimated the *otaku* population to be 1.72 million-strong with a market size of ¥411 billion.[5] This number

---

[5] Nomura Research Institute, Ltd., "New Market Scale Estimation for Otaku: Population of 1.72 Million with Market Scale of Yen411 Billion" in the Nomura Research Institute (NRI) News Release [downloaded on 5 Dec 2014], available at https://www.nri.com/global/news/2005/051006.html.

Low-rise multi-storey buildings now house the leading Japanese popular culture retailers in Japan (and the world).

The iconic Sofmap, a recognised giant in popular cultural retailing, offering both mainstream and niched product, a must-stop for *otaku* pilgrimages.

does not include overseas markets, mainstream consumers who consume *otaku* products but do not identify themselves as *otakus* and closet *otakus* who hide their identities for various reasons. According to this study, the industries that the *otakus* engaged in are also multi-faceted, including comics, animation, idols, games, PC assembly, audio–visual equipment, mobile IT equipment, autos, travel, fashion, cameras and railways.[6] Nobuoka quoted the following figures from Kitabayashi's study to indicate the respective population and market sizes of different kinds of *otakus* (2004 figures): *manga otakus* (1 million and ¥100 billion); anime *otakus* (200,000 and ¥20 billion); idols otakus (800, 000 and ¥60 billion); games *otakus* (800,000 and ¥78 billion); PC assembly *otakus* (50,000 and ¥32 billion).[7] A decade later, Japanese Internet portal *My Navi* conducted an early 2014 survey of 5,663 individuals about to graduate from college or postgraduate school in March of 2015 and 39.5% of the respondents self-identified themselves as *otakus*.[8]

Methodology

The methodology for this chapter is three-folds. First, I employ textual analysis with interpretation of textual documents and secondary materials. Second, I utilised onsite observational studies of major Japanese popular cultural production and consumption centres in Tokyo, including locations like Akihabara and Ikebukuro during my summer 2014 fieldwork. Third, I performed the role of a collector of material artefacts, acquiring and amassing popular culture products in order to understand practitioners' motivation in consuming these items. The acquisition of material items facilitate my understanding of how fans acquire their social value and capital in their networked communities. The ability to display the latest figurine or to boast about the acquisition and experience of attending a balloted sold-out concert connotes social

---

[6] *Ibid.*

[7] Nobuoka, Jakob, *Geographies of the Japanese Cultural Economy Innovation and Creative Consumption* (Sweden: Uppsala University Geografiska Regionstudier NR 83), 2010, p. 76.

[8] Baseel, Casey, "Are you *Otaku*? Roughly 40 Percent of Japanese College Students Say, 'Yes!'" dated 1 Feb 2014 in the Rocket News 24 website [downloaded on 5 Dec 2014], available at http://en.rocketnews24.com/2014/02/01/are-you-otaku-roughly-40-percent-of-japanese-college-students-say-yes/.

status and fan pride. It is a form of social ritual performed for acceptance by others within the community. Materialistic possession also drives individual incentives to consume the product through personal ownership and when this personal ownership becomes viral through social network promotion or internet publicity, a sense of collective identity and cultural resonance results. The question is whether such collective consumption repeated over many times and many products from either Japan or Korea constitute a source of soft power?

While I focus on the consumption aspects of popular culture in Japan, specifically the major centre of Tokyo, I acknowledge the importance of the role played by the state in cultural policy formulation and the social context of consumption in anthropological studies. They are as important as the historical narrative. Because I was based in Hong Kong between 2010 and 2014, I was able to study overseas consumption of Japanese popular culture in one of the two major overseas markets for J-pop (Hong Kong and Taiwan). Here, it adds a comparative element to my study as I observe how overseas fans (primary consumers for Japanese popular cultural exports) consume cutting-edge Japanese popular cultural products. This chapter cannot avoid having no discussions of Korean popular culture (Kpop or Hallyu), given that there are temptations and tendencies for scholars interested in East Asian popular culture to compare between the two. In the presentation of my previous papers on Japanese popular culture, audience questions in the Q&A sections often inevitably raise enquiries and feedback for such comparisons.

Significance

Roblyn Simeon's journal article prefers to define this industry as a "contents industry" (including hardware to cultural exports) which makes up approximately ¥13 trillion (US$130 billion) yearly retail sales and has become Japan's ranking business sector by 2006.[9] When sectorally segmented, the 2006 figures for the popular cultural industries' market size are in the following: the visual media (¥4,833.8 billion), publishing and

---

[9] Simeon, Roblyn, "The Branding Potential and Japanese Popular Culture Overseas" dated 2006 in the *Journal of Diversity Management* 1, 2, 2006, p. 13.

newspapers/image and text (¥5,789 billion), music and audio (¥1,914.1 billion) and video games (¥1,144.2 billion) make up a total of ¥13.7 trillion.[10]

"A" for anime of Anime, Comics, Games (ACG) industries

The economic resilience of the creative industries was pointed out by Sugiura Tsutomo who noted:

> According to Yoshimoto Mitsuhiro (2003), in the 1990s, when the Japanese economy had long been in depression, the number of employees in all creative industries increased by 16% from 1.2 million in 1996 to 1.4 million in 2001, while that of all industries decreased by 4.3% from 60.9 million to 58.3 million. In terms of revenues, creative industries as a whole earned 28 trillion (US$280 billion) in 1999, robust gain of 86 percent from Yen 15 trillion (US$150 billion) in 1989, whereas all service industries earned Yen 202 trillion (US$2,020 billion) in 1999, a gain of 69 percent from Yen 119 trillion (US$1,190) in 1989.[11]

According to Sugiura, the Japanese *anime* market rose from ¥4.6 billion (US$46 million) in 1975 to ¥200 billion (US$2.0 billion) in 2002, more than 60% of the global *anime* market (Marcadal 2006).[12] At least from 2006, Japanese *anime* industry already makes up more than 60% of global output of cartoons.[13] In terms of practical contribution to the economy, Otmazgin and Ben-Ari provide some figures in their publication: *anime* industry has about 450 production companies, 5,000

---

[10]Nobuoka, Jakob, *Geographies of the Japanese Cultural Economy Innovation and Creative Consumption* (Sweden: Uppsala University Geografiska Regionstudier NR 83), 2010, p. 71.

[11]Sugiura, Tsutomu, "Japan's Creative Industries" in *Soft Power Superpowers* edited by Watanabe Yasushi and David L. McConnell (Armonk NY and London England: ME Sharpe), 2008, p. 130.

[12]Sugiura, Tsutomu, "Japan's Creative Industries" in *Soft Power Superpowers* edited by Watanabe Yasushi and David L. McConnell (Armonk NY and London England: ME Sharpe), 2008, p. 133.

[13]Simeon, Roblyn, "The Branding Potential and Japanese Popular Culture Overseas" dated 2006 in the *Journal of Diversity Management* 1, 2, 2006, p. 13.

animators.[14] Given the promising size and growth of the industry, the state is keen to be a stakeholder here. Other than the central government, local governments are keen to promote *anime*, for example, the Tokyo Metropolitan Government sponsors the Tokyo International Anime Fair which in 2007 drew over 200 firms and 100,000 participants with an increasing number of foreign participants.[15] MEXT provides grants for outstanding Anime films limited to three awards annually.[16]

"C" for comics of ACG industries

The symbolic event for the *manga* industry is the Comiket convention in Tokyo where in 2003, it was estimated that more than ¥1 billion is

The large iconic Sofmap billboard featuring the *anime* flavour of the month in Akihabara.

---

[14]Otmazgin, Nissim and Eyal Ben-Ari, "Cultural Industries and the State in East and Southeast Asia" in *Popular Culture and the State in East and Southeast Asia* edited by Nissim Otmazgin and Eyal Ben-Ari (London and NY: Routledge Taylor and Francis Group), 2012, p. 19.

[15]Choo, KuKhee, "Nationalizing "cool": Japan's Global Promotion of the Content Industry" in *Popular Culture and the State in East and Southeast Asia* edited by Nissim Otmazgin and Eyal Ben-Ari (London and NY: Routledge), 2012, p. 96.

[16]Choo, KuKhee, "Nationalizing "Cool": Japan's Global Promotion of the Content Industry" in *Popular Culture and the State in East and Southeast Asia* edited by Nissim Otmazgin and Eyal Ben-Ari (London and NY: Routledge), 2012, p. 93.

Another iconic anime in the 1980s with its own café franchise in Akihabara, one of the perennial stops in a typical *otaku* pilgrimage.

transacted and exchanged in this event (an amount higher than the money spent at World Cup).[17] Comiket is described by Nobuoka as a "temporary innovative space, only present for a few days throughout the year" that is "also cyclical since the event reoccurs every year and also is becoming part of global cultural practices".[18] This transitional space provides *gentei* limited temporal space as a small window of opportunity for the fans to acquire their limited edition collections and fulfil other material yearnings. The experience of queuing up and attending the event for fans from Japan and overseas is an attractive one as these fans swagger and show off their insider information or the latest acquisitions. The consumption experience at this event also feeds the subjective of the two-dimensional world that *otakus* live in as they read and visually experience their favourite comic book contents.

In overseas markets, by 2004, English translations of *manga* became the fastest-growing sector of US-based publishing industry with yearly

---

[17] Macias, Patrick and Tomohiro Machiyama, *Cruising the Anime City* (Berkeley, CA: Stone Bridge Press), 2004, p. 119.
[18] Nobuoka, Jakob, *Geographies of the Japanese Cultural Economy Innovation and Creative Consumption* (Sweden: Uppsala University Geografiska Regionstudier NR 83), 2010, p. 62.

A Gundam figurine can be found standing in front of the Gundam café entrance. A favourite corner for fans to pose with their favourite robotic character.

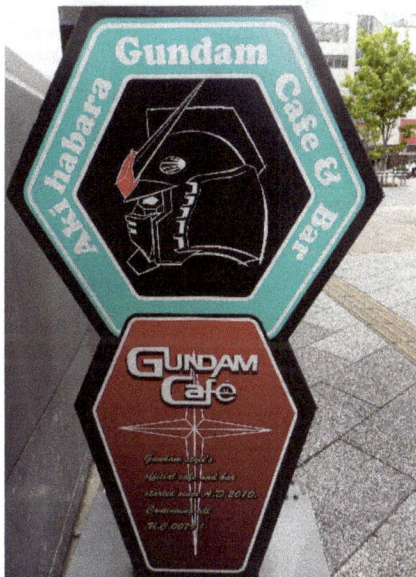

For mature adult fans, the Gundam café is also a bar for drinks.

Large billboards promoting game retailers at Akihabara (photo taken during fieldwork in summer 2014).

For the hardcore fans, visitors and overseas tourists alike, there are retailers at street corners in Akihabara trading in fandom products. This photo that the author took in Akihabara during summer fieldwork 2014 shows a retailer specialising in dealing with second-hand products related to the popular singer-idol group AKB48.

sales volume of approximately US$120 million.[19] Three years later in 2007 in the US alone, *manga* for all age groups expanded by 10% in sales, attaining US$220 million and almost an estimated 1,500 titles were released.[20] In North America, there are 1.5–2 million *manga* fans with sales of ¥300 billion (according to 2007 media statistics).[21] Domestically, in the decade of the 1990s, the *manga* industry produced 12 magazines with more than one million readers and approximately 50 magazines with 150,000 to a million copies circulated and by 2001, over 3.2 million different *mangas* came into circulation.[22] In practical contribution to the economy, in 2012, the *manga* sector hired about 4,000 cartoonists and 28,000 assistants.[23] Outside Japan, *anime* and *manga*-derived characters have become mainstream popular cultural icons and images. Sugiura noted that the French group Daft Punk used *anime* by Matsumoto Keiji creator of Uchu senkan Yamato (Space battleship Yamato), while Hollywood movies like *Kill Bill* (Quentin Tarantino) derived ideas from *manga*.[24] Sugiura made the following observation about the gaming industry:

> One English Web site devoted to the popular game Final Fantasy has received more than 59 million hits as of June 27, 2007, an indication of how many fans this game has attracted. In fact, according to BusinessWeek

[19]Macias, Patrick and Tomohiro Machiyama, *Cruising the Anime* City (Berkeley, CA: Stone Bridge Press), 2004, p. 19.

[20]Tiffany, Laura, "Embracing Japanese Pop Culture" dated 11 May 2008 in NBCNews. com website [downloaded on 21 Nov 2014], available at http://www.nbcnews. com/id/24546355/ns/business-us_business/t/embracing-japanese-pop-culture/.

[21]Nobuoka, Jakob, *Geographies of the Japanese Cultural Economy Innovation and Creative Consumption* (Sweden: Uppsala University Geografiska Regionstudier NR 83), 2010, pp. 67–68.

[22]Nobuoka, Jakob, *Geographies of the Japanese Cultural Economy Innovation and Creative Consumption* (Sweden: Uppsala University Geografiska Regionstudier NR 83), 2010, p. 67.

[23]Otmazgin, Nissim and Eyal Ben-Ari, "Cultural Industries and the State in East and Southeast Asia" in *Popular Culture and the State in East and Southeast Asia* edited by Nissim Otmazgin and Eyal Ben-Ari (London and NY: Routledge Taylor and Francis Group), 2012, p. 19.

[24]Sugiura, Tsutomu, "Japan's Creative Industries" in *Soft Power Superpowers* edited by Watanabe Yasushi and David L. McConnell (Armonk NY and London England: ME Sharpe), 2008, p. 134.

Rowley 2005), more than 35 million copies of the Final Fantasy series has been sold, and its online version has more than 300,000 subscribers worldwide.[25]

"G" for the gaming industry

In terms of revenue, Pokemon alone, is retailed in more than 140 countries with profits of over US$15 billion by August 2003.[26] Spin-off for Pokemon which started off as a card game and then taken over by Nintendo as an electronic game include movie franchises. Within Japan, online game titles like World of Warcraft attracted 8.5 million participants online as of 27 March 2007, while portable game sets like Nintendo DS sold 35.61 million consoles by end 2006.[27] Overseas, by 2006, global sales of its movies amounted to a profit of US$91 million (the North American market generated US$85 million).[28] The gaming industry hires around 18,500 in 146 mainly small-scale firms.[29]

Spin-Offs Related to the ACG

Figures for the ACG industries alone do not tell the whole story. The prevalence of a mixed media format in which products are simultaneously launched as animation, comics, games and other paraphernalia implies there is an informal economy beyond the original ACG products. The informal economy can be based on franchises granted to independent producers carrying the local or/and overseas original brand name or design or fan-based products. Some of these products are lifestyle

---

[25] *Ibid.*

[26] Allison, Anne, *Millennial Monsters* (Berkeley, LA and London: University of California Press), 2006, p. 193.

[27] Nobuoka, Jakob, *Geographies of the Japanese Cultural Economy Innovation and Creative Consumption* (Sweden: Uppsala University Geografiska Regionstudier NR 83), 2010, p. 69.

[28] Allison, Anne, *Millennial Monsters* (Berkeley, LA and London: University of California Press), 2006, p. 236.

[29] Otmazgin, Nissim and Eyal Ben-Ari, "Cultural Industries and the State in East and Southeast Asia" in *Popular Culture and the State in East and Southeast Asia* edited by Nissim Otmazgin and Eyal Ben-Ari (London and NY: Routledge Taylor and Francis Group), 2012, p. 19.

choices as popular cultural symbols are designed onto functional items which are then used by consumers in their daily lives. In such cases, lifestyle (the functionality of the products) is integrated with design aesthetics and cultural symbolisms (the ability to look cool when carrying such symbols around as a source of status). Sometimes, aesthetic symbolism even trumps functionality when an object used in daily life is not used for the primary purpose for which it was created but as a decorative item or accessory.

There are spin-off products from ACG that have become industries by themselves, including the toy manufacturing and *manga*-recycling sectors. Akihabara also feed other industries like the comics (*manga*)-recycling industries when unwanted and used *manga* books and volumes are recycled into toilet paper.[30] There are also independent firms ("indie" companies) that engage with small-scale musical or visual production assignment. There are also tourism-related venues for domestic and foreign tourists and visitors. In the 1990s, one of the more popular museums related to Akihabara was the Tetsuwan Atomu museum, featuring robotic displays and Atom Boy memorabilia.[31]

Toys based on manga and anime

Toy products, not included in the traditional ACG industry, is another spin-off industry. In Mandarake, which is the top-ranking retail chain store in used *anime* and *manga* headquartered in Nakano, more than a million items line the shelves, and some 45,000 *manga* titles, *anime* DVDs and toys are traded on a weekly basis.[32] The now ubiquitous and addictive capsule toys "Gashapon" are purchasable by turning a knob after inserting coins and then waiting for a toy to fall out. The innovative feature about this product is encouraging addictive desires to collect the

---

[30]Macias, Patrick and Tomohiro Machiyama, *Cruising the Anime City* (Berkeley, CA: Stone Bridge Press), 2004, p. 28.

[31]Allison, Anne, *Millenial Monsters* (Berkeley, LA and London: University of California Press), 2006, p. 62.

[32]Macias, Patrick, "10 of the Best Otaku Shops in Tokyo" dated 1 Feb 2012 in theguardian.com website [downloaded on 21 Nov 2014], available at http://www.theguardian.com/travel/2012/feb/01/top-10-otaku-shops-tokyo-anime-manga.

Photo of Gashapon machine outside a popular idol products retailer in Akihabara (taken during author's fieldwork in Akihabara in summer 2014).

entire range of figures in the capsules derived from popular *anime* and *manga* series, including the rare pieces.

The Gashapon toy retailing model is now well known through East Asia. The intense demand for these small toys contained in plastic capsules spawned another industry far away in China. Japanese companies like Bandai making Gashapon hired Chinese artisans well skilled in painting miniature objects (e.g. rice grain painting) and housed them in factories to make Gashapon products on a large scale. Eventually, another idea emerged when small and medium-sized enterprises (SMEs) like Kaiyodo with their own independent product identities decided to team up with other industrial players like sweets confectioner Furuta Seika to produce Choco Eggs (Easter egg-shaped chocolates with hollow interiors encapsulating mini animal figurines) that sold 6 million units within months (by 2004, candy toys became an annual US$500 million industry and Gashapon itself became a US$310 million industry by 2004).[33]

---

[33] Macias, Patrick and Tomohiro Machiyama, *Cruising the Anime* City (Berkeley, CA: Stone Bridge Press), 2004, pp. 40–43.

The success of all-girl bands in Akihabara have sparked off successive generations of imitators and innovators. The author saw a large billboard featuring idol wannabes in idol discovery searches.

Other creative ideas

Akihabara is also a generator of creative ideas in the Japanese popular cultural retailing industry. Nobuoka describes the "essence of Akihabara" as a "place for exchanging, promoting and testing ideas".[34] An early creative business model found in this district is plastic boxes hosted in Akiba shops and rented out to individual retailers to sell their products. Sometimes, these boxes capitalised on the *natsukashii* sentiments (nostalgia) for things used, rustic (*shibui*) and old. I have seen this retail business model replicated in Singapore and Hong Kong. The most well-known creative franchise in Akihabara is probably the AKB48 product line. Starting off as an idol group in Akihabara (AKB is short form for "Akihabara"), they now have an iconic café in the area and regional franchises in Jakarta (JKT48), Shanghai (SNH48) and other cities/regions.

---

[34] Nobuoka, Jakob, *Geographies of the Japanese Cultural Economy Innovation and Creative Consumption* (Sweden: Uppsala University Geografiska Regionstudier NR 83), 2010, p. 38.

The Creative Ecology

Akihabara is a "space where different cultures, technologies and prac-tices can meet, interact and develop".[35] It provides the platform for differ-ent sources of cultural and lifestyle influence to cross-pollinate and hybridise into unique products that are later introduced to the mass consumption market. As the origin of innovative retail business models and fashionable products, Akihabara also belongs to a space at the top of an architecture of ideas. The creative ecology of Akiba in this sense func-tioned in the same manner as Silicon Valley where creative ideas are fermented in garage-size units resulting in products that first served the consumption desires and needs of *otakus*. These products are sometimes the result of collaboration between different units specialised in their own fields but collectively working towards a final product. Sometimes, these collaborations become bigger units or get acquired by larger firms like Bandai. Some successful product ideas started small and fermented in humble units, but when they were picked up by a progressive *otaku* crowd, then mainstreamised for the general crowd of domestic consum-ers they eventually proliferated to become an internationally-known product line. Sometimes, Akihabara also gives space for subcultures to exist and interact with the main ecology of the district, eventually fea-tures of these subcultures would be subsumed into popular culture industry, hybridising with more mainstream cultures to generate ideas and products that become acceptable to the mass consumers. An exam-ple is the gothic movement with its sado-masochistic tendencies and deliberate display of social rejection and ostracisation co-existing with Lolita and Kawaii movements in Akihabara to evolve new hybridised products, images and ideas like Gothic Lolita fashion or Kawaii figurines adapting gothic features that become palatable to more mainstream consumers.

This narrative of de-marginalising different subcultures or innovative minority ideas related to Akihabara's production ecology contributes to the organic *laissez-faire* growth of creative ideas with little intervention and inputs from the state. At the same time, while the fermentation of ideas in Akihabara is organically conceived with little state intervention, when the select few ideas are actualised into popular products and gain traction with

---

[35] *Ibid.*

domestic and overseas consumers, the government becomes a stakeholder in its success and offers funding for the promotion of cultural items. Here Choo Kukhee's writing is instructive:

> The Agency for Cultural Affairs (Bunkacho), a subdivision in MET, oversee the cultural promotion of the content industry. The budget for Bunkacho in 2010, under the title "Cultural Transmission and Realization of Culture Arts Nation," was 102 billion Japanese yen. The areas of promotion included those to cultivate artistic creativity (14 billion Japanese yen), to preserve and utilize cultural artifacts (41.5 billion Japanese yen) and to transmit "excellent" Japanese culture abroad (41.4 billion Japanese yen).[36]

Some scholars notice the looming state presence. For example, Nobuoka detected the presence of state involvement in Akihabara:

> In the Akihabara article, I touch upon how policy makers have begun to show interest in these topics and how subcultures have undergone a shift from being unnoticed or overlooked to becoming top issues for foreign trade and innovation policy. This shift can be notice in acts, such as Doraemon becoming a cultural ambassador, or when a former minister during his election campaign called himself a fan of manga in an opening ceremony in Akihabara.[37]

Indeed, in the case of Akihabara, the government is beginning to go beyond utilisation of cultural symbolisms to reorganising cultural spaces and economic geography of Akihabara itself although it is still early to tell how this process will evolve and the impact it will have on the popular cultural industries in Akihabara. METI also has another initiative that includes Akihabara (Town tourism, Electrical Town as well as Town management stakeholders). There are initiatives for Tokyo's creative clusters to be slowly cultivated by state agencies, e.g the initiative of Creative

---

[36]Choo, KuKhee, "Nationalizing "Cool": Japan's Global Promotion of the Content Industry" in *Popular Culture and the State in East and Southeast Asia* edited by Nissim Otmazgin and Eyal Ben-Ari (London and NY: Routledge), 2012, p. 92.
[37]Nobuoka, Jakob, *Geographies of the Japanese Cultural Economy Innovation and Creative Consumption* (Sweden: Uppsala University Geografiska Regionstudier NR 83), 2010, p. 71.

Tokyo under the care of Ministry of Economy, Trade and Industry. In this initiative, the supporters of Creative Tokyo propose utilising Japan's cultural capital to contribute to Japan's economy, attract foreign talents (including international creative personalities) and investments, accentuate businesses that reflect Japanese culture and lifestyle, boost domestic consumption, support overseas operations of Japanese firms, encourage information exchange, all with the aim of making Tokyo the most important creative hub in Asia.[38]

Literature Review

Fan-driven "democratization"

Ian Condry details the concept of "collaborative creativity" in his important publication on the *anime* industry, noting that the creative process links studio productions with fan-created products.[39] In the field of *anime*, Condry quotes other scholars like William Kelly who argues that Japanese popular culture form is a distinctive entity that is forged through collaborative ventures between fans and producers.[40] Condry points out that a major point of debate faced by *manga* publishers and *anime* studios is that they tend to disagree with the concept that "free publicity" through non-official distribution is more important than illegal downloading and streaming.[41] Amongst the many English-language literatures that I came across in Japan, Ian Condry's publication probably contained one of the most succinct explanations behind the origins

---

[38]Ministry of Economy, Trade and Industry (METI), "The Creative Tokyo Proposal" undated in the METI website [downloaded on 9 Dec 2014], available at http://www.meti.go.jp/policy/mono_info_service/mono/creative/creative_tokyo/about/sengen_en.html.

[39]Condry, Ian, *The Soul of Anime* (Durham and London: Duke University Press), 2013.

[40]William, Kelly, *Fanning the Flames: Fans and Consumer Culture in Japan* (Albany: State University of New York Press), 2004; Condry, Ian, *The Soul of Anime* (Durham and London: Duke University Press), 2013, p. 21.

[41]Condry, Ian, *The Soul of Anime* (Durham and London: Duke University Press), 2013, p. 24.

and success of Japan's most successful idol Miku Hatsune. Condry's narrative about Miku Hatsune's origins and her success is one good example of fan-driven creative production:

> Released in 2007 by Crypton Future Media, a small company in Sapporo, Miku Hatsune started out as a voice character in the music synthesizer software Vocaloid, which allows users to enter lyrics and melody that the soft can "sing." Cyrpton released an illustration and some body characteristics (height, weight, etc.) to go with the character, but interestingly, the company allowed the image to be used by anyone. Many Vocaloid users created songs and uploaded them to the Internet — for example, to the video-sharing website Nico Nico Douga (literally, "smile video"). Many of the uploaded songs were made into music videos with either moving or still images of the Miku character. This is an excellent example of how a character can be a "platform of creativity..."[42]

Sharing is an effective marketing and distributional tool in this sense and the availability of digital technologies increases the speed and geographical reach by which such cyber products can reach their audiences. Sharing itself is also another ritual as fan clubs, official and unofficial, seize upon the latest gossips and news and proliferate them through smartphones, blogs and websites. When fans subtitle, create their own decorative items for concert, develop specific dance moves for use during concert, translate foreign language products into their own language, they are developing a code through which fellow fans within the same community can speak to each other. Sharing bits of information such as concert dates, store discounts, limited edition product sales when gathered together create a collective narrative that contribute to identity building and coherence of the fan club, group or tribe dedicated to a particular idol, group or product. In some genres of Japanese popular culture, fans even integrate performance into the collective ritual of identity building. In the arena of cosplay, for example, Kazumi Nagaike and Kaori Yoshida argued that fan gatherings "not only functions as a science for fans' social activities, but also as a cultural arena for

---

[42] Condry, Ian, *The Soul of Anime* (Durham and London: Duke University Press), 2013, p. 63.

self-experience".[43] The proliferation of popular cultural information through word of mouth is facilitated by the use of social media which enables the sharing of experience to be disseminated easily and cheaply.

Of course, not all information-sharing is cohesively harmonious, sometimes information is manipulated by networked individuals for showing off social status. Outside the communities themselves, fan groups and clubs work as active collaborators with the mass media and social media outfits to shape the form and contents of popular culture. Regardless of whether there are disagreements or common accolades amongst the fans, technology is an effective mediator to transmit fan information and news to a large audience within a short period of time. In the past, television played that role but with the advent of smartphones and social media software, the process has become interactive, allowing fans to have disproportionate access to large circles of dedicated fandom.

Vocaloid fandom as case study

Other than the information exchange that act as the software to lubricate the interactions and communications between fans in a club, hardware infrastructure is equally important. This include physical assets such as publicity materials, events and conventions attendance and fan-made merchandise, such as those depicted by Ian Condry in the quotation below.

> "But the phenomenon around Miku shows that the character, more than the music software, is the platform on which people are building. I was one of the seven thousand people who attende3d the sold-out, one-day "Vocaloid-only" fan convention at the Sunshine City department store complex in the Ikebukuro section of Tokyo in November 2010. Almost five hundred fan groups had gathered to sell their wares- mostly CDs but also DVDs, books of drawing (irasuto), posters, videogames, jewelry, costumes, manga, and more. These activities cannot be explained only by capabilities of the voice synthesizer software, or in academic terms, the affordances of a computational platform. Rather, the creativity grows out of social energy arising from a collective interest in Miku."[44]

---

[43] Nagaike, Kazumi and Kaori Yoshida, "Becoming and Performing the Self and the Other: Festishism, Fantasy, and Sexuality of Cosplay in Japanese Girls'/ Women's Manga" dated Autumn 2011 in *Asia Pacific World* 2, 2, 2011, p. 23.
[44] Condry, Ian, *The Soul of Anime* (Durham and London: Duke University Press), 2013, p. 63.

Three important general points follow from the quotation above. First, fans of Miku get to participate actively in the maturity of the product by adding more biographical, aesthetic and artistic details to her basic existence. Second, through collective social events, fans gather and develop common-interest groups and their own networked ecology, exchanging information and personal creative works with each other. Third, the allowance by the production company of wide personalised use of the images essentially democratises and frees up the appropriation of Miku's original image in public space, an issue with implications on intellectual rights since it challenges the notion of artistic rights to a creative work. But the common thread that runs through all three points is that successful and cutting-edge Japanese popular cultural products rely on fan-based and fan-driven consumption. In essence, Condry is arguing about the importance of the social network between fans and how they are able to innovate products. One good example of the importance of this network to creative productivity is fan-subbing which Condry defines as:

> ...the translation and dissemination of anime online by fans — a controversial practice that illuminates debates about culture, economy, and intellectual property in the digital era. Fansubbing refers to the practice whereby hundreds of fan groups digitize the latest anime broadcasts, translate them, add subtitles, and make the media available online.[45]

The Otakus

In some ways, fan-driven trends represent the "democratization"[46] of popular cultural consumption in Japan as fans actively participate in shaping the outcome of the products personally, contributing their value-addedness in creating new innovative items. Nobuoka argues that consumption satiates a particular desire for a product and satisfy the emotive needs of "novelty, adventure and defining self" as part of lifestyle

---

[45] Condry, Ian, *The Soul of Anime* (Durham and London: Duke University Press), 2013, p. 161.

[46] Nobuoka describes this trend in cultural geographical terms, indicating "how users managed to contribute to innovation and dynamism by creating places and spaces that have become important institutions in the cultural economy". (Source: Nobuoka, Jakob, *Geographies of the Japanese Cultural Economy Innovation and Creative Consumption* (Sweden: Uppsala University Geografiska Regionstudier NR 83), 2010, p. 31).

choices and the process of consumption.[47] It is a form of experience-based consumption and not just material accumulation and/or ownership. One group of consumers stand out amongst the fans in driving popular cultural trends — the *otakus*. Originally stereotyped as a group of nerdy individuals who rather spend their time in their idol-plastered bedroom playing electronic games, the *otakus* have become a major group of consumers in Japan due to their willingness to collect their idols' paraphernalia. Their consumption and fan inputs into content-based aspects of their favourite comic book, game or animation essentially shapes and drives the popular cultural trends. Some management literature classify them as a rising group of important consumers, alongside other products of Japan's demographic and social changes like the elderly, single women and freeter/"parasitic" singles living with their parents. *Otakus* have moved into the position of governing taste and, through this route, made their impact on shaping lifestyle choices, fashion sense and social status determinants. In playing these roles, *otakus* have accumulated cultural capital credentials. Producers have correspondingly made it their careers to track and predict *otaku* trends and fashion. *Otakus* may fulfil the role of being "creatives", defined by Nobuoka as "people who are creative", differentiating this group from the creators who produce, manufacture and make the products.[48] Producers therefore may selectively extract the creativity of *otakus* for their product designs.

Otakus have also spawned industries that are relatively recession-proof. Even the economic bubble burst in 1989 that started a long-lasting recession, which Abenomics is climbing out of, could not stop the growth of *otaku* consumption. Because of the resilience of this market, other stakeholders started to notice the *otakus* and connected with them through marketing research, intellectual studies, and tapped into their knowledge and consumption patterns for exports.[49] The *otaku*

[47]Nobuoka, Jakob, *Geographies of the Japanese Cultural Economy Innovation and Creative Consumption* (Sweden: Uppsala University Geografiska Regionstudier NR 83), 2010, p. 37.

[48]Nobuoka, Jakob, *Geographies of the Japanese Cultural Economy Innovation and Creative Consumption* (Sweden: Uppsala University Geografiska Regionstudier NR 83), 2010, p. 27.

[49]Macias, Patrick and Tomohiro Machiyama, *Cruising the Anime City* (Berkeley, CA: Stone Bridge Press), 2004, p. 15.

culture spawned and mainstreamised in the 1990s was a different model from the Bubble Economy man in the economically booming 1980s. The idealised male individual worked in finance or for an advertising agency, wearing Italian suit, drove a foreign luxury car, a gym member and goes clubbing.[50] The *otakus* spawned an alternative lifestyle that created their own universe of consumption. Besides games, *anime* and comics as well as the large array of paraphernalia that came with these three categories of products, *otakus* also indicate their own preferences for food, converse in their own *lingo franca* and terminologies related to popular culture and form their own circles (*sakuru*), clubs and associations both in reality and online. *Otaku* consumption represents a deep integration between culture, lifestyle choices and the economic system.

Fans including the *otaku* fandom and their consumption habits created demand for retailers to satisfy. Akihabara reflected the contextual changes in the Japanese's economy. After serving consumers faithfully in retailing electronics throughout the 1970s and 1980s, the post-bubble economy period saw customers optimising their budgets and shopping at malls in the suburbs instead of travelling to the Tokyo city to buy common electronic goods.[51] Tokyo as a stakeholder for adapting to changes in domestic consumption patterns and local economic development in Akihabara is visible. Kukhee Choo covered this ambition in his writing:

> With locations such as Akihabara and concentrated Anime studios along the Central train line, Tokyo is indeed the global center of information on Anime. One of the most prominent examples of Tokyo establishing itself as a hub to promote Anime has been the construction of a life-size Gundam Robot status in Odaiba, Tokyo Bay, in the summer of 2009. Under the banner "Green Japan," Gundam was used as part of a bid for the 2016 Olympics Games that ended in failure.[52]

---

[50]Macias, Patrick and Tomohiro Machiyama, *Cruising the Anime City* (Berkeley, CA: Stone Bridge Press), 2004, p. 15.

[51]Morikawa, Kaichiro, "Otaku and the City: The Rebirth of Akihabara" in *Fandom Unbound Otaku Culture in a Connected World* edited by Mizuko Ito, Daisuke Okabe and Izumi Tsuji (New Haven and London: Yale University Press), 2012, p. 134.

[52]Choo, KuKhee, "Nationalizing 'cool': Japan's Global Promotion of the Content Industry" in *Popular Culture and the State in East and Southeast Asia* edited by Nissim Otmazgin and Eyal Ben-Ari (London and NY: Routledge), 2012, pp. 96–97.

Popular culture could be appropriated for economic growth as well as public campaigns to attract global events to come to Tokyo. While the bid for the Olympics failed the first time round, Tokyo succeeded in the second attempt when it successfully won the right to host the 2020 Olympics and Doraemon became the official mascot for the games. The state mechanism capitalised on *anime* characters that are already well known and established and utilised them for national initiatives. At the grassroots level, however, the directional trends and consumption habits/lifestyles remain the purview of a grand narrative that is made up of individual preferences and product evaluations by large numbers of dedicated fandom, including the *otakus*.

In the process of the urban construction of Akihabara as the retailing and intellectual centre for Japanese popular culture, *otakus* were not stand-offish consumers but took part in shaping the production process, fashion trends and creative conceptualisation of the products they consumed. The very idea of creative products connotes that value lies not in the material base used to make them but the value-addedness of innovation implemented in shaping these materials or decorating them to create symbolic designs that reflect certain cultural inclinations or lifestyle choices. Therefore, consumer inputs like the ones offered by *otakus* are very important in such cases. Azuma Hiroki's volume *Otaku Japan's Database Animals* is arguably one of the most important works on contemporary otaku culture in the English language. In an interview with *Moe Manifesto* writer Patrick Galbraith, he made the following comment on the sophisticated nature of *otaku* fandom:

> As consumers, they want to know how the work is produced, so that they can break it down and reconstruct something else... What otaku are doing can also be seen in the remixing culture of hip-hop music, for example.[53]

Essentially, what Galbraith is arguing is that *otaku* fans add a value-addedness to the process of Japanese popular cultural production. They consume but, at the same time, want to direct the consumption pattern, the production process and the marketing directions. Because *otaku* consumption is a collective effort of many different individual preferences,

---

[53] Galbraith, Patrick, *The Moe Manifesto* (Tokyo, Rutland, Vermont and Singapore: Tuttle Publishing), 2014, p. 172.

the process is not hegemonically-led but consists of contesting ideas that will eventually produce a general trend through aggregation of these preferences. Similarly, the opinions and views of *otakus* are not guided or led but each contribution of ideas when uttered becomes a component of the grand narrative that will then become the dominant ideas and concepts for each evolving stage of fandom and this will subsequently be displayed in Akihabara's gaudy district.

While male *otakus* have dominated academic and media discourses on the relationship between consumption and lifestyles, they are not the only group or players in the popular cultural universe. Celia Lury's persuasive publication *Consumer Culture* argues that individuals are not completely autonomous in their consumption decision-making process. They receive marketing influence from popular cultural producers (especially their marketing arm) and react in response — an impact–response relationship. But, in reacting, Lury noted that instead of a hegemonic response, consumer adopt multiple identities in consuming the product. In the case of Hello Kitty, she indicated that "Sanrio made a concentrated effort to tie together within a single individual different modes of self-presentation that chronologically correspond to girlhood, female adolescence, and womanhood: 'cut', 'cool' and 'camp'...".[54] Hello Kitty is morphed into different self-identities by discerning consumers who appropriate the image that best satisfies their public image-making priorities.

Polycentrism and Cross-Pollination

Other than fan contributions, Condry also agrees with Tsutsui that sources of influence on Japanese producers of creative works are now global in scope:

> In Japan, animators drew inspiration from Disney and from the animated Popeye and Betty Boop shorts by the Fleischer brothers, amongst others. The emphasis on characters with personalities is not uniquely Japanese, therefore, but the linking of characters to particular actors

---

[54]Lury, Celia, *Consumer Culture* (Cambridge UK and Massachusetts: Polity), 2011, p. 163.

and performances — such as Mickey Mouse's borrowing from Buster Keaton in Steamboat Bill — tends to be more common in U.S. animation. This can be taken to extremes when animated characters are inextricably linked — for example, Robin Williams as Genie in *Aladdin* or Eddie Murphy as Donkey in *Shrek*.[55]

There are three implications arising from the long quotation above. First, it indicates the dynamic nature of cultural influences, often a process of receiving influence and trendspotting pulses, indigenising these pulses and then re-influencing others. The following section elaborates on this point. The second implication is the presence of certain universal commonalities amongst different popular cultural products, in this case, the association of characters with personalities, but this can also be found in US popular culture, although in unique ways (e.g. association with Hollywood stars).

The argument of whether Japanese popular culture is universalistic or particularistic can be resolved without taking sides. It is neither universal nor particularistic and this view may even be applicable to the general idea of cultural transmission itself since all forms of cultures cannot be clearly delineated from each other. Popular cultural trends often travel between different consuming markets. Japanese popular cultural products are translated and marketed to US consumer and audiences and *vice versa* and, in the midst of this exchange, these two groups of product co-influence each other. Such exchanges have been described variously in popular cultural literature, including the processes of cross-pollination of ideas, polycentrism, cross fertilisation, etc. But they all essentially refer to the same phenomenon of learning from each other, influencing trends cross-culturally or indigenising and imitating/emulating features to fit the local contexts.

Regional reception

Japanese popular culture's past successes with regional audiences, particularly in East Asia is well-studied. Some scholarly works have used the term "resonance" to describe the positive reception of regional audiences,

---

[55] Condry, Ian, *The Soul of Anime* (Durham and London: Duke University Press), 2013, p. 99.

arguing that content-based signifiers and symbols become associated with objects in the viewers' daily lives, thereby identifying their lifestyles and cultures with those found in Japanese popular culture. Other terminologies had been used in scholarly works to describe this scenario, including Leung Y.M. who argued that this is a form of hyber-reading, arguing the transnationality of the Japanese *Ganbaru* spirit in Japanese TV dramas as something reflecting the life experiences of the audiences in reality.[56]

The Cyberspace Future

What is the future shape of cyberidolism? On 22 October 2008, a Japanese male Taichi Takashita set up a webpage to appeal for support for the legal recognition of a marriage with an *anime* character Mikuru Asahina.[57] Takashita's rational was that he lost interest in the three-dimensional world and wanted to live his own life with his two-dimensional counterpart, and his public petition was supported by 3,000 people within two months, many of whom had their own preference of *anime* characters for marriage.[58] The *otakus'* obsessions, hobbies and interest have spawned new innovative lines of products one after another. Some of the *otakus* have given up being interested in the three-dimensional lives and realities that they live in and switched to a preference for the two-dimensional world. Nobuoka believes in the compatibility of the pragmatist school with the Akihabara experience received by *otakus*, fans and visitors and emphasises it is not the objective reality but the individuals' own subjective understanding or experience of reality that drives creative ideas in Akihabara amongst

---

[56]Wong, Chi Hang, "From Passive Receivers to Distributing Consumers: The Changing Role of TV Drama Audiences in Hong Kong" dated Dec 2010 in *The Journal of Comparative Asian Development* 9, 2, 2010, p. 225. This article quotes Leung's original source: Leung, Y.M., "Ganbaru and its Transcultural Audience: Imaginary and Reality of Japanese TV Dramas in Hong Kong" in *Feeling Asian Modernities: Transnational Consumption of Japanese TV Dramas* edited by Koichi Iwabuchi (Hong Kong: Hong Kong University Press), 2004, pp. 89–106.
[57]Condry, Ian, *The Soul of Anime* (Durham and London: Duke University Press), 2013, p. 186.
[58] *Ibid.*

all its stakeholders.[59] The cosplayers, the *otakus*, the *manga* reader, the gamer, the figurine collector and the *anime* consumer are all engaged in their own subjective interpretation of reality when they consume fantasy and make-believe products found in Akihabara. The two-dimensional world is the subjective reality where *otakus* engaged in this experience lived in.

The growing preference for a two-dimensional existence is also facilitated by the fact that *otaku* fans are now linked globally through cyberspace. Morikawa succinctly describes this trend succinctly:

> Propelled by the spread of the Internet, communities of interest that do not depend on shared geographical locations or blood ties are growing in numbers and influence. These communities manifest themselves in various forms, including online portal sites and web forums devoted to particular interests and tastes.[60]

This meant that fans do not need to physically travel to Akihabara to connect with other fans with similar interests. It also meant that foreigners can now participate in the democratic shaping of Japanese popular culture from its centre and core. Foreigners or individuals based outside Akihabara in other parts of Japan are able to get their voices heard through online portals and forums. Fandom had become truly global in participation and performance. It also meant that any possibility of attempts at state regulation or dominance/monopolistic behaviour by one single corporation is diminished. The whole process makes consumption and fandom trends more reactive to global pulses. It is important to note that the *otaku* and popular cultural communities, both online and in actual reality, are fluid and constantly evolving to adapt to external contexts and dynamically-changing fashion trends.

---

[59] Nobuoka, Jakob, *Geographies of the Japanese Cultural Economy Innovation and Creative Consumption* (Sweden: Uppsala University Geografiska Regionstudier NR 83), 2010, p. 59.
[60] Morikawa, Kaichiro, "Otaku and the City: The Rebirth of Akihabara" in *Fandom Unbound Otaku Culture in a Connected World* edited by Mizuko Ito, Daisuke Okabe and Izumi Tsuji (New Haven and London: Yale University Press), 2012, p. 152.

Akihabara as a Constant Reference Point

But one location remains relatively constant in terms of popular cultural consumption and this is the J-pop Mecca of Akihabara. In the constantly dynamic consumer tastes evolving according to global, regional and local contexts and trends, Akihabara remains the constant centre and continues to create value to the popular cultural industry. For the retailers, they need to carry innovative products that fit the trends and fashion senses of different groups of popular cultural consumers. For the producers, it remains a source of inspiration for consumer-driven ideas that they can translate into new products. For the consumers, it is a place where they can demonstrate and display their creative identity and exercise their power of showing preferences for different products offered in Akihabara.

As one of the few global nucleuses that reflect the trend physically, and universally recognised as the centre of the Japanese popular cultural universe, according to Morikawa Kaichiro, a design theorist and professor at the School of Global Japanese Studies at Meiji University, Akihabara was shaped by *otaku* tastes in the 1990s when the retail outlets evolved from electronics retail to retailing personal computers as well as games.[61] The Comic Market also expanded in the 1990s with fanzines retailed throughout the year, along with the figurines that became popular when Evangelion became a hit and spawned a following.[62] Messe Sanoh (games retailer), Kaiyodo (figurine manufacturer at Radio Kaikan) and Toranoana (fanzine and comic seller) were the pioneering J-pop cultural retailers that moved into Akihabara.[63] By 2009, at the peak of the *moe* (positive vibes towards made-belief cute-looking characters) movement, Akihabara became a *bishojo* retailing area. Akihabara became the public space where private interests like *bishojo* were openly displayed, the analogy

---

[61] Galbraith, Patrick, *The Moe Manifesto* (Tokyo, Rutland, Vermont and Singapore: Tuttle Publishing), 2014, p. 159.

[62] *Ibid.*

[63] Galbraith, Patrick, *The Moe Manifesto* (Tokyo, Rutland, Vermont and Singapore: Tuttle Publishing), 2014.

is equated with an *otaku* bedroom expanding into the streets of Tokyo.[64] An *otaku* fan naturally felt freer in this environment.

Akihabara did not only cater to *otakus*. Another range of products that arose was the emergence of cute or *kawaii* products popular with Japanese popular cultural consumers as well. The originators of the trend was attributed to girls in the 1980s who wanted adorable and cute idols that were not only sweet but had a strong fighting spirit and motivation.[65] This preference gave rise to a whole new empire of product merchandising that started innocently from the emergence of letter-writing trends that undergirded product design booms characterised by the strong success of Hello Kitty for example.[66] Christine R. Yano calls the Hello Kitty popular cultural globalisation "pink globalization" (feminine, cute and sexual) equated with the global spread of *kawaii* products and franchises.[67] By 2002, in the US alone, Kitty products trawled US$100 million in earnings from its branded product lines and an additional US$400 million in licensing fees.[68]

Men were not left out of the pink or *kawaii* globalisation. Out of this *kawaii* culture, Akihabara spawned its own variant, the maid cafes in which women dressed in maid costumes served tea and snacks to mainly male *otaku* customers. The maid café appropriated from the *kawaii* movement evolved with the tastes of *otakus* and then became mainstream when their popularity increased with tourists, non-*otaku* customers and regular consumers. Founded in 2008,

---

[64] Galbraith, Patrick, *The Moe Manifesto* (Tokyo, Rutland, Vermont and Singapore: Tuttle Publishing), 2014, p. 160.

[65] Okazaki, Manami and Geoff Johnson, *Kawaii! Japan's Culture of Cute* (Munich, London and NY: Prestle), 2013, unpaginated introduction.

[66] *Ibid.*

[67] Shiraishi, Saya S., "Doraemon Goes Abroad" in *Japan Pop!* edited by Timothy J. Craig (Armonk NY and London England: M.E. Sharpe), 2000, p. 154.

[68] Yano, Christine R., "Monstering the Japanese Cute" in *In Godzilla's Footsteps* edited by William M. Tsutsui and Michiko Ito (Hampshire England: Palgrave MacMillan), 2006, p. 154; Shiraishi, Saya S., "Doraemon Goes Abroad" in *Japan Pop!* edited by Timothy J. Craig (Armonk NY and London England: M.E. Sharpe), 2000, p. 154.

This is a photo of Radio Kaikan that hosted some of Japan's cutting-edge popular culture-related figurine producer.

MailDreamin with five branches in Akihabara, male to female ratio has grown to about six to four and tourists from Asia and particularly from France became the bulk of foreign consumers.[69] Maid cafes also innovated their own indigenous designs for customer satisfaction, including *kawaii* versions of household doorbells to give customers the impression that they are entering a residential area instead of a café joint.

Soft power element

Pink globalisation shaped the lifestyle goods consumption patterns for legions of fans. The maid cafes become constructed environments that create the fantasy of being in a comic book environment or *manga* world. The Japanese Ministry of Foreign Affairs (MOFA) has even appointed Lolita

---

[69] Okazaki, Manami and Geoff Johnson, *Kawaii! Japan's Culture of Cute* (Munich, London and NY: Prestle), 2013, p. 94.

models "kawaii ambassadors" due to their immense appeal.[70] In fact, Tokyo's *Diplomatic Bluebook 2006* mentioned:

> Japanese culture is currently attracting attention around the world as 'Cool Japan'. In order to increase interest in Japan and further heighten the image of Japan, Ministry of Foreign Affairs (MOFA) is working with the private sector through overseas diplomatic establishments and the Japan Foundation to promote cultural exchanges while taking into consideration the characteristics of each foreign country.[71]

In 2009, Japan's Minister of Land, Infrastructure, Transport and Tourism Fuyushiba Tetsuzo appointed Hello Kitty as a goodwill ambassador to advocate tourism to Japan from China and Hong Kong.[72] The focus on East Asian economies is strategic, as they represent economic growth for Japan in the near future. In East Asian economies like Indonesia, economic growth is giving rise to a consuming class that is urbanised and modern, resonating with the lifestyles portrayed in Japanese *manga* and *anime*.[73]

Rising rivals

Akihabara faces other rising popular cultural centres in Tokyo like East Ikebukuro. Currently, Ikebukuro specialises in products differing from Akihabara such as Boy's Love products (in the Otome Road of East Ikebukuro or more mainstream products found in Sunshine City). Besides more mainstream emerging rivals, Akihabara also faces threat from gentrifications and mainstreamization of the district into a financial/

---

[70] Okazaki, Manami and Geoff Johnson, *Kawaii! Japan's Culture of Cute* (Munich, London and NY: Prestle), 2013, p. 113.

[71] Lam, Peng Er, Japan Too Going After "Soft Power" in East Asian Institute National University of Singapore (EAI NUS) Background Brief No. 336 (Singapore: EAI NUS), 2007, p. 2 quoting MOFA, Japan, Diplomatic Bluebook 2006, p. 208.

[72] Tsutsui, William, *Japanese Popular Culture and Globalization* (Ann Arbor MI, USA: Association for Asian Studies, Inc.), 2010, p. 66.

[73] Shiraishi, Saya S., "Doraemon Goes Abroad" in *Japan Pop!* edited by Timothy J. Craig (Armonk NY and London England: M.E. Sharpe), 2000, p. 302.

Photo of a prominent and successful multi-storey maid café joint in Akihabara (second building from the right). This joint offers multi-lingual services with some floors of the maid café dedicated to customers speaking different languages.

Ikebukuro's Hello Kitty Gift Gate. A *kawaii* gateway in East Ikebukuro cementing mainstream appeal in Ikebukuro as the next centre of popular culture in Japan.

Ikebukuro also has large-sized gaming centre that are not found in Akihabara, drawing mainstream gamers to the district.

Skyscrapers hosting offices, hi-tech incubators, showrooms and mainstream executives (salarymen) have popped up in Akihabara that seems to be preparing for the post-popculture era should Akihabara shift from being a retail district to a financial/business centre, just as the shift happened from electronics retailing to the pop cultural scene in the 1990s.

Akiba Square is the entrance to a gleaming new skyscraper which houses offices, galleries and mainstream non-*otakuish* tenants, as well as a highly-institutionalised Tokyo Anime Center for visitors (domestic and foreign). It remains to be seen whether this represents the new mainstream face of Akihabara or the new evolution phase after the organically-developed *otaku*-based growth origins of the district.

business/retail sector. One can already find skyscrapers hosting hi-tech companies and showrooms slowly creeping upon the main street.

Concluding Remarks

Singapore is unlikely to have the same critical mass of *otaku* fandom and a specialised district like Akihabara, given the diverse pluralistic offerings of popular cultures in Singapore, such as Hollywood productions, K-pop, Bollywood, Mat Rock, Cantopop, Mandopop, just to name a few. But it is likely to have a core community of diehard hardcore *otaku* community who are willing to consume Japanese popular culture and following the trends set in Akihabara and other creative economic districts in Japan. Given the cyberspace connectivity that fans around the world now possess, the Singapore J-pop community is not isolated but connected with their counterparts around the world through the internet and social media. This ensures the sustainability of interest in Japanese popular cultural products. It will also pique Singaporean fans' interest in the latest offerings of J-pop products by viewing them first before they are available in Singapore. I took on the role of a fan and carried out observational studies in Akihabara in the next chapter on location in the creative district.

13

The Creative Economy in Japan

Introduction

The idea of Cool Japan is a nationwide campaign to promote the creative products emanating from Japan. When I arrived in Japan on 17 January 2016, I was greeted by a campaign poster promoting traditional arts and crafts in Japan. Cool Japan includes both traditional handicrafts (*mingei*) and contemporary popular cultural products (J-pop products). The term often includes hybridised products that incorporates both traditional and contemporary designs, often updating traditional handicraft and artisanal designs for contemporary audience. Cool Japan products can be intangible in the form of images to concrete items like figurines, *manga* or decorative items. In addition to the fluidity and comprehensiveness of genre of products, sometimes, the variety of a certain product can be dizzyingly large, spoiling the consumers with many choices. This caters to Japanese consumers who want to have a large number of choices but at reasonable prices. Japan is well-known for its fickle-minded consumers, who may have deterred some foreign companies from retailing products in Japan, although the market in Japan can be rewarding if retailers are able to offer good quality well-priced products.

Cool Japan products and items range from high-tech items like game sets with chips that can operate guided missile systems to low-tech products with a sense of aesthetics that appeal to Japanese consumers. Some of these products focus on youths and cater to their needs while others innovate creative products out of ideas. Many designs emerged from ergonomic needs and other functional purposes while others highlight aesthetic priorities to appeal to Japanese senses. Besides advertising commercial retail services, popular cultural designs also serve an important social function. Popular cultural characters and designs are featured in public signs and posters because they are cuter, more attractive and less jarring when conveying public campaign messages or when they are performing functional roles like pointing out public directions for commuters.

Traditionalism

High-tech applications are only one aspect of the creative industries and Cool Japan campaign in Singapore. Japanese designs, creative and popular cultural industries have also retained strong traditional elements, drawing from nostalgic designs and pre-modern customs and rituals for incorporation into contemporary designs and products.

Retail space

Because spaces are limited in Japan, every inch of it is optimally maximised for retailing or manufacturing cool products that appeal to customers. In the case of the *manga* café, the core idea is selling private space to the consumers so that they can enjoy private time with their favourite comic books or savour a delicious cup of coffee. This is a commodification of private time and space for consumers. In the organized chaos of Tokyo's urban layout, creative advertising is practiced to capture the attention of consumers. This is particularly since high rental rates demand the need to capture the attention span of individuals in human traffic passing by the retail area.

Besides retail space, Japanese companies also try to create aesthetically pleasing architectural designs to attract and draw customers to consume.

A robotic mechanical arm hidden behind the strands of noodles lifts the *soba* up and down in an inviting gesture for patrons and guests to come into the restaurant (photo taken on 18 January 2016).

Cross-Pollination of Culture with American Popular Culture

I arrived in Japan at a time when *Star Wars 7: The Force Awakens* was making its way regionally across East Asia. At many drinks vending machines I encountered in Tokyo, I witnessed an intense promotion of BB8 from *The Force Awakens*. This indicated that Japanese popular cultural consumers continue to indulge and be influenced by US popular culture which has widespread appeal in East Asia. Since the post-war era, Japan has received cultural influence from Hollywood movies, but they have also influenced the American audience with

A simple innovation, a high absorbent pad that allows the user to flap the umbrella against it to absorb excess rainwater or melted snow to prevent untidy wet floors in the building. This was particularly useful during the heavy snowfall that I experienced during my trip on 18 January 2016.

their own cultural products. This is sometimes known by cultural scholars as the "cross-pollination" of cultures. Both *Star Wars* and *Godzilla* are part this process of cross-pollination. *Star Wars*, by George Lucas' own admission, was influenced by Akira Kurosawa's films, Samurai outfits and other early iconic Japanese popular cultural products. *Godzilla* and other films of that era from Japan were acquired because of their low costs for screening in drive-in theatres where audiences may consist of dating couples whose attention may not be totally focused on the film itself!

The hotel that I put up at the fringe of Kabuki-cho is considered an essential location for hardcore *Godzilla* fans making the pilgrimage to Tokyo. The hotel lobby also featured a historical chronology of

A billboard by the public roadside advertising a *manga* café. *Manga* cafés are popular with consumers who want to have private time reading quietly the latest *manga* borrowed from the café's in-house library (photo taken on 18 January 2016).

Godzilla works from the 1950s to the 2000s. Godzilla is a good example of the contextual importance of creative products emanating from Japan. Scholars and commentators have argued that *Godzilla* is a social response to the atomic bombings and post-war nuclear tests that saw radioactive ashes falling onto Japanese fishing boats (the Lucky Dragon incident).

Hotel Gracery featured a Godzilla head at the top of its building overlooking the city district of Shinkuju in Tokyo armed with sharp talons. Visitors go to the building to see this magnificent site. This particular version of Godzilla features the 1950s version. At the base of this Godzilla head, there are a number of bas-reliefs that feature images of Godzilla from the retro era.

Sofmap is a major player in the *manga* and *anime* distribution supply chain. Variety is a major feature of the *anime* and *manga* industry. Sofmap offers a wide variety of popular cultural products for the mainstream manga fans and also niche subcultures like BL, moe fans and other members of the *otaku* communities. The photo features a branch outlet of Sofmap at Shinjuku. The main retailing outlet in Akihabara is the Mecca for animation and *manga* fans within Japan and outside (photo taken on 18 January 2016). The photo also shows the complex maze of buildings layout in the Shinjuku district in Tokyo. Some designers, architects and other stakeholders in urban planning characterise Tokyo's layout as "organized chaos".

My first encounter with a large Godzilla in Tokyo was in 2014 when Roppongi Hills featured a large Godzilla sculpture from waist up that was able to spew smoke, cry out loud and release laser light beams. The Roppongi Godzilla is modelled after the Hollywood version as opposed to the 1950s version of Godzilla found on the top of Hotel Gracery.

The owner of this building recreated the facade of an old theatre that used to stand in this location. This was near the site of the theatre that used to feature the iconic Japanese popular singer Hibari Misora (photo taken on 19 January 2016).

Another feature that characterises the Japanese popular cultural retail industries is the diversity that they offer. For the hardcore *Star Wars* fans, there are niche retail spaces that distribute vintage figures and this draws *Star Wars* fans all over the world to these retail spaces. Engaged in this fandom, I performed the role of a fan collector and was impressed by the diversity of vintage products available in Japan. An example of the niche product they offer included personally signed autographed pictures of the *Star Wars* actors for Jango and Boba Fett. These shops are highly specialised retail distributors for high value-added popular cultural products. Offering the *gentei* or limited edition *Star Wars* figures proved that Japanese retailers are not only focusing on *gentei* Japanese popular cultural character goods but also iconic American ones. In other words, these are highly specialised supply chains to cater to a group of fans who are willing to pay more for what they want.

More European and American design influence in Tokyo's Shinjuku skyline with a gothic church design (probably a wedding hall) and a large Coca Cola Billboard behind it.

The US is not the only Western country to influence Japanese Popular Culture or creative products. During more than two centuries of *sakoku* isolation policy, pre-modern Edo Japan interacted with two groups of foreigners, the Dutch and the Chinese. This part of history has been integrated into Japanese lifestyles, including wine-drinking, western culinary cuisines and even designs of household items. This photo shows a restaurant featuring such stylised designs of two Dutchmen drinking wine by the grapevine.

Akihabara

The creative cultural district of Akihabara remains the nucleus of Japanese popular cultural consumption.

Another example of hybridised culture is a stylised ninja as shown in the figure, swinging around New York City at Times Square. The image appears to be borrowed and adapted from the movie *Spiderman* starring Tobey Maguire (photo taken on 16 January 2016).

A major marketing concept in the Japanese creative industry is *gentei* or limited edition. Japanese covet items that are limited in circulation and therefore there is a tendency for collectors and consumers to value these products.

A major component of Japanese popular culture is its culinary traditions and pop food.

While the pop foods featured above are created with youth in mind particularly in fashionable districts like Akihabara, Japanese cuisines continue to retain traditionalism in their food presentation. Sometimes, innovation in designs, technologies and lifestyle goods may not just mean moving deterministically forward but can also include looking

Another image that bears some semblance to iconic New York images such as the I Heart New York design. In this picture, it is replaced by I Heart Kabkicho (photo taken on 16 January 2016).

back into the past for inspirations. Even though Japan has developed cutting-edge packaging technologies, a restaurant I patronised continued to use leaves for food presentation. The sense of aesthetics for nostalgia ensures the survivability and sustainability of traditional packing practices. Another example of traditionalism in Japanese culinary presentation is the use of cast iron vessel to cook the rice, ensuring even distribution of heat and no rice grain is charred in the process. It is a practice carried forth from the Edo period despite electronically controlled rice cookers with precision temperature controls. The hybridization of Japanese culinary culture is not merely along East–West fusion but it also involved indigenization of other Northeast Asian cultures. The "horumon" dish *motsunabe*, consisting of the hotpotting the intestines of cow with vegetable and herbs, was originally a Mongolian cuisine

Mobile billboards featuring the latest pop albums in Akihabara with trucks plying the public roads (photo taken on 19 January 2016).

Akihabara remains attractive to electronics geeks and buffs who can purchase micro parts that they need and then construct their technologies at home. There are also platforms in the incubator sections of Akihabara located on the other side of the train station that provide equipment facilities for geeks and entrepreneurs to make their own machines. This platform also brings together human talents to collaborate on projects based on their respective expertise (photo taken on 19 January 2016).

successfully and permanently indigenised in Japanese culinary culture. Japanese innovation involved using the fatty intestines. Another example of intra-Northeast Asian hybridization is the *yakitori* dish. The Japanese version of the *kebab* uses miso sauce to flavour the meats. *Miso* is traceable back to Tang dynasty, China's monastic order which prepared *miso* for its monks' culinary needs. Here, it is applied to barbeque meat for extra flavour. The *ramen* is another dish that originated from southern China but has been indigenised and further innovated upon by Japanese noodle makers. Innovations are extremely sophisticated as *ramen* retailers offer customers options and choices in noodle width, level of spiciness, choice of toppings, amount of spring onions, and to top it all up, an *onsen tamago* or egg cooked by dipping in water that resemble the temperatures found in natural hot springs. Readers who want to understand the importance of *ramen* noodles as a theme in Japanese popular culture should watch the movie *Tampopo*.

The retention of traditionalism and time-tested ways of doing things is a testimony to identity formation and authenticity.

A good example of how creativity is used to enhance the identity of a local community. This plaque embedded in the ground in Ueno depicts a stylised panda design which symbolises the location's renowned zoo that hosts panda in its enclosures. It encapsulates the identification of the location with one of its most famous attractions (photo taken on 18 January 2016).

This chapter discussed the production and trendsetting process of Japanese popular culture in Akihabara, Tokyo. Creative production must go hand in hand with fandom reception to complete the process of popular cultural consumption. In the next chapter, a Singaporean otaku fan's perspective on Japanese popular culture consumption in Singapore will be discussed.

14

Japanese Popular Culture from the Perspective and Opinions of a Fan Living in Southeast Asia

Yeo Kai Yeat

Limitations of the Following Chapter

Before I begin on the chapter, I would like to emphasise on the fact that the following ideas and content are solely based on my own past and present experiences with the Japanese popular culture. But I assure the reader that the information is correct based solely on my personal experiences. Most of my experiences come from my previous trips to Japan, including trips down to *anime*-based events and conventions, visits to popular locations such as Akihabara, Ikebukuro and Nakano Broadway. The motivation in using these experiences is mainly on the fact that it shows us something not a general Japanese culture fan will see, but more of what a fan who has delved deep into the culture experience. It is also to be noted that this chapter focuses more heavily on the Animation side of Japanese popular culture, as that is where most, if not all, of my interest in Japanese popular culture stem from.

Due to the fact that the chapter is based highly on personal opinions, it is very likely that certain viewpoints, thoughts and opinions can be biased.

Pop Culture from an *Otaku* Point of View — a Fan Perspective

As far as I can remember, the very first Japanese Animation that I have watched was *Nintama Rantarō* when I was still very young, perhaps around eight years old when the Chinese dubbed version of it was aired in the early hours of the day. However, back then, I did not have any knowledge about the Japanese Popular culture, or anything related in that sense, and in all honesty, I believed that *Nintama Rantarō* was actually a Chinese animation because of the dubbing. However, the art style, design and content really appealed to me.

What really startled me then was an undubbed episode of *School Rumble*, where the content of the episode really attracted me. The content was funny, the artwork felt very different and last but not least, the voices of the characters. It lit a fire within me that started this little fandom of mine.

What is Unique and Different About Japanese Pop Culture that Attracted Me More Than Other Forms of Popular Culture?

At first, what attracted me to Japanese popular culture more than the other forms of culture was definitely the Animation part of Japanese Anime, Comics, Games (ACG), and from it, the character design. Albeit the fact that the art of the characters were not good representations of its realistic counterparts, I felt some strong sense of attraction to wards them. Above that, animation styles for certain scenes that have a lot of actions and movements were also at a higher level as compared to other forms of popular culture.

As some of the Japanese animations are adaptations of their *manga* counterparts, out of curiosity and interest in wanting to know the full progress of the storyline, or to find out how much the animation has deviated from its *manga* counterpart, I had also started delving into reading Japanese *manga*.

Moving on, most, if not all, Japanese animations come with a unique opening (theme) and ending (theme) that belong to this genre called Anisong (short for Animation music/song). Although not actually knowing the lyrics of these songs back then, constantly listening to those catchy tunes caused a continuous growth in the interest I have in the Japanese popular culture.

While some of these songs are performed by a Japanese pop (J-pop) singer, others, notably character songs, are performed by voice actors/actresses (*seiyuus*, 声優) who are responsible for bringing life into the characters in the Japanese Animation. I started to have an interest in *seiyuus*, and my fandom grew towards it. Some *seiyuus* have their radio shows, where they will host and talk about certain themes and topics, where fans could also send in their fanmails, and if selected, their mail would be read by the artistes and have questions on their mail answered, which I would tune in to listen to, and sometimes write to. Sometimes they will also have live telecasts on the Japanese Youtube counterpart, *Nico Nico Douga*, which I would tune in to those that starred the artiste who I'm a fan of.

As Ian Condry have pointed out in his publication, *The Soul of Anime*, that Japanese *anime* has started to get the fans involved, rather, give fans more opportunities to indulge into the *anime* experience outside of the mainstream media type, via meet and greet sessions, forward *anime* screening events, talk shows, conventions, music concerts (or lives(ライブ)).[1]

During these events, certain production team and cast members of the show (sometimes the producer, the author, artistes and the voice actress (or *seiyuu*) behind the voices of the characters) will appear during the screening to give a talk about their thoughts and feelings during the production of the *anime*. During this time, fans get a chance to meet with the voices behind the characters, know more about an *anime* title, and also the creator's and voice actor's feelings and thoughts behind it. It allows fans to be able to enjoy the title more.

---

[1]Condry, Ian, *The Soul of Anime* (Durham and London: Duke University Press), 2013, pp. 113, 161–184.

Fans, like me, now are just as interested in meeting the people behind the title. Japanese *anime* has already, I would say, evolved into a level where it is not just about the animation that is shown on medium anymore; this, today, is what really attracts me to Japanese popular culture more than the other types of popular culture.

Although other forms of Popular Culture also do have these types of meet and greets, concerts, it is their style and the sheer amount of available events that are tied towards Japanese popular culture, paired together with a bit of personal preference that made me more interested in Japanese popular culture than its counterparts. The Japanese popular culture industry puts in a lot of effort to continuously make sure that a series lives on even after the screening ends and keeps its popularity up. I will talk about my consumption of these in another section below.

Globalisation of ACG to a Fan

Firstly, I would like to fix my idea of Globalisation I would be using in this context, which is mainly the interaction and integration amongst people, companies of different countries, driven by trade, investment assisted by information technology.[2] Globalisation in this context and chapter I am writing about is when it is easier for people to interact together, trade, consume and communicate about Japanese popular culture, where contents from Japan become easily available in other countries, or rather, specifically in Singapore, my home country. As I have been a frequent attendee for various events, local and overseas, I do believe that I have some placing in my opinions and ideas about the various situations.

Observations of Local and Overseas Events, Attendee Demographics

Local events in Japan

Personally, I do not think that there is a huge market that comprises fans travelling to the origin, Japan, yet, just to consume Japanese popular

---

[2] Globalization101, "What Is Globalization" undated [downloaded on 5] available at http://www.globalization101.org/what-is-globalization/.

culture, but I will be mentioning about certain overseas events, and some of my experiences from these events.

Firstly, twice a year, there's a major convention called Comic Market (or Comiket for short), where fans or circles who have created their works are allowed to participate, and interact with other circles, and most importantly, sell their user created products. As of 2006, Comiket has known to attract more than half a million attendees in a single half-year session.[3] It is a grand event that was born out of the Japanese ACG industry. I have attended the event twice, during the year 2013 and 2014, both during the winter season.

Queue at Tokyo Big Sight, location for Comiket, during the winter session of Comiket for the year 2014, roughly four hours before the opening.

---

[3] McCarthy, Helen, "Manga: A Brief History" in *500 Manga Heroes & Villains*. Hauppauge, New York, USA: Chrysalis Book Group, 2006, p. 14.

As mentioned before, consumption of Japanese popular culture has evolved from just the consumption of the product itself, but into the consumption of the chances and possibilities like meet and greets, live concerts, talk shows, etc. The actual process for someone overseas like me to have a chance to attend these events is actually not a simple one.

The following is a standard process in obtaining an entrance ticket to some of the live concerts, meet and greet events (which requires tickets), *but it does not represent all the possible ways of getting a chance to attend the events.*

Most of these events require tickets, which can only be obtained via the usage of a e-ticket balloting account, which requires a Japanese phone number, a Japanese address, and/or a Japanese credit card. Not all the balloting sites work with overseas credit cards. For certain ticket ballots, ballot slips and codes need to be obtained and there are times these slips can only be obtained if and only if the fan purchased a certain product related to the event from a Japanese ACG store inside Japan itself. It is also good to take note that there are some ballots where credit cards and online payment are not accepted as a form of payment, where payment of the ticket has to be done in a convenience store in Japan, within days of the announcement of the ballot results, which is technically not very possible for a fan who is away from Japan during the announcement of the results.

Although there exist middle-man services that help overseas fans with these procedures, all these actually carry a fee, which can be quite hefty depending on the tediousness of the process. In my situation, it is with the help of Japanese acquaintances and friends that I'm able to complete the process.

Next, attending the actual event. Without a doubt, most if not all of the event attendees are Japanese themselves. From my personal experience, I have managed to see and meet some foreigners attending the event, but they are really rare, also, the medium language for all these events is Japanese. From the process of attaining the tickets to what we can see in the events, we can see that these local events are marketed more towards their local population, meaning that the demographics of the attendees are expected to be fully Japanese, once in a while having some foreigners. From experience, it can be also noted that there are times where artistes ask the attendees if there is anyone from overseas, albeit the fact that the event is not targeted at them. This, however, brings up another topic on consumption of overseas fans and the appeal of overseas events.

In conclusion, personally, although there exists an avenue for fans to visit and attend events in Japan, there are still some difficulties which make it hard for fans to do so, but there are still opportunities for fans to do so due to the existence of overseas events, which I will be talking about next.

Overseas Events in Singapore, and Certain Things Fans Do for Their Artistes

Singapore is one of the countries in Southeast Asia that has a lot of Japanese popular culture-related events. To break it down, in the recent years, there is a major Japanese Animation convention, called Anime Festival Asia (AFA) held near the end of the year annually, where Japanese guests, exhibitors, artistes and performers attract over more than half a million attendees.

There are also other well-known cosplay events that are held annually such as Cosfest, EOY Cosplay Festival, etc. There is a notable event called Singapore Toy, Games and Comic Convention (STGCC), which comprises popular culture from not just Japan, but also the West.

I have been a frequent attendee of these events especially AFA. For simplicity and to prevent confusion, I will be using mainly my observations and experiences from attending AFA to talk about the local events. I have attended the first AFA back in 2008. To the best of my memory capabilities, back at the time, AFA was a rather small convention with few local exhibitors and exhibitors from Japan. The stage was a part of an open area inside the exhibition hall, and people without stage passes could enjoy the concert. Since then, AFA has continuously grown bigger and bigger, starting with more exhibitors, a greater array of guests that represents Japanese Popular Culture such as producers of certain Japanese Animation, voice actors/actresses behind the voices of those animations, and last but not the least, authors of certain Japanese Light Novel series and many more.

With more overseas guests and vendors, there exists a bigger range of "goods and service" which fans could consume. Certain fans would queue overnight just to be able to get into the venue first and be able to get what they want. The need for consumerism is something I will be mentioning about at the end of this chapter.

It has seen observed that, there are translators and interpreters to ensure that attendees have a method to communicate with the guests, and that they have a better understanding and clarity of the featured popular culture content. The medium of language used for communications is the countries' national language, even in advertisements, Facebook and websites.

Adding on, depending on the guests and artistes that were invited to grace the event, there have been times when fans from overseas travelled over to Singapore to attend AFA, and I have actually managed to make friends with some of them. What we can see here is that the local scene of Japanese Animation has been growing bigger and bigger, also to mention that in my own belief, with the growing success of the Japanese popular culture scene, more and more events have been appearing, for example, CharaExpo in the year of 2015.

For certain local fans like me, when the artistes that we like are invited for an event, some of us would write fan letters for them, given that we have a chance to deliver the letter to them, be it via an autograph or some meet and greet sessions. Fan letters can include certain details like some greeting messages, expressing the fan's joy for them visiting Singapore, where some might also write about their own personal experiences and thoughts, with others leaving messages hoping that the artistes or guests will come again in the near future. Some fans might go an extra mile as to design and decorate flower stands for their artistes just to show their support for them.

Additionally, although there are ways and methods for fans to deliver their mails and letters to Japan, these local events also provide an extra avenue, and a closer opportunity for fans overseas to meet, communicate and interact with the artistes. All these would not have been very much possible without globalisation. With globalisation, Japanese popular culture market can expand overseas.

In terms of opportunities, in my opinion, partially due to AFA and the appeal of the Japanese ACG market in Singapore, Sea*A (Southeast Asia * Anime), a J-Pop singer group comprising three Singaporeans and a Malaysian, where they debuted with the song DREAM SHOOTER under HoriPro (Hori Productions) for the television anime, Cardfight!! Vanguard in 2011 (Disclaimer: Sea*A have been disbanded since June 2013, but one remaining member, Valerie, has since been with Asian Pop Collective, and is still singing J-pop songs.)

For some Japanese ACG artistes, due to the overwhelming response, they receive from overseas fans, some artistes have opened themselves out to the overseas market, one of which is Risa Oribe (more known as LiSA), who on 4 July, 2015 opened her official fanclub in both English and Chinese, and has allowed non-Japanese to be able to sign up for her fanclub. It is noted that participation and memberships of fanclubs of Japanese ACG artistes have been something that has always been a Japanese-Only privilege, due to various reasons like the requirement of a Japanese mobile contract, and/or an address of an actual residence in Japan.

These, in my opinion, I believe are opportunities and chances that were made possible due to the responses in overseas events. Without the responses from the fans that was made possible due to globalisation, the above would not have been a reality.

Networking, and Knowing More People

Through the attendance of events both locally and overseas, I have met and connected with many people. We connected mainly via exchanging social networking services (SNS) like Twitter handles, LINE IDs and Facebook for some. Through these, in my opinion, various possibilities became available for overseas fans. The local Japanese fans could help the overseas fans in various matters such as obtaining event tickets, and the overseas fans could help the Japanese fans when they are interested to visit overseas events. These, I believe, were made possible via globalisation.

Fans could also get together to produce works which they distribute to others to promote their artistes, or arrange gifts, congratulatory flower stands for their artistes.

On matters such as fan gatherings, especially those with both local and overseas fans, I believe that even though there are times (most overseas fans that I know were able to communicate in Japanese, but there were still some that did not have the ability to) where language proves to be a barrier in communication, the fans love it and interest for Japanese popular culture creates an avenue, topics for them to communicate, using certain tools like translators. In terms of language, it is not really an issue for these fans to get to know each other and to connect in my personal opinion although it is definitely better when both sides of fans have a common language for communication.

Consumerism and Consumption

In terms of economics, consumption refers to the "using up of goods and services using an exchangeable value".[4]

Before proceeding further, I will talk about some of the reasons why I consume these goods, and why I feel that there is a "need" to undergo the consumption of these goods.

As mentioned, as more people are interested in the people behind the *anime* itself (typically voice over actors and actresses), there is also a growing market for merchandise and goods behind these people. Just like mainstream media and mainstream popular culture (i.e. J-pop, Idols), goods related to voice actors and actresses are on the rise too.

Whenever there is a release of goods, the concept of 限定 (limited) and 特典 (bonus gift) is something that is commonly seen from the sale

---

[4]"Consumption" undated [downloaded on 22 Sep 2015] available at http://dictionary.reference.com/browse/consumption.

of these. If fans buy the related goods early, most of the time they are rewarded with a shop limited bonus, and the concept of 限定 works where certain items are only sold at a specific event, or only for a specific period. Most of the time, the concept of both 限定 and 特典 works together, whereby purchasing certain goods in a limited time entitles them a limited bonus. Sometimes milestones in purchases also entitle you these bonuses. This promotes fans to consume the goods and merchandise. Also as mentioned in the previous section, there are also cases whereby fans are given the chance to ballot for an opportunity to meet with the voice over actors and actresses in three events.

Moving on to other aspects, in Japanese ACG industry, apart from merchandise by official sources and producers, we can also see a lot of user-created goods sold at places like Animate, Tora no Ana, Gamers, etc. Japanese producers are not against fans making their own goods adapted from official sources (in the forms of little merchandise like key chains, or more popularly, *doujinshi*), and earning a profit out of it. These fan-made goods are also items that certain fans feel a need to purchase, to show their deep interest about a certain series. It is also noted that some of these fan-made goods are targeted towards the more mature, adult population with an age restriction.

Personally, I feel that the consumption in Japanese and overseas markets do have their differences. Fans in both sides readily consume what is available to them in their own countries with an increasing number of fans importing the goods from Japan itself. However, what is available to them in the two markets actually differs.

Although in recent years, what is available in Japan would likely be available in Singapore (with regard to mainstream items such as published *manga*, Japanese popular culture magazines, figurines, model kits and less limited edition items). There are still certain goods that are not locally available to overseas fans. These include goods such as Music CDs, (or more commonly known to fans as Singles and Albums, where Singles refer to music CDs with fewer tracks, and Albums which are compilations of the music done by the artiste/series), un-dubbed and un-subtitled original versions of the Japanese Animation, various merchandise, etc. As an example, most of the Japanese Animation Discs sold in Singapore are either subtitled by a local publishing company or dubbed from another country. These, I believe to the best of my reasoning, are due to the fact that the languages of the two countries are different, and the importers feel that having more localised content would be more appealing to the overseas fans.

However, this might actually not be the case in my opinion. As I have mentioned before, the goods in Japan have the concept of 限定 (limited) and 特典 (bonus gift), and these are not available in the localised forms of the goods (although it can be noted that there are times where local companies will include their own bonuses and gifts to boost sales). Without the special gifts, certain fans might not see the need or lose some desire with regard to consuming the goods, where some of the fans might actually choose to import the goods directly from Japan or choose not to consume at all. Certain products that are targeted at mature and adult audiences are also not available in certain overseas markets due to the individual countries' law and censorship.

These in turn create a difference in the Japanese and overseas markets, where although there is an overseas market for Japanese popular culture, fans end up consuming straight from the local (Japanese) market.

There is also that famous debate about fan subbing, and the following are my honest opinions and observations with regard to this matter. I would like to emphasise on the fact that even though I appreciate the fact that fan-subs exist and also do appreciate what they are doing to help with the community, infringing copyright and profiting from it is something that should always be frowned upon. Also from Ian Condry, *The Soul of Anime*, fan-subbers view their act as a contribution to the industry by coding subtitles into releases and sharing it with others to download for free.[1] This actually infringes laws of copyright, where distribution of one's work is not allowed unless authorised.[5]

Adding on to the fact, there are fan-subbing groups coming forward for donations in the idea that they need funds to be able to support their

---

[5]Copyright Law of Japan, Copyright Research and Information Center CRIC, undated [downloaded on 5 July 2015] available at http://www.cric.or.jp/english/clj/ocl.html.

servers that are hosting the episodes they are releasing. However, this is strongly arguable, as it has been noted that the actual cost for fan-subbing is near to zero, as fan-subbers should not be profiting from their work. Japanese *anime* companies have been using their need for donations as a point that fan-subbers are profiting from their work.

However, we cannot deny the fact that fan-subs are driven by the rising demand for overseas *anime* fans that are unable to access the episodes due to various reasons, and those affected by the language barrier, *vice versa*, fan-subs are also motivated by their need to spread their content to enable others to equally enjoy what they love. The interlocking supply and demand of fan-subs created by subbers and fans has enabled the fan-subs to be able to thrive till today in my opinion.

On the other hand, I would also like to say that fan-subs have actually helped promote Japanese ACG to the rest of the world. Some countries, due to media restrictions, have been unable to receive certain *anime* episodes. As there are also times whereby releases on distributable media are slow or late (Even in Japan, most Blu-Ray and DVD releases take about 4–6 months for the full release, even though at times DVDs and Blu-Rays are released in parts, where typically the first contains a single episode and the rest contains 1–2 episodes each). One might also be able to buy and import the media from Japan itself, but the lack of proper subtitles prove to be a strong deterrence against overseas fans, thus, even with fan-subs, the offset caused by their "piracy" might not be something of a very substantial amount. Most of the time, fan-subbers also do encourage fans to buy the official release if they liked the title, which I believe they actually do. Also together with the concept of *gentei and tokuten* as mentioned before, fans will still buy the official release if they are interested in collecting the goods.

In conclusion, the rise of fan-subs is caused by the rising demand for consumption of Japanese popular culture and due to various issues and reasons such as locality, timing and language issues, consumption of Japanese popular culture in overseas market has been affected. But in my opinion, I feel that it has been more of a benefit than a negative with regard to the overseas market of Japanese popular culture, although I would still like to emphasise that piracy should always be frowned upon.

Based on my observations, the varying attraction levels in consumption based on ethnicity, religion and culture are not very evident to me. However, it is very evident when we talk about gender. From what I see and what I personally consume, I would like to believe that the male gender are generally more interested in goods and products that contain the elements of "moe", loosely meaning elements of cute, endearing, products with elements of *shounen* (少年), which is a genre that is targeted towards young males, most of the time containing elements of hot-bloodedness and action. Whereas for females, they tend to prefer products that either have emphasis on romance, or *shoujo* (少女), which is a genre that is targeted at young females. I have also observed that there exist another spectrum of female fans that are attracted towards products that contain handsome/appealing boys or males with male on male contents. These groups of fans are also referred by others as fujoshi (腐女子).

In conclusion, I feel that there is not much of a difference in the pattern that local and overseas fans consume, where the difference is more in the form of what is available for them, and how it might be possible that community subtitlers might have helped promote consumerism. Lastly, I have also briefly categorised how consumption attraction differs by the gender.

15

Another Fan Perspective: The Japanese ACG (Anime, Comics, Games) Popular Cultural Products

Sim Zhi Ya

The first thing that comes to my mind when "Japan" is mentioned is probably their *manga* or *anime*, two prominent Japanese entertainment products that enjoy worldwide popularity. The term "*manga*" refers to Japanese comics while "*anime*" refers to animations. Both are often cited as important features of Japan's cultural soft power globally with many events and merchandise spinoffs dedicated to promoting them all over the world. *Manga* and *anime* have given rise to the otaku culture with cosplay events and other promotional activities.

Some techniques still used in drawing contemporary *manga* and *anime* were pioneered by Osamu Tezuka, a *mangaka* (*manga* artist) who was later dubbed the "godfather of manga". He realised that the majority of *manga* works produced during his time were drawn from an artistic "two-dimensional perspective" and it was difficult to convey the feelings and plot of the story effectively to the readers compared to three-dimensional moving images. Thus, he started to introduce cinematic techniques into *manga* drawings and capture the *manga* characters' facial expressions in greater detail. His work has inspired many other genres of *manga* and is said to exert a fundamental influence on the *manga* industry even today.[1]

So what makes *manga* so appealing to people? Firstly, *manga* has a variety of different genres. They have genres such as "shoujo" which are targeted at teenage girls, "shounen" for teenage boys, mature *manga* which are more for adults and many more. Other than these genres targeting specific age groups, there are more genres specific enough for individual preferences such as romance, comedy, adventure, sci-fi, etc. This wide range of genres ensure that there is something suitable for everyone no matter what age or gender. *Manga* also usually employ a more sophisticated form of drawing style compared to western comics, which makes it more attractive, especially for older readers. Secondly, *manga* also appeals to the readers' fantastical and whimsical side. Most *manga* either have a storyline which borders on the fantasy including individual characters possessing magical powers or storylines that appeal to the majority of readership which are imaginative and unlikely to happen in reality. This allows readers to escape into the virtual world, in that way, *manga* becomes a form of stress relief or escapism. The storylines are usually well-thought out and detail oriented to make it relatable to the reader. Occasionally, there are values and moral lessons strategically integrated into the storyline and thus have the ability to educate its readers instead of merely providing entertainment. Lastly, good *manga* content and themes are timeless. They will appeal to readers long after they have been released, even when some of the *manga* classics are decades old. Some evergreen examples are *Sailor Moon* and *Dragon Ball*, both of which are *manga* series popular in the 1990s but still hold appeal for a large number of people today.

As an avid reader of romance *shoujo manga*, I feel that the greatest appeal of these category of *manga* is how female readers can relate to the storylines and content. Most girls at one point of time have probably dreamt of being swept off their feet by a white knight in shining armour and romance *shojou manga* tends to depict just that but with a more realistic storyline set in everyday scenarios which makes it relatable to readers. The story is also usually told from the female protagonist's

---

[1]Thorn, Matt, "A History of Manga," in *Manga-gaku* [downloaded on 30 March 2016], available at http://www.matt-thorn.com/mangagaku/history.html.

perspective which further resonates with the reader's life experience. Although most readers are aware that such stories are unlikely to happen in real life, the thrill of reading them is enough to give satisfaction and fulfil fantasies.

However, *manga* series do not just stop when the series have finished its run. Often, popular *manga* are serialised and turned into *anime*. Although *anime* can be inspired by many different genres such as games and novels, the majority of them are still adapted from *manga*. Similar to *manga*, *anime* offers a wide variety of genres to cater to different groups of people. It is a good alternative to *manga* drawings as some popular culture fans prefer watching the scenes in motion, especially animated action or fighting scenes which can sometimes be difficult to decipher in two-dimensional *manga* depending on the drawing styles. However, some argue that *manga* storylines usually become diluted when the *manga* is turned into an *anime*. This may be due to producers having different ideas from the original *mangaka* and thus directed the *anime* in a different way from its *manga* original work, or because the numerous graphics needed to produce the *anime* require some scenes to be deleted, causing the original *manga* version of highly developed storyline to be diluted. In addition, since *anime* productions are based on *manga*, popular *manga* series, which are yet to be completed are usually first animated and the story progression and endings may differ from their original *manga*. Animating a *manga* before it is completed also raises another issue which is that the plot progression may be a lot faster than the *manga* and hence, producers will slot in filler episodes in the *anime* version that are completely unrelated to the storyline.

Personally, most people I know read both *manga* and watch its *anime* version as well. The order depends on which medium piques their interest first. Those who read the *manga* first and watch the *anime* later may feel that it is a natural progression that after reading the still images, watching it later in animation will give the storyline more dimension and may shed light on details which may have been missed while reading the *manga*. On the other hand, those who watch the *anime* and continue on to the *manga* may prefer the more detailed storyline which *manga* may offer. Furthermore, *anime* are usually released only once a week and enthusiasts of a particular *anime* may choose to read the *manga* while waiting for new episodes of the anime to be released. Additionally, if an anime covers the content or storyline up to a certain point in the original storyline of the *manga* series it was adapted from, some popular cultural fans may go on to read the *manga* to continue following the rest of the plot. With a strong fan base, popular *anime* series are not just confined to the small screen. There are *anime* films as well, which are very popular. Some of these *anime* and *anime* films have gained popularity not just in Japan, but overseas as well. One example is the 2001 Japanese animated film "Spirited Away" which won an academy award for the category of best animated feature.

Anime and *manga* are not just limited to two-dimensional drawings or animation. There are also dramas and live action movies with human actors adapted from them as well, although the storylines are usually tweaked to fit reality. These adaptations bring *manga* and *anime* to life and makes it more relatable to the audiences. Both serve to further cement the popularity of Japanese culture. Popular *manga* and *anime* such as Hana Yori Dango, Itazura Na Kiss and Hana Kimi have been translated and adapted into drama series not just by Japanese production companies but by production companies from other East Asian countries as well such as Taiwan and Korea.

However, *manga* and *anime* have also led to negative impacts such as the formation of the *otaku* culture. *Otaku* originally referred to people who are obsessive over popular culture. It had a negative stigma and *otakus* are often regarded as people who have lost touch with reality, preferring to immerse themselves in the virtual world of *manga* and *anime* instead. In extreme cases, some *otakus* see themselves fully-integrated as part of the virtual world of the *manga* and thus enact scenes from the *manga* in real life. One example is the incident committed by Miyazaki Tsutomu, nicknamed "The Otaku Killer", who was a serial killer thought to be influenced negatively by violent and slasher *anime*.[2] However, in our modern day, the usage of this term has lost much of its original negative connotations and it is used by many fans of Japanese *anime* and *manga* all over the world to identify themselves.

---

[2]Ryall, Julian, "Nerd Cult Murderer Executed," dated 17 June 2008 in *The Telegraph*, available at http://www.telegraph.co.uk/news/worldnews/asia/japan/2144503/Nerd-cult-murderer-executed.html.

Due to their popularity, *manga* and *anime* have been commodified and heavily commercialised. Merchandise such as keychains, figurines and toys are spin-offs from popular *manga* and *anime* series and they boost the economy in the creative cultural sector. These merchandise are usually targeted at fans and an entire franchise could be created if the *anime* or *manga* series is popular enough. This can include games, novels, toys and hobby items. In fact, themed cafés and restaurants are set up such as maid cafés where waiters dress like maids to fulfil the customers' cosplay interests. These eateries are not only attractive to fans, they appeal also to the general population as a novel idea. There are also theme parks and marathons dedicated to *anime* such as the One Piece theme park in Japan and the One Piece marathon that was recently held in Singapore which are both dedicated to the exceptionally popular anime series "One Piece".

It comes as no surprise then that cosplay culture has grown in tandem with the rise of *anime* and *manga* products. Cosplay literally means costume play and it refers to the practice of dressing up and pretending to be a fictional character in *anime* and *manga* series. It ranges from simple to incredibly detailed versions of *anime* or game characters. Cosplay is used to show appreciation to the *anime* characters and have become a hobby for many. Previously, cosplay was more limited to *anime* characters but in recent years, characters from western comics and movies have been popular cosplay options as well. Cosplay has seen increased popularity around the world as the events for promoting cosplay has increased and are still rising rapidly. There are also full-time cosplayers who do engage in this activity as a paid job. It is common for well-known cosplayers to be part of a fan base and receive invitations to the different events which are influenced by Japanese pop culture. They are regarded as celebrities in the *otaku* community.

In Singapore alone, there are many cosplay events which serve as a platform for fans to show their passion for a *manga* or *anime* character.[3] Cosplayers usually put in a lot of effort for weeks or even months before

---

[3] Gurveen Kaur, "Singapore's Anime Instinct: Japanese Pop Culture is Still an Attraction," dated 11 June 2015 in *The Straits Times*, available at http://www.straitstimes.com/lifestyle/singapores-anime-instinct-japanese-pop-culture-is-still-an-attraction.

each event to get the perfect costume, props and imitate the manner-isms of the characters they are portraying. Non-cosplayers *anime* also play an integral part at these events and can usually be seen taking pho-tos with cosplayers and also patronising the various merchandise stores set up for the events. The events also usually draw crowds from neigh-bouring countries, be they fans or curious foreigners, which can also serve as a form of tourism for Singapore. Stores specialising in cosplay and *anime* merchandise such as Otaku House and CosAsia are also emerging. Although they still remain relatively uncommon, these stores serve as one of the few avenues for *manga* and *anime* enthusiasts to shop and support their hobby.

While the *manga* culture is strong in Singapore, it is often quite dif-ficult to purchase *manga* from a retail store. Firstly, there are only a few retail stores that carry *manga* such as Comics Connection and Kinokuniya, and they only carry limited *manga* series. As such, it is dif-ficult for people to search for and purchase *manga*. Secondly, the price of each volume of *manga* can be expensive, ranging from S$8 to S$12 each. Considering that most popular *manga* have a long storyline which spans many volumes, it can be an expensive hobby to collect these *manga*. Thirdly, not many *manga* series are translated into different languages, which makes the selection of *manga* sold in retail stores very limited. As such, many *manga* fans read freely-available *manga* on web-sites which scans, translates and upload different *manga* for fans all over the world. It is a more accessible, cheaper and convenient option.

That said, it is also the prevalence of internet which has led to increasing popularity of *manga* and *anime*. The convenience of having hundreds of *manga* series available on the go via smart phones or lap-tops has led to an emerging trend of people accessing *manga* on the internet instead of having the hardcopy version. Furthermore, *manga* is preferred over books as the still images in a *manga* is more stimulating than pages of words in a book.

Future Trends

Nevertheless, from my own perspective as a fan of both Korean and Japanese popular cultures, the popularity of Japanese culture does pale in comparison to the "Hallyu Wave" especially in Singapore. One of the reasons could be the failure of the Japanese government to capitalise on the popularity of *manga* and *anime*. Since these entertainment products are part of Japanese culture, it was mainly for internal consumption in Japan and the government was not fully aware that their culture had gained popularity worldwide in the 1990s. This is in contrast to the South Korean government. When the first signs of the "Hallyu Wave" started around 2008, the Korean government was quick to respond to the rising demand for more Korean merchandise and that resulted in an explosive popularity of Korean products and entertainment which led to what is now dubbed as the "Hallyu Wave". The Japanese government has since tried to popularise *anime* and *manga* once again through a "Cool Japan" movement and to project a cool image of Japan. From my opinion as a consumer, such efforts met with minimal success as many artists did not wish to participate in this movement. Moreover, in my own personal view, what was thought to be "cool" by the Japanese government differed from the public and the video made for this particular movement actually went viral for being uncool.[4]

Manga and *anime* are still hugely popular around the world and Singapore is no exception. With the many genres each medium (i.e. *manga* and *anime*) has to offer, there is no doubt that there are fans from all ages and gender attracted to its various offerings. The many events available all year round also serve to promote the *manga* and *anime* culture. Whether the popularity of *manga* and *anime* can continue to rise or will plateau or even peter off will depend on the continued efforts of the Japanese government in promoting pop culture and the relevant artists involved in the creative production process. Although it may seem difficult now since many Singaporean pop culture consumers are fixated on the "Hallyu Wave", if the Japanese government and artists choose to focus on the fashionable trends and collaborate together to combine and share their resources, the popularity of *manga* and *anime* will surely increase and may even rival that of the "Hallyu Wave".

---

[4] "Japan's Soft Power, Squaring the Cool" dated 16 June 2014 in *The Economist*, available at http://www.economist.com/blogs/banyan/2014/06/japans-soft-power.

16

Perspective from a Passionate Consumer of Japanese Pop Culture

Alvin Teo

Introduction

First and foremost, I have to confess that Japanese pop culture has greatly influenced me throughout my life. My first encounter with it was when I received my first copy of a "Pokemon" game as a gift when I was still schooling in Kindergarten. In my view, what sets Japanese pop culture apart from other countries is the uniqueness in their ideas. This can be seen in many industries that produce Japanese popular culture (pop culture for short).

My Thoughts on the Anime Industry

Uniqueness of anime

The term "Anime" essentially refers to animated films mostly catering to the Japanese consumer market. "Naruto" and "Bleach" are some of the more commonly known examples that have even been well-received overseas. Since Japanese animated films are hand drawn, it allows authors to have more freedom and control over expressing themselves graphically. The long-running series *One Piece*, where characters obtain superpowers through consuming special fruits, is a prime example of a story conceptualised in an unrealistic setting and subsequently produced into a TV show with live actors and then turned into a full-length movie. The origin of Japanese animation was heavily inspired by western animated cartoons such as the Mickey Mouse franchise but the Japanese *anime* industry further developed the techniques used in animation, showing exceptional improvements in quality over time.[1] Anime has now become a type of entertainment associated with some distinctive Japanese features and widely recognised all over the world. Although "Animes" are usually associated with younger audiences and viewerships, newer "Anime" genres are breaking through this stereotype by integrating darker and more mature themes such as the popular series "Death Note".

Japanese versus western animation

Compared to its western counterpart, cultural differences are visible in how different countries interpret the concept of *anime* and produce animation. From my own visual experience, the most successful cartoons in the US are inclined towards parodic and comedic themes with very simple stylised designs. Examples of such genres are *South Park* and *Family Guy*. On the other hand, Japanese *anime* covers a wider variety of genres, including fantasy and science fiction genres and includes more realistic character drawings. Although some may point out Japanese overemphasis on exaggerated drawings of physical features like eyes and body shapes, with unlikely proportions as well, Japanese *anime* and *manga* artistic styles also often display more aesthetic diversity than western animation.

Entering the global market

In the past, *anime* was mostly produced for the Japanese consumer market and contains mainly Japanese cultural themes. However, there is a rising trend for more Japanese animation studios to penetrate the global

---

[1] Lu, A. S, "The Many Faces of Internationalization in Japanese Anime". *Animation* 3, 2, dated 2008 in pp. 169–187.

market. A notable example is the *anime* "Plastic Memories" where many of its background scenes were derived from actual backdrops and landscapes in Singapore.[2] There are also more superhero-themed *anime* works emerging on the *anime* scene such as *One Punch Man* which is similar to western comic heroes that are gaining popularity globally as there are many new movies produced based on comic heroes such as the latest "Deadpool" movie.

More than just entertainment

Certain "Anime" works have more than just pure entertainment value. In the past, I vividly remember my primary school teacher making a case that Studio Ghibli animated films are really meaningful and he often played it during classes for our multimedia experiences and analyses of the film's themes. One film that was especially memorable for me was "Hotaru no Haka" or "Grave of the Fireflies" (1988). Studio Ghibli is one of the animation studios that used animation as an effective medium to discuss the relationship between human and the environment.[3] Viewers like myself still remember the messages that the film was trying to portray, such as anti-war sentiments implied by the sad tone and feel of the film and its theme of warfare in the film. Other movies like "Princess Mononoke" (1997) also raised the importance of eco-friendly practices by showing the dark consequences of environmental damage on human societies.

Thoughts on the Video Game Industry in Japan

Characteristics of Japanese video games

Sony's PlayStation series and the Nintendo game consoles are some of the most popular video gaming devices in the world. An estimated total

---

[2] Hayato, A. "[ANIME] Plastic Memories Anime Features Locations in Singapore?!" dated May 2015, AFA Channel! Availabale at http://www.afachan.asia/2015/05/plastic-memories-anime-features-locations-in-singapore/.

[3] Lahiri, H. "Reality through Fantasy: Miyazaki Hayao's "Anime" Films" dated 28 Sep 2014 *The Asia-Pacific Journal: Japan Focus*, available at http://apjjf.org/2014/12/39/Hiranmoy-Lahiri/4191/article.html.

of 157 million sets of PlayStation 2 consoles were sold worldwide, making it the best-selling console in the world.[4]

Typically, Japanese video games have a single-player format featuring little interaction with other players. In fact, some companies have developed dating simulation games that allow the users to have a realistic interaction with virtual characters. The demand for such games comes from fans who are passionate about gaming with virtual characters. There were even instances where the fans would organise birthday celebrations for their favourite virtual characters.

Japanese video games in the global market

However, in my opinion, the video gaming industry in Japan is in decline. Many Japanese video games are not translated into the English language, actively marketed or sold overseas, and so they are not as competitive internationally largely due to cultural barriers.[5] On rare occasions, some Japanese video game companies have produced games based on domestic market conditions and local fans' preferences that were unexpectedly successful overseas such as "Dark Souls".[6] The game is famous for being notoriously challenging although Japanese gamers find it enjoyable. Alternatively, some Japanese video game companies decided to collaborate with western companies in order to penetrate foreign markets. An example is the production of the popular "Kingdom Hearts" game which was created by Square-Enix in partnership with Disney.[7] As the world becomes increasingly globalised, strategies focusing only on the domestic market are not enough. Popular overseas

---

[4]Statista, Video Game Consoles Lifetime Unit Sales Worldwide as of 2015", undated in Statistic, available at http://www.statista.com/statistics/268966/total-number-of-game-consoles-sold-worldwide-by-console-type/.

[5]Coskrey, "The Tricky Path Abroad for Japanese Games", dated 27 Sep 2014 in *The Japan Times*, available at http://www.japantimes.co.jp/life/2014/09/27/digital/tricky-path-abroad-japanese-games/#.VxnPyDB96Ht.

[6]Byford, S. "Japan Used to Rule Video Games, So What Happened?" dated 20 March 2014 in *The Verge*, available at http://www.theverge.com/2014/3/20/5522320/final-fight-can-japans-gaming-industry-be-saved.

[7]Brookey, R. A., *Hollywood Gamers: Digital Convergence in the Film and Video Game Industries* (Bloomington: Indiana University Press), 2010.

gaming companies are now trying to enter Japan's video game market. "League of legends", a competitive e-sports game, with a prize pool of US$2.13 million up for grabs in its largest-scale international competition,[8] was recently launched in Japan. An estimated 67 million players participate in the "League of legends" gaming sessions every month.[9] With such a huge player base overseas, it could possibly draw more Japanese gamers into the online gaming platform in a market which is currently dominated by console gaming in the domestic market.

Thus, Japanese video gaming companies will need to target the global market while differentiating themselves from global competitors by incorporating Japanese cultural values and aesthetic uniqueness into their game content and design in order to level the playing field with their western counterparts.

Barriers hindering the progress of Japanese video games

A recent trend in the western video game industry is the increased releases of games produced by independent developers (Indie games).[10] The appearance of virtual game stores such as Steam decreased production costs for game developers. As customers are more used to purchasing digital copies through virtual game stores, there is less demand for hard copies and other costs related to physically distributing the games to the end consumers. As a result, there are now many Indie games in the western video game market, which is increasingly the main reason for purchasing a video game console in the West.[1] However, Japan has not caught on to the trend yet. Buying digital copies of console games

---

[8]Miller, K. K., "Want to be a Professional Gamer? Time to go to School!" dated 19 Feb 2015 RocketNews24, available at http://en.rocketnews24.com/2015/02/19/want-to-be-a-professional-gamer-time-to-go-to-school/.

[9]Riot, "Our Games" undated in *Riot Games*, available at http://www.riotgames.com/our-games.

[10]Byford, S., "Japan Used to Rule Video Games, So What Happened?" dated 20 March 2014 in *The Verge*, available at http://www.theverge.com/2014/3/20/5522320/final-fight-can-japans-gaming-industry-be-saved.

has not been generally accepted by gamers in Japan. Owning and keeping physical copies of the game remains a part of the gaming culture in Japan.[1] Hence, this is probably where the bottleneck for creative innovation exists in the Japanese video game market. Japanese game developers have to be part of a huge conglomerate such as Square-Enix in order to produce a video game. Independent developers have trouble releasing their games in the market as they are unable to bear the initial cost of producing the games without the help of virtual game stores distribution.

Next generation of portable gaming

Buying digital content such as train schedules on mobile phones has been a norm in Japan even before smartphones were introduced into the Japan market.[11] After smartphones were adopted by most Japanese consumers, they became receptive to the idea of purchasing applications for their phones. In 2013, Japan became the world's top ranking country in smartphone application store revenues and the main reason for its success in this business is due to the popularity of mobile phone games. The convenience of playing mobile games without the need to buy another device proves to be more attractive for consumers in the casual gaming market. The shift in consumers' tastes in terms of portable gaming is potentially fatal to portable handheld gaming companies such as Nintendo. In order to survive the market changes, they would either need to create a more compelling reason for people to buy and use a handheld device or follow the market trend and change their core business to produce mobile games instead.

Thoughts on the Pop Idol Groups in Japan

Uniqueness of Japanese idol groups

On one side of the Akihabara train station lies the location of Japan's very first idol group's specialised theatre facility. Producer Yasushi

---

[11]Neghishi, M., "Japan Tops World in Mobile Apps Revenue," dated 11 March 2013 in *WSJ*, available at http://www.wsj.com/news/articles/SB10001424052702 30333020457925122169260 6100

Akimoto revolutionised the concept of idol girl groups in 2005 with the creation of one of Japan's largest and most successful idol girl groups, AKB48.[12] The concept behind his idea was to allow fans to meet their idols every day through a rotational system of public appearance amongst their members. Apart from performances, AKB48 regularly hold handshake events and fan meetings all across Japan as part of their promotional activities. Other than handshake interactions between the idols and their fans, AKB48's success can be mainly attributed to the high level of participant involvement through voting contests for the most popular member of the group. The attraction of the AKB48 idol group lies in the amount of efforts and hard work put into their performances perceived by their fans and the proximity of the idols' reach to their fans rather than merely focusing on their good looks or abilities to sing. Despite gaining fame within Japan, cultural barriers prevented AKB48 from attaining global popularity. An example would be the closure of the AKB48 theatre and cafe in Singapore after only a short span of one year. In comparison, it seems much easier for Singaporeans to accept the idols from the US or South Korea. Interestingly, the concept of AKB48's voting system is now adopted by other countries such as South Korea in their "Produce 101" reality show on the theme of choosing idol groups.

My Experiences in a Japanese Exchange Programme

Appreciation of the differences in cultures

I was first introduced to a Japanese exchange programme in 2014 by a friend who is a huge fan of Japanese culture as well. As part of the programme, we had the opportunity to act as a guide to show our Japanese friends around Singapore.

What I presumed would be a tour guide experience turned out to be an opportunity for me to befriend Japanese visitors from different parts of Japan. These visitors are mostly high schoolers, although

---

[12]Galbraith, P. W., and J. G. Karlin, *Idols and Celebrity in Japanese Media Culture* (Houndmills, Basingstoke: Palgrave Macmillan), 2012.

we occasionally chaperoned students from middle schools or technical colleges as well. These students, usually in their second year of high school or third year in junior high schools, make up one of the largest segments of Japanese outbound travellers.[13]

Despite their schooling age, the students whom I interacted with were mature in their thinking and were constantly conscious of their behaviour in public places. The programme, which emphasises conversational English, gave them an opportunity to recall their classroom lessons back in Japan to converse with foreigners like me. I found the exercise useful in this form of applied learning for enhancing their conversational skills in the future. Other than the common tourist spots, most were interested in finding out about typical Singaporean lifestyle habits and checked out the common hangouts for youths like themselves.

The programme not only allowed me to learn more about their way of life, it was also a journey of discovery in our cultural similarities and differences. On one occasion, I took my group to a local hawker centre and introduced them to the sugarcane drink which is not commonly found in Japan. Similar to our local tastes, they appeared to enjoy the refreshing and sweet taste of the juice. However, from my exchange experiences, most Japanese have a bad impression of the durian taste and often the act of eating durians became a dare or challenge for members within the group. What we take for granted in Singapore such as the food found in hawker centres and food courts is unique and interesting for people coming from other places.

Streets of culture

The majority of Japanese visitors expressed a keen interest to visit the cultural spaces in Singapore such as Chinatown. They were awed by the unique architectural structures reflecting traditional culture, a strong ethnic culture as well as the local food that can only be found in

---

[13] Society for Serviceology, In Mochimaru, M., K. In Ueda, and T. In Takenaka, *Serviceology for Services: Selected Papers of the 1st International Conference of Serviceology*, 2014.

Singapore. Similarly, when I first visited Japan, I was astonished when I stepped into the Akihabara's street which is THE haven for Japanese pop culture.

Influence of Japanese Pop Culture in Singapore

In recent years, Japanese pop culture has spread all over the world. Growing local passions and affinities for all things Japanese have led to several adaptations based on our own local cultural preferences, such as the recent Cherry Blossom (Sakura) display at "Gardens By the Bay" in March 2016. There is also an increase in Japanese movie offerings like "Detective Conan" screened in local cinemas. The annual "Anime Festival Asia Singapore" is also becoming increasingly popular with roughly 85,000 visitors in 2013.[14]

Many fans of Japanese pop culture in Singapore are bridging the gap by learning Japanese language and attending Japanese cultural events such as the annual "Natsu Matsuri" or Summer Festivals that are held locally in Singapore.

As the world becomes increasingly globalised, we can expect more Japanese pop culture to be integrated into more aspects of our society, such as we have seen from Taiwan's recent political practice of adapting *anime* culture into their political campaigns to appeal to the electorate.[15] As for now, let us continue to appreciate Japanese pop culture that dedicated artists and other creative workers in Japan have created for us to enjoy.

---

[14]Low, P., "Anime Fest Gets Bigger, Better", dated 5 Dec 2014 in AsiaOne Singapore News, available at http://news.asiaone.com/news/singapore/anime-fest-gets-bigger-better.
[15]Ashcraft, B., "When Politicians Campaign with Anime", dated 18 Jan 2016, available at http://kotaku.com/when-politicians-campaign-with-anime-1753552178.

17

Conclusion

In this publication, politically, we noted the significance of Singapore and Japan having a close political, geopolitical and security relationship in the region. This relationship is intertwined with the common interests of the East Asian region, which is the maintenance of peace and security for economic development. The relationship is also beneficial to ASEAN, with Singapore as a platform to express the concerns, worries, anxieties, suspicions and friendship of all major powers, middle powers and small states in the region. While political and security represent the "hard" aspects of bilateral cooperation, both countries are also engaged in "softer" economic cooperation which had catalysed economic development in the region, with Singapore as a nimble, fast-mover promoter of free trade agreements in East Asia and Japan as a major builder of production networks in the Southeast Asia. Both roles are contributive to the formation of an economic community in Southeast Asia.

Economically, Singapore and Japan are likely to intensify their respective roles as nodes within the East Asian economies that can provide economic developmental training to other economies in the region, promote free trade by institutionalising structures and regulations to break down barriers, stimulate technological cooperation to disseminate technological knowhow to the Southeast Asian region in the latter's industrialisation process, enhance connectivity between economies in the region through encouraging production networking first set up by Japan in the past few decades. Both countries are likely to promote a form of loose, open, market-driven regionalisation that foster greater economic interdependence between different economies in East Asia. Singapore is likely to add value to that process by being the neutral economic platform for all major economies to work together. In the management realm, guest chapter contributor **Kong Tuan Yuen** remains convinced that, in the globalisation era, Singapore or Southeast Asian companies will apply various management techniques to meet their own needs of manufacturing and management processes. The Toyota Production System (TPS), Lean production, Total Quality Management (TQM) and other techniques can be applied appropriately according to management needs. In Kong's view, selected elements of Japanese business management techniques are still major areas of study, research, training and implementations in Singaporean local companies.

Socially, given the closeness in ties and friendship between the two countries and the comprehensiveness of such exchanges, one can extrapolate and expect relations between the two peoples to intensify. For two societies to have *sustainable* ties, they must be able to stand the tests of economic difficulties, political turbulences and geopolitical challenges. The two peoples' understanding of each other's societies help create a substratum of goodwill and generosity that helps to overcome environmental difficulties, unexpected externalities and shocks inherent in the world system or economy. It is this reservoir of goodwill that act as a buffer to absorb shocks in the international system, be they economic or political in nature. This chapter discussed mainly institutional forms of people-to-people exchanges within the rubric of non-governmental, non-profit and volunteer organisations. Much of the exchanges mentioned in this chapter are ethically conscious and purposeful, e.g. directed towards natural disaster recovery or law enforcement. They are also functional, like the world of the Japanese expatriate community in Singapore, i.e. salaryman who bring their families along to conduct productive business activities for their companies and firms.

Culturally, the elements of popular cultural and lifestyle goods consumption as well as appreciation for Japanese traditional culture were discussed in the volume. They are by no means comprehensive discussions but serve to survey some aspects of the embeddedness of Japanese culture in the local landscape. The two chapters on social exchanges through tours and travels as well as cultural exchanges focus on how contemporary Japanese culture is manufactured and produced in Japan before it is exported to Singapore. The commodification of culture is not possible without a complex cultural ecological system to produce such goods for the Singaporean and global consumers. In terms of cultural tourism in Japan, when it comes to appreciation of Japanese culture, arts, traditions and designs, both contemporary and tradition, the element of authenticity cannot be satisfied unless the traveller or tourist is willing to read up and research on some fundamental aspects of Japanese culture in general. Efforts made in pre-departure research on the cultural features of the travels in Japan can deepen people-to-people exchanges when Singaporeans and Japanese encounter each other in their travels.

Besides the chapters with broad overviews, the volume also contains snippets and perspectives from Singaporeans from all walks of life. In the social exchanges, **Aomi Poh** recounted how Japan's culture results in a society-centric society. The concept of harmony, their collectiveness, loyalty and the *ganbaru* spirit results in a group-oriented country which is highly commendable. Employees stay motivated by working together to achieve the company's goals, and even when the company is undergoing restructuring, employees stay on and work towards overcoming hardships. Employees put in their best for the companies they are working for. This is also reflected in their language, in which 社会人 (*shakai-jin*) is used to address someone who have started working, and contributing back to society. Poh's exchange trip with Japan was an eye opener for her into Japan's societal and management trends. **Hilda Tan** was equally circumscribed about her lessons from an exchange trip to Japan. In her view, in retrospect, Tan's most important lesson garnered from her exchange trip is that each system and policy has its own challenges and disadvantages. There is and will never be a right or perfect answer. She argues that it is important to be open and learn from others and willing to adapt to the ever-changing external environment.

Finally, **Soh Hui Shi**'s take on the partnership between Singapore and Japan have certainly come a very long way since Singapore achieved its independence in 1965. In light of the celebration of the 50 year-relationship between Singapore and Japan, such as the upcoming Super Japan festival that will be held in Esplanade (Esplanade, 2016), Soh is sure that it is a possibility that many Singaporeans yearn to such activities organised on a regular basis to learn more about the Japanese popular and traditional cultures. In Soh's view, it will also be ideal for such organised activities to encourage the Japanese community in Singapore to interact with locals more extensively. Through this, she argues that the exchanges will foster a stronger understanding of each other's culture and ensure that they have a better integration into our society.

The volume ended with narratives from three Japanese popular cultural fans. While Singapore is unlikely to build up the same critical mass of *otaku* fandom to have a specialised district like Akihabara, there is a core community of diehard hardcore *otaku* community who are willing to consume Japanese popular culture and follow the trends set in Akihabara and other creative economic districts in Japan. Given the cyberspace connectivity that fans around the world now possess, the Singapore J-pop community is not isolated but connected with their counterparts around the world through the internet and social media. This ensures the sustainability of interest in Japanese popular cultural products. It will also pique Singaporean fans' interest in the latest offerings of J-pop products by viewing them first before they are available in Singapore.

Yeo Kai Yeat, a self-professed Japanese popular culture fan, tackled a wide range of relevant issues in the volume. He noted the rise of fansubs are caused by rising demand for Japanese popular cultural products although he did not condone the idea of piracy. He believes that the male fans are generally more interested in goods and products that contain the elements of "moe", loosely meaning elements of cute, endearing, products with elements of *shounen* targeted at young males most of the time, containing elements of hot-bloodedness and action. In Yeo's view, female fans tend to prefer product that either has emphasis on romance, or the *shoujo* genre. There are also female fans who are attracted to products that feature handsome/appealing boys or males, with male on male contents known as *fujoshi*.

Sim Zhi Ya critiqued how *manga* and *anime* are still largely popular around the world and Singapore is no exception. In her view, this is due to the many genres each medium (i.e. *manga* and *anime*) offered for fans from all ages and gender. Sim also indicated the many events available all year round to promote the *manga* and *anime* culture. She argues that, if the Japanese government and artists choose to focus on the fashionable trends and collaborate together to combine and share their resources, the popularity of *manga* and *anime* will surely increase.

Taking a macro perspective, **Alvin Teo** spotted the trend of localisation of Japanese popular culture even as it reaches different parts of the world. Growing local passions and affinities for all things Japanese have led to several adaptations based on Singaporean cultural preferences, such as the recent Cherry Blossom (Sakura) display at "Gardens by the Bay" in March 2016. Teo noted that the annual "Anime Festival Asia Singapore" is also getting increasingly popular with roughly 85,000 visitorship in 2013. He also detected spin-off effects of Japanese popular cultural dissemination. Many fans of Japanese pop culture in Singapore are bridging the gap by learning Japanese language and attending Japanese cultural events such as the annual "Natsu Matsuri" or Summer Festivals that are held locally in Singapore.

Finally, **Janice Kam** reminds us of how far we have come in Singaporeans' encounters with things Japanese. She reflected on her childhood and adulthood where Japanese stores and services were, and still remain, a ubiquitous presence in her life experiences. Gazing into the near future, from a broader perspective, it may be possible to see a more equitable partnership between Singapore and Japan since the former has evolved from a learner economy adapting from Japanese management practices and economic features to a model from which Japanese could pick out best practices for indigenisation. This is especially the case in the financial sector where Singapore has become a leading financial centre in the region and a successful advocate of free trade with other nations in the world. Japan is known to have an interest in studying these integrated resort. Singapore's ability to attract global foreign talents as a migrant and heterogeneous society is also a case study for Japan's homogenous society seeking for solutions to cope with an ageing society that needs more manpower.

www.ingramcontent.com/pod-product-compliance
Lightning Source LLC
Chambersburg PA
CBHW070758300326
41914CB00053B/724